Best wishes,

The First Resort

Fun, Sun, Fire and War in Cape May,
America's Original Seaside Town

Ben Miller

A bustling scene on the boardwalk around 1920, in front of the entertainment pier that was next to convention hall
Cape May County Museum

Dedication

I DEDICATE this book to my beloved Nana, Dorothy Cann. She spent summers in Cape May as a child, returned in 1941 to work in the Congress Hall ballroom and then introduced her own family to the resort she had grown to love so much.

My Nana passed her enthusiasm for Cape May down through the generations, just like any other treasured family heirloom. I've made the trip hundreds of times, but every time I smell that salty air as I reach Exit Zero, I still think of my Nana.

I love you Nana and I am truly grateful for all that you've done for me and the unconditional support you've shown me throughout my life.

The First Resort

ISBN 978-0-9799051-8-6

Library of Congress Control Number: 2009926199

Published by Exit Zero Publishing, Inc.,
109 Sunset Boulevard, Suite D,
Cape May, NJ 08204
www.exitzero.us

*Book edited and designed by
Jack Wright
Exit Zero Publishing*

Left: A nod to Cape May's Dutch origins – the city got its name from explorer Captain Cornelius Mey
Don Pocher

Right: A Saturday afternoon at Cape May Yacht Club
Don Pocher

The early days of Cape May's Beach Patrol, which was founded in 1911
Don Pocher

Contents

Acknowledgments

FIRST and foremost, I'd like to thank my wife, Andrea. While I was researching and writing this book she saw little more of me than the top of my head bent over a laptop computer. I couldn't have written this without her support and patience.

Secondly, I'd like to thank my mom, who continued the traditions my nana started so many years earlier, bringing my brother, my sister and me down to Cape May year after year. My mom always made our weeks in Cape May memorable and set an example for me to follow with my own kids. I'd also like to thank my dad for the many hours he spent exploring the city with me when I was growing up. From our morning walks on the mall to the hours upon hours we spent on the beach, my dad always put us first... even though he probably would have rather been sitting in the shade, enjoying a good book.

I absolutely need to thank Jack Wright, who made all this possible. Jack gave me the opportunity to write for *Exit Zero* a few years ago and offered me the chance to share my love of Cape May through this book. Jack had faith in me when others didn't and that is something I will never forget. I still won't try haggis, but am grateful to him nonetheless.

I'd also like to thank the family and friends who have put up with untold numbers of unanswered phone calls and texts while I was writing. Hopefully, they will forgive me and enjoy the book. Since most of them have spent considerable time in Cape May with me at some

BEACH BUDDIES The author (sitting) on Cape May beach in 1979 with his brother Chris Miller, sister Jen Miller Jones and two friends, Kevin and Kyle Collura. *Ben Miller*

ON THE PROMENADE Opposite page: Ben Miller's niece, Madalan Jones, and his cousin, Abbey Cann, take a walk following the author's marriage to Andrea Fedak at the Cove in September, 2007. *Ben Miller*

point, maybe the book will also bring back some good memories.

It would be a crime if I didn't take a moment to thank Don Pocher, whose extensive postcard collection was the inspiration for "The Way We Were" columns in *Exit Zero* magazine, which ultimately paved the way for this book. Don's also been a constant source of support and information about old Cape May and has graciously shared many pieces from his personal collection for use in this book. The words only go so far — thank you, Don, for supplying the images that help to tell a richer, deeper story.

Next, I'd like to thank the friends in Cape May who have given of their time to talk with me and share so many stories. It's been won-

derful seeing the city through your eyes. Specifically, I'd like to mention Sandy Miller, Doug and Anna Marie McMain, Chip and Barbara Masemore, Harriett Sosson, Mark Kulkowitz, Archie and Stephanie Kirk, Ed and Diane Hutchinson, Bonnie and Lance Pontin, Sandy Montano, Bill Cole, Harry Bellangy at the Greater Cape May Historical Society, Pary Woehlcke at the Cape May County Historical Museum, Margo Harvey and the team over at the Mid-Atlantic Center for the Arts and the great people at Cape May Point State Park.

I'm sure there are others who've helped me along the way and I hope you will accept my apologies for not mentioning you specifically — my sincerest thanks for your assistance!

— *Ben Miller*

CHAPTER ONE

A Visit From Henry Hudson

COTTAGE COMMUNITY
Opposite: An early settlement on Cape Island
Cape May County Museum

HUDSON'S DARK DAY
Previous page: In 1610, just a year after he spotted land at the tip of New Jersey, Henry Hudson and his crew faced a mutiny in the Hudson Bay
National Archives

THE CAPE MAY story began on August 28 of 1609, when Sir Henry Hudson spotted land at the tip of New Jersey, where the Atlantic Ocean meets the Delaware Bay. Hudson was the captain of a Dutch sailing vessel *De Halve Maan*, or *Half Moon*, and his first mate, Robert Juet, recorded his discovery.

According to Juet's log, Hudson and his crew sailed around the cape and continued a short distance up the coast into the Delaware Bay. There, they met a number of obstacles that forced the *Half Moon* to abruptly halt the exploration and reverse course. Heavy seas proved too rough for the vessel, coupled with the bay's strong tides and hidden underwater obstacles.

Juet's notes document that Hudson's ship became grounded on a sandbar. The crew had no choice but to spend the evening in the Delaware and wait for the next high tide. As they remained anchored in the bay a powerful early morning storm battered the ship. The *Half Moon* was dragged off the sandbar before being pushed out of the bay and propelled around the cape.

Hudson and his crew escaped unharmed and continued on their voyage. They had been hired by the Dutch East India Company to find a water passage to the East Indies. By the time of Hudson's trip, the people of Europe had come to realize Christopher Columbus's monumental mistake when he claimed the Americas to be the easternmost tip of the Indies. They knew that the area was actually a separate, unsettled continent.

Each country clamored to be the first to explore the uncharted land and claim it as a sovereign territory, so Hudson's financial backers in Holland tasked him with a secondary mission. He was to map the territory and determine if any part of the New World was inhabitable.

When Hudson returned home with news of his adventures around the cape the Dutch leaders and noblemen were quick to respond. They recruited a number of sailors to return to the New World and explore it further. The most prominent of those sailors was a weathered skipper hired by the New Netherland Company. His name was Captain Cornelius Jacobson Mey, and he sailed the *Blyde Boodschap*, or *Glad Tidings*.

Though it's been lost in history over the years, there were two other explorers who also charted the area in the early 1600s.

The first was a sea captain from England who entered the Delaware Bay almost immediately after Hudson sailed away. That voyager was Samuel Argall, who later gained fame as the man who kidnapped Pocahontas.

Argall mistook the region as an eastern portion of Virginia and named the bay after the new governor of the Virginia colony, Lord De La Warre. With the exception of his charting a small portion of the "De La Warre Bay", Argall recorded little of his visit before he continued on to the English settlement at Jamestown.

Following Argall was Captain Cornelius Hendricksen, who traveled around the cape and up the Delaware River to Philadelphia in 1616. He captained the ship *Onrust*, or *Restless*. Hendricksen was also Dutch and worked for the New Netherlands Company.

In reviewing the earliest history of Cape May it is important to note that Hudson's discovery in 1609 occurred more than 10 years before the Pilgrims arrived on the *Mayflower*. Captain Mey's initial exploration of the "Cape Mey" peninsula occurred in 1621, the same year as the first Thanksgiving in Plymouth, Massachusetts.

There were no European settlers in the entire mid-Atlantic region, with the exception of the few surviving Jamestown colonists. The land was primarily inhabited by indians of the

CAPE CURIOSITY
The Legend Of Captain Mey

CAPTAIN Cornelius Jacobsen Mey was born in the late 16th century in a small Dutch town called Schellinkhout. Little is known about Mey's childhood or his family, with the exception of his older brother, Jan Jacobszoon May van Schellinkhout. Both brothers grew up to become well-known sailors and each one has been remembered in the name of a land they helped discover. The elder brother lent his name to Jan Mayen Island, in the Arctic Ocean.

The brothers' exploits were so similar that some historians have had a difficult time distinguishing between them. This led to the mistaken belief that Henry Hudson explored Jan Mayen Island in 1609, before Captain Jan Mey. Hudson's own diaries prove that the trip never happened. He was in the area of Cape May at that time - the confusion probably lies in a melding of the two brothers' stories.

Cornelius Mey made his first trek to the new world in 1614, when he was a young navigator on the *Fortune*. By the 1621, he had become skipper of the *Blyde Boodschap*. It was on this trip that Mey discovered the small peninsula that would bear his name. Mey and his crew had sailed from Sandy Hook, down the coast and up the Delaware River on the other side. Once he reached the western side of Cape May, Captain Mey had grown enamored with the climate and likened it to that of his homeland.

He returned to Holland, where his reports and maps led his benefactors to believe they could build a new colony, which they called New Netherland. The Dutch West India Company assumed control over New Netherland and appointed Captain Mey as their first Director General in 1623.

Just one year into the job, Mey grew weary of managing the struggling colony and returned to Holland. Little is known of his travels beyond that.

Lenni Lenape tribe. A sub-division of the Lenni Lenape, the Kechemeche indians, lived in the area of Southern New Jersey, which they referred to as Scheyichbi, or 'land along the water.'

The Kechemeche were a peaceful tribe who spent much of their lives hunting and farming. They lived in wigwams that were single-room dwellings with a domed roof, as opposed to the teepees that were favored by other tribes.

Thick woods covered the entire peninsula in the early 1600s, so the Kechemeche used an ancient method of hunting deer and other large stock. They positioned archers from the tribe on the outskirts of groves and then lit multiple fires in the woods. The dense smoke would act as a cloaking agent, disguising the scents of the hunters and confusing the deer. The flames would then chase the animals out into open clearings, where the archers would be waiting with their bows and arrows.

The fires also proved useful for the women of the Kechemeche tribe, who farmed the land. The burned ashes replenished the earth with important nutrients that made farming more productive. Additionally, the large sections of the woods cleared by the flames provided more land for the planting of crops.

The area that is now Cape May Point was home to the majority of local indians, due to the prevalence of both salt and fresh water. Another factor that drew the Kechemeche indians to the Point was the existence of smooth quartz crystals, now known as Cape May Diamonds.

Indians believed the crystals to have mystical powers and they used them to barter for goods and services between other tribes and early settlers. They also used a form of wampum made by stringing shells with small beads.

Local lore includes tales of Captain Mey disembarking his ship to meet with the Kechemeche people and exploring the land on foot. Some volumes have gone on to note that the indians pre-

FROM THE ARCHIVES
The Lenapes

From *South Jersey, A History, 1664-1923*
THE old enemies of the Deerslayer, the Lenni Lenapes of the Algonquins, came down from Ottawa, and in their wanderings reached the shore of the Delaware Bay at the point that is now Cape May. Here they rested, for, unlike the refugees from the flood, they had no ark, and before them stretched too wide a river to cross. The Lenni-Lenapes, or Delawares as they were often called, were hunters, and were attracted to this region by the great variety of game and birds. Wilson, the ornithologist, says: "If birds are good judges of excellent in climate, Cape May must have the finest climate in the United States, for it has the greatest variety of birds." Living in Cape May were the Kechemeches, a subdivision of the tribe who gave to New Jersey the name Schaakbee, or Scheyichbi, and to the River Delaware that of Whittuck. With noiseless tread they roamed, two hundred years ago, over a spicy carpet of pine needles, through a wilderness of dense forest, destined to echo in future years with the hum of the sawmill.

sented Mey with ornate wampum and led him through the land, though no historical data has ever been found to substantiate that claim.

All that was definitively recorded about Captain Mey's first visit to the cape was his love of the area and especially the climate, which he found to be similar to that of his native Holland. Mey chose to name the peninsula after himself, calling it Cape Mey.

The name was transcribed on to charts, maps and other documents, but the 'e' was mistaken for an 'a' almost immediately. This led to many of the old records showing both Cape May and Cape Mey, though the entire mass of land between Cape Cod and Henlopon was officially known as New Netherlands.

In 1623, Captain Mey was appointed Director General of New Netherlands and a series of voyages were arranged to bring Dutch settlers to the new province, although the first ship to bring pioneering families to New Netherlands was actually filled with Flemish settlers from Belgium.

The ship *Nieu Nederlandt*, or *New Netherland*, set sail in March of 1624. Later that year, six more sailing vessels were sent from Amsterdam, loaded with supplies and additional settlers. Upon reaching the Dutch colony, clusters of people were scattered across the entire province to establish small villages and trading posts.

The Dutch settlers were much different from the English pilgrims in that their trip to the New World was based primarily on financial gain. Commercial ventures like fur trapping, trading and bartering drove their expansion in the province; little time was devoted to settlement.

They moved up and down the Delaware and Hudson rivers like nomads. It was not until the Swedish and English pioneers began moving to New Netherland in the late 1620s that the Dutch began to focus on establishing homesteads.

The Cape May area was of special interest to three directors of the West India Company: Samuel Godyn, Albert Burgh and Samuel Blommaert. They favored whaling as a means to invigorate the quiet Cape area and bolster trade. The three men invested in a plan to develop the area, along with their company.

In May of 1630 the first land transfer on the cape took place between members of the Lenni Lenape tribe and representatives of the West India Company. The transaction gave the Dutch company ownership of the Cape May peninsula. History has recorded the deed as providing, "The eastside of Godyn's Bay, or Cape de May, reaching four miles from the said Cape towards the bay and four miles along the coast southward and another four miles inland, being sixteen square miles."

Along with the Dutch signatories the deed was signed by 10 Kechemeche tribesmen who lived in Cape May. It was a precarious situation for the indians since their long-held beliefs precluded them from owning or possessing any of the land. When the sale occurred they were under the impression that they were only selling right to use the land for hunting and fishing.

Had the West India Company pressed forward with their plan to establish a whaling port in Cape May, the Kechemeche would have been shocked by their displacement. Fortunately for the indians the principal backers of the development pulled out four years later and transferred their stakes to the West India Company.

A few lone fishermen did attempt to demonstrate whaling as a viable option, but their efforts proved fruitless and the company's plan was abandoned. No whaling port was ever constructed by the West India Company in Cape May. The Dutch settlers all but abandoned the Cape May area and moved north to their fledgling city of New Amsterdam, which later became New York.

PIVOTAL MOMENT
Left: This famous painting depicts the signing of a treaty of friendship between William Penn and the Lenni Lenape indians
Benjamin West

SHIP OF DISCOVERY
Right: The *Half Moon* in New York Harbor
National Archives

CHAPTER TWO
Puritans, Indians, And Diamonds

AFTER THE Dutch pioneers moved to the north, Cape May was again left to the Kechemeche indians. It remained that way until the late 1630s, when English Puritans began relocating from the New England states.

Like the Indians, the English pioneers recognized the importance of both fresh water and salt water, so they chose to establish their first settlement, just north of Cape May Point. They constructed rudimentary structures for their homes, far enough from the shoreline to prevent flooding.

The English were joined by a small group of Swedish settlers in the early 1640s, who also saw the land's potential for fishing, whaling and farming. Neither faction endeavored to go beyond the coastal areas along the Delaware Bay until an English traveler named Robert Evelyn arrived in 1643.

Evelyn was an adventurer who relished the opportunity to visit uncharted lands. He was the first European to survey the Cape May peninsula from the Delaware Bay to the Atlantic Ocean. He later wrote a narrative of his explorations that provide a vivid picture of what he found.

He spoke of wild cedar swamps, forests of oak and pine and a wide profusion of animals inhabiting the land. Specifically, Evelyn mentioned bison, bears, wolves, wild turkey of a very large size and deer. He also noted the plentiful fishing in the ocean and in freshwater streams, along with small game like raccoons, foxes, mink and beavers.

As he made his way across Cape May, Evelyn encountered the Kechemeche indians. He described an aggressive confrontation between 50 indian men and his party of 15 explorers. According to Evelyn's notes, there was "bickering" back and forth, but no violence. Even though they greatly outnumbered Evelyn's party, the natives were fearful of the muskets the group carried.

FROM THE ARCHIVES

An Indian Deed

From *South Jersey, A History, 1664-1923*
THE following [synopsis of an] Indian deed, believed to be the only one that has been handed down, was found among the papers of Jacob Spicer, and is now in the possession of Charles Ludlam, Esq., of Dennisville.

It was given on January 1st, 1687 by Panktoe to John Dennis, for a tract of land near Cape Island, viz: "Beginning from the creek and so running up into the woodland, along by Carman's line to a white oak tree, at the head of the swamp, and running with marked trees to a white oak by a pond joining to Jonathan Pine's bounds. All the land and marsh lying and between the bounds above mentioned and Cape Island."

The witnesses were Abiah Edwards and John Carman. Panktoe's mark bore a striking resemblance to a Chinese character.

A BITTER STRUGGLE
This page, left: The French and Indian War, also known as the War of Conquest, lasted from 1754-1763
National Archives

DRESSED FOR THE BEACH
This page, right: Early Cape May settlers frolic in the waters off the Point in the late 1700s
Cape May Point State Park

The extensive exploration of the Cape May peninsula led to an eventual migration of settlers eastward and south, towards the Atlantic shore. It also established the notion that a portion of Cape May was an island. This was the point when the term Cape Island began to be widely used.

In August of 1664 England sent a flotilla of warships into the harbor of New Amsterdam and forced the Dutch governor to relinquish control of New Netherland. Now under English control the northern portion was renamed New York and the southern province was called New Jersey, which was then split in half from east to west, with the Cape May area considered West New Jersey.

In the years following the English conquest of the province, migration eastward on Cape Island continued. The year 1685 marked the official founding of Cape May County, which brought a semblance of law and order to the area. The new county employed public servants to act as early policing authorities and establish a system of government based on local justices of the peace.

Land ownership began to take more precedence over simply settling an area. Historical documents show a purchase in 1688 of 95,000 acres of land by an English gentleman named Daniel Coxe. Prior to his purchasing the land Coxe had been appointed governor of the province, a title he held from 1687-1691.

The Coxe transaction included a large portion of what is now Cape May County, beginning at Cape Island and going north. It was the earliest known case of land speculation in the region as Coxe bought the land with the intention of dividing it and selling parcels to the early settlers.

Coxe never actually visited his property in Cape May, nor did he ever journey to the Americas. His decision to buy the land was based on two factors — commercial interests and a desire to institute the Church of England in West New Jersey. As a deeply religious man Coxe felt it was his duty to bring the church to the colonies.

Like his predecessors Coxe took great pride in the fact that he did not cheat the indians out of their land. Although he had already paid the English pioneers as part of the original sale, he also made a second payment to the Lenni Lenape indians to ensure they were treated fairly.

One year after he purchased the property Coxe sold the first two parcels on Cape Island to Humphrey Hughes (206 acres) and William Jacobs (340 acres). More sales followed, including one to a whaler named Thomas Hand, whose family name is synonymous with Cape May history.

Hand purchased William Jacobs' entire property, which encompassed the east side of the island, including Schellenger's Landing, the site of Cape May's modern fishing docks. The official record, noted in early 1699, notes the land parameters as being "between Randall Hewitt and a pint athwart Cape Island."

Around the turn of the century, whaling became an important part of life in much of the coastal areas around Cape May. Whales were plen-

FROM THE ARCHIVES

Indian Murder

New York Weekly Journal, **August, 1736**

CAPE May, July 17-Yesterday the Coroner's Inquest view'd the body of an Indian man, said to be kill'd by Joseph Golden, an English inhabitant, here. Isaiah Stites being present and seeing the whole difference, gave his evidence to the inquest, the substance whereof was, that Golden having hired the said Indian with another Indian man and woman to pull some flan was to give them three quarts of rum for their labour; with which they got drunk and quarrel'd with Golden, who then bid them begone from his house, but they refus'd going and gave him ill language whereupon a quarrel ensued and many blows passing on both sides, Golden got a small stick or cudgel to drive them away but the two Indians fell upon him and got him down, beat him very much, and twisted his neck, so that he seemed in danger of his life. Stites endeavoured to part them; at length Golden (with Stites' help) got on his legs, and then took a larger stick in his hand to defend himself, bidding the Indians to keep off; but one of them coming violently at him, he struck him on the head, knock'd him down, and he died without speaking a word more. Is appearing that there was no difference between Golden and the Indians before that sudden quarrel, and that they had put him in fear of his life, before he struck that blow, the Coroner's Inquest found it manslaughter.

tiful in the local waters and early colonists valued the oil that was derived from their blubber. Contrary to popular belief, however, whaling was not the major industry for residents of Cape Island.

Due to the convergence of the Delaware Bay and the Atlantic Ocean, waters were rough off the Cape May shore. Those who did choose to make a living by whaling found it difficult and dangerous. Just as the Dutch settlers before them, most English colonists decided it was not worth the risk.

Instead, colonists on Cape Island primarily engaged in farming. The land was found to be well suited for agriculture. Crops were planted over the viable areas of the peninsula and the revenue fueled the continuing growth of Cape Island.

The completion of Cape May's first road in 1707 enabled farmers to peddle their wares beyond their immediate neighbors. That first road stretched from Cape May to Burlington, nearly 100 miles to the north.

Another consequence of the new road was the infusion of more religion into the Cape May area. Prior to the road being built the only organized religion that was openly practiced was among followers of the Church of England.

That changed in June of 1712, however, when the Baptists built their 'Cape May Church,' with Nathaniel Jenkins as their first pastor. Following suit in 1714, the Presbyterians constructed the Cold Springs Presbyterian Church and appointed Reverend John Bradner to lead the congregation.

In 1716 the Quakers chose to build a meeting house in Seaville, on the northern end of Cape May County. Their building remains standing today and is still being used regularly by the Quakers for worship and meetings.

The colonies of Cape May County and Cape Island, in particular, continued to thrive. Whaling in the northern parts of the county and farming on Cape Island had come into their own. A new road was constructed in 1721 that was reputed to

be much easier to navigate and smoother than its 1707 predecessor.

Early colonists on Cape Island found a variety of ways to recreate and unwind from their daily work. In the summertime contests were arranged for corn husking and wood chopping, a variety of games were played and rudimentary sporting events were held. Winter brought ice skating and sleigh riding, as well as large feasts shared in front of roaring fireplaces that not only cooked the food but provided warmth and light.

When the French and Indian War broke out in 1754 the majority of Cape Island residents were blissfully unaware. Few newspapers made their way down to the island and the majority of news that was received came in the way of gossip from travelers. Even as the colonists received word of

the hostilities there was little alarm since they felt secluded from the other English colonies.

After the French and Indian War ended, in 1763, it was the possibility of a much different war that gained the attention of Cape Island colonists. The British parliament began imposing restrictions on the colonies, like the infamous Stamp Act of 1765 that regulated a stamp tax on all legal documents, newspapers and even playing cards.

It was the first major attempt by the British government to tax the colonists and it was met with wide protests, as the call of "No taxation without representation" was heard throughout the colonies. The stamp tax was repealed one year later, but the seeds of revolution had already been planted.

CAPE CURIOSITY

Cape May Diamonds

THE AREA now known as Sunset Beach in Cape May Point has become famous over the years for its abundance of Cape May Diamonds. Unlike traditional diamonds, which require expensive exploration and mining efforts, the Cape May variation are plentiful and free for the taking.

Of course, they are not actually diamonds; they are polished quartz stones, washed nearly 200 miles down the Delaware River by the force of the waters and propelled on to the beach by the tides. As the diamonds make their journey they are constantly rubbed against one another, along with other rocks, which accounts for their smooth finish.

Local legend claims that Cape May Diamonds are washed ashore due to the interruption in the bay's current from the sunken hull of the SS Atlantus. In reality, the beach has been covered by the quartz crystals for hundreds of years, long before the concrete ship was built.

The original inhabitants of Cape May, the Kechemeche indians, discovered the gems in the 1500s and used them for jewelry. They also traded the stones with other tribes and European settlers. The Indians believed the diamonds possessed mystical powers, giving strength to those who wore them.

It was this belief that led the Kechemeche people to routinely collect the diamonds and store them for their own use. When the settlers caused the indians to move from the area, they carried piles of the stones with them for protection during their journey.

In later years unscrupulous individuals took advantage of the Cape May Diamonds' resemblance to the real thing. They would polish and cut the stones and sell them to diamond brokers who were unable to tell the difference.

Today's modern technology has made the practice virtually impossible, though there are still a few people who continue to try and pull off the deceit. They are typically thwarted by gem-scan equipment or by jewelers who are thoroughly trained to spot the difference.

A History Of The Old Brick Church

The New York Times, May 3, 1896

FAMOUS OLD
NEW JERSEY CHURCH
A Presbyterian Congregation
Formed 182 Years Ago

CAPE MAY, NJ – The one hundred and eighty-second anniversary of the founding of the Presbyterian Church at Cold Spring, three miles north of Cape May, will soon be celebrated by appropriate exercises. A few years previous to 1714 the peninsula of Cape May County was settled by colonists from the vicinity of New Haven and from Long Island.

From Long Island came John Townsend and his brother, Richard, who had come over from England. Richard was a bachelor, but John's descendants made up in numbers for Richard's deficiency. The Cape May County and Long Island Townsends claim John as their paternal ancestor. The Townsends were Quakers.

The colonists from New Haven were mostly Presbyterians. Some of them had heard Jonathan Edwards preach more than once, tradition says. The settlers were whalers and are said, in old historic papers, to have made splendid livings.

The Cold Springs Presbyterian Church was under the care of the Philadelphia Synod, which was organized in 1704. The records say the church was under the care of the New

Brick Church, Cold Spring, N.J.:

Cold Springs Presbyterian Church, or Old Brick as it is known, was built in 1823. It replaced an older house of worship that was built on the same spot, on Seashore Road, just north of Cape May, in the early 1700s *Don Pocher*
Opposite page: Cold Spring Church photographed some time in the 1970s *National Archives*

Brunswick Presbytery from 1740 until 1752. It was turned over to the New York Presbytery in 1752, where it remained until 1839, when the West Jersey Presbytery was organized.

The first regular pastor of the church was the Rev. John Bradner, who was ordained May 6, 1715. He lived on his own estate, consisting of 200 acres. Mr Bradner removed to Goshen, Orange County, NY, in 1721. He sold his estate to the church, and the property is still used for the pastor's parsonage.

After Mr Bradner left it, the church had no regular pastor until 1726, when the Rev. Hughston Hughes became its settled minister.

From him nearly all of the Hugheses in the vicinity descended. Mr Hughes was pastor one year, and was dismissed because "of his too free use of intoxicating drinks."

The Rev. Samuel Finley, who in 1761 became the fifth president of Princeton College, was a pastor of the church for some years before entering upon his college duties. He was a graduate of the "Old Log College," in Pennsylvania, and he was buried near it.

The Rev Daniel Lawrence became the head of the flock in 1752. He was a Long Islander, and was born in 1718. Before entering the ministry he was a blacksmith. His learning was gathered

at the "Old Log College" before mentioned. He became a preacher in 1745. Mr Lawrence served the church until he died, April 13, 1766. He was buried in the cemetery back of the church, and upon his tombstone are the following lines:

In yonder sacred house I spent my breath,
Now, silent, mouldering here I lie in death;
Those silent lips shall wake and yet declare,
A dread amen to truths, they published there.

The first church was a small log building. In 1764 it was replaced by a frame and shingle building. This was removed in 1824, to give place to the present brick structure. Surrounding the church is a graveyard, where the dead of Cape May for two centuries are buried.

The present church was built by Thomas H. Hughes, the only Congressman who has made his home in Cape May.

One of the early members of the church is said to have been Jacob Spicer, second, a son of Jacob Spicer, who came to Philadelphia with William Penn. Mr Spicer was one of the compilers of the Colonial laws of New Jersey. He was born in 1716, and died in 1765. He was buried by the side of his father in the Cold Spring Church yard.

Another family of the time was the Leamings. The family came from Connecticut, and has been honored continuously with public offices to this day.

The last pastor of the church, who was noted, was the Rev Moses Williamson, who was the head of the flock from 1831 to 1873. Mr Williamson received Henry Clay when he visited Cape May, in 1847, and Clay spoke highly of his oratory.

The present pastor is the Rev D. H. Laverty. The church has a membership of 400 and is prosperous.

CHAPTER THREE
From Revolution To Recreation

20667

THE YEAR 1766 saw the British parliament's repeal of the Stamp Act, but the damage in the colonies had been done. The citizens of Cape Island were split along the lines of allegiance, with many of them standing behind the British rulers. The island was still somewhat secluded from the rest of the colonies, shielding the people from much of the dissension.

There were, however, a growing number of residents who wanted to break free of what they felt was a tyrannical rule. They listened intently to people like Samuel Adams, the popular colonial essayist and future founding father of America. He rallied the people together at a pivotal point in history, when the divide between colonists and the British government grew intolerable. Adams professed,

"For if our trade may be taxed why not our lands? Why not the produce of our lands and everything we possess or make use of? This we apprehend annihilates our charter right to govern and tax ourselves... If taxes are laid upon us in any shape without our having a legal representation where they are laid, are we not reduced from the character of free subjects to the miserable state of tributary slaves?"

The British parliament and colonial governors were aware of the rising resistance to their rule, even in areas like remote Cape Island. Local sailors on the cape were accused of sneaking goods into the port without paying the proper taxes. Though the captains vehemently denied any smuggling claims, the government persisted with their indictments.

In November of 1770 a British tax collector named John Hatton was reassigned from Salem, Massachusetts to Cape Island. Local citizens felt Hatton was an angry, self-important man who took his duties as a tax collector to mean he was above the average populace. The local captains took great offense to his demeanor and considered him a threat to their livelihood.

History recounts a confrontation between Hatton and a group of local fishermen who refused to let him inspect their ships. Hatton was attempting to board a vessel, *Prince of Wales*, when he was attacked by the ship's crew and thrown off.

Other fishing boats surrounded the ship and assisted in the operation, showing both their support for the *Prince of Wales* captain and defiance of the British rule.

Hatton promptly reported the incident to his superiors and the men responsible were formally charged, though they were never prosecuted. In a surprising twist, an arrest warrant was issued for Hatton himself, only one month later. It seems a local man, Jedediah Mills, accused Hatton of threatening to "wound, maim or kill him."

Britain responded to the growing dissension among colonists with more taxes and levies, like the Tea Act of 1773. This act was particularly notorious amongst the colonists since it was enacted solely to help the East India Company. The move demonstrated a tone of contempt on the part of parliament, along with an appeasement of British-backed companies at the expense of colonists.

New England settlers organized the famous Boston Tea Party to protest the move and, as a result, parliament ordered the Boston port closed. Their action meant that all merchant vessels already en route to Boston would be redirected around the cape and up the Delaware River to Philadelphia. The decision proved to be a big concern to the people of Cape Island, since many of the local citizens had come to resent the British-backed government by this point.

Ships destined for Philadelphia typically traveled through the Delaware Bay and up the river, with the assistance of a river pilot who was often a resident of Cape Island. Wanting to support their fellow countrymen and deeply resentful of the British government, many pilots simply refused to work the river, leaving the merchant ship captains to navigate the treacherous Delaware River on their own.

American history notes the Second Continental Congress organized on May 10, 1775, the same day a small group of Vermont citizens overtook the British-controlled Fort Ticonderoga in New York. It was an eventful day with the Continental Congress voting to create an army of 20,000 men, under the command of General George Washington.

On September 21, 1775, a battalion of light infantry soldiers from Cape May County was assembled, to comply with the congressional edict. An election was held at Cape May Court House to appoint officers to oversee the battalion and a force of local sailors were tasked with protecting the waters off Cape May's coast.

Those elected to office that day proclaimed that all citizens of Cape May County between the ages of 15 and 50 would be expected to join the revolution and fight with the colonists. The only exception that was made involved 'conscientious objectors' who believed their religious principles forbade any fighting. Those who were exempted were required to pay a monthly fee for the privilege.

Britain reacted to the revolutionary movement with a strong military response. They sent droves of soldiers to the colonies to stamp out the revolution and also hired 17,000 Hessians (German mercenaries) to join the Brit-

THE FATHER OF
OUR COUNTRY

APPEALED FOR SOLDIERS AS FOLLOWS

TO ALL BRAVE, HEALTHY, ABLE BODIED, AND WELL
DISPOSED YOUNG MEN,
IN THIS NEIGHBOURHOOD, WHO HAVE ANY INCLINATION TO JOIN THE TROOPS,
NOW RAISING UNDER
GENERAL WASHINGTON,
FOR THE DEFENCE OF THE
LIBERTIES AND INDEPENDENCE
OF THE UNITED STATES,

TAKE NOTICE,

FROM THE ARCHIVES

Attack On A Tax Man

From the archives of the State of New Jersey

Proclamation by Governor William Franklin, Esquire, Captain General, Governor and Commander in Chief in and over the Province of New Jersey, and Territories thereon depending in America, Chancellor and Vice Admiral in the same, &c.

A PROCLAMATION

Whereas I have received information from John Hatton, Esq, Collector of His Majesty's Customs, for the Port of Salem, &c, in the Province of New Jersey, That on the Eighth Day of November Instant, a Boat's Crew, consisting of Nine Persons, from on Board the Ship Prince of Wales, Patrick Crawford, Master, then riding at Anchor near Cape May, armed with Guns, and other offensive Weapons, in an hostile manner, boarded and re-took, from the said John Hatton, a certain Pilot-boat, late the Property of Jedediah Mills laden with Goods, known to have been clandestinely discharged out of the said Ship Prince of Wales, which said Pilot-boat and her Cargo the said John Hatton had on the same Day seized and taken Possession of, by virtue of his said Office: And that after the Boat's crew had boarded the said Pilot-boat, they most cruelly beat, and dangerously wounded the said John Hatton, his Son, and a Mulatto Slave, and robbed the said John Hatton of four Spanish Dollars, three Guns, two Hangers, one rifle barrell'd Pistol, a Pair of Shoebuckles, and other small Articles. One of the said Nine Persons, who appeared to have Command of the said Boat's Crew, was called Smith, and is a short, thick, well-set Man, supposed to be between thirty and forty Years of Age, and has a fresh cut on the right Side of his Head and Face, made with a Cuttlass in the said Affray. Another of the said Persons is named Hughes, and is now in His Majesty's Gaol at Cape May. The other seven Persons are supposed to be Sailors, belonging to the said Ship Prince of Wales, whose Names are unknown

I have therefore thought fit to issue this Proclamation, hereby requiring, and strictly charging and commanding all Officers, Civil and Military, and other his Majesty's Liege Subjects within the said Province of New Jersey, to use their utmost Endeavours to seize and apprehend the said Offenders, or any of them, so that they may be brought to Justice. And I do hereby promise His Majesty's most gracious Pardon to any one of the Persons concerned in the said Assault and Robbery (except the aforesaid Smith) who shall inform against and prosecute to conviction any one of more of his Accomplices.

Given under my Hand and Seal at Arms, at the City of Burlington, the Seventh Day of November, in the Eleventh Year of His Majesty's Reign, Anno Domini 1770.

- William Franklin
GOD SAVE THE KING

FROM THE ARCHIVES
A Naval Battle

The Pennsylvania Ledger, July 6, 1776

By accounts from the Capes we are informed; that a brig from St Thomas's with 400 barrels of powder, arms, dry goods and coming into our Capes on Saturday last, was chased by the King Fisher, and run aground off Cape May. Captains Barre and Weckes sent their boats to assist in unloading her; having taken out all the arms, cannon, 160 barrels of powder, and some dry goods, as much as their boats would hold – they discovered the men of war's boats coming to her, upon which they opened the remainder of the powder, and spreading some doubled canvass upon it they laid on the canvass live coals, and left her – one of the man of war's boats having got alongside, they had hardly boarded her before she blew up.

ish militia. The Hessians had a reputation for being particularly aggressive, due in part to the fact that many were criminals who were forced to fight for their freedom.

Upon hearing of Britain's actions the resolve of the American colonists grew even stronger. The revolution was in full effect and on Cape Island nearly all the citizens rallied around their new colonial confederacy. They supported their men in service under General Washington and helped monitor British naval activity in the Delaware Bay.

On July 2, 1776, the State of New Jersey adopted its first constitution, with the approval of all five Cape May delegates. Two days later, the Second Continental Congress adopted the Declaration of Independence, declaring that the American colonies were no longer under British control.

The war raged on and the brave men from Cape Island continued to fight on the Pennsylvania battlefields. At home, their families worked to preserve local produce, seafood and other supplies so that they could be sent to the soldiers. Off the coast, in the Delaware Bay and Atlantic Ocean, local sailors repeatedly engaged British ships.

The revolutionary battlefields never reached Cape May, though many lives were lost over the course of the war. Through skirmishes on the Delaware Bay and on the war's front lines in Pennsylvania, Cape Island felt the painful losses that come from war.

By the time hostilities ceased in 1783 the people of Cape May were relieved to see their lives return to normal. Farmers were glad to return to their plantations and the sea captains were grateful to use their boats for fishing, rather than battle.

Once again, prosperity reigned on Cape Island, though the dynamic of the village was soon to change. Word of the charming seaside village began to spread after the war, particularly amongst the wealthy families in the new United States capital of Philadelphia.

Visitors started making their way to Cape Island to enjoy the ocean breezes, paying local residents for room and board. Seeing the opportunity before them, two prominent Cape May citizens took advantage of the situation and built guest houses to accommodate the travelers.

The first was a gentleman named Ellis Hughes, who is often credited as the father of Cape May hospitality. Hughes was a carpenter by trade but in 1791 he sought permission from the local government to operate an inn. He was joined by Ephraim Mills, a former river pilot who opened Cape Island's second inn with his wife, Mary.

Hughes drummed business for his hostelry with an advertisement he placed in *The Philadelphia Aurora*. While Mills continued to provide guest lodgings for many years his inn never reached the height of popularity that Hughes enjoyed.

As time went by and Hughes received more requests for lodging, he added on to the original building. Large bays were constructed, similar to a rudimentary barracks. People slept on cots or directly on the floor, with blankets and sheets acting as privacy curtains. He named his expanded hostelry The Atlantic House.

The Atlantic House was the first true hotel on Cape Island, although its facilities and amenities were a long way from what today's visitors would expect in a hotel — guests were provided with little more than a roof over their head and a warm meal.

Even so, some of Philadelphia's most prominent citizens flocked to Cape Island and helped establish it as America's first seaside resort.

CAPE CURIOSITY

Cape May Point's Religious Birth

BECAUSE of its expansive beaches on both the Atlantic Ocean and the Delaware Bay, along with a large freshwater lake, the area of Cape May Point was the site of Cape May's first settlement. Even before the pioneers first visited the area, Kechemeche indians took advantage of the Point's many amenities.

During the Revolutionary War, however, one of the area's most attractive features was effectively removed. In an attempt to dissuade British sailors from landing on Cape Island and using the fresh water from Lake Lilly to supply their ships, American nationalists changed the flow of the water into the lake.

To ensure that the British Navy would not be able to use the pure water, small groups of patriots assembled and dug channels, connecting the lake with the ocean. Once completed, the salt water of the Atlantic Ocean flowed into Lake Lilly and tainted the water supply.

Though it inevitably killed off all freshwater species living in the lake at the time, it also accomplished the mission of making the water undrinkable. After the hostilities were concluded, and the Americans claimed victory, the channels were eventually filled in. Even without the influx of salt water to the lake, it still took years to restore the ecological balance and make the water fresh again.

Nearly one hundred years after the Revolutionary War ended, a man

by the name of Alexander Whildin also saw great potential in the Point. In 1885, Whildin decided the location was perfect to develop into a new Christian-oriented town.

He named his new village Sea Grove and nearly all the trees and sand dunes were removed to make way for the development. In contrast to the morally-sound atmosphere Whildin hoped to foster, hundreds of immigrants were employed in the construction, with brutal work schedules and very little pay.

According to Cape May Point historical records, the laborers who built the planned spiritual resort were forced to live in small tents, while working 80-hour weeks. In the end, their hard work proved to be without cause. As the New Cape May scheme did many years later, the righteous resort of Sea Grove failed to stay afloat.

In 1881, only six years after its conception, the community was all but gone, most of the properties vacant. The Sea Grove Association, founded by Whildin and well-known merchant John Wanamaker, was disbanded. All their holdings were sold at public auction and the initial investors in Whildin's plan lost a great deal of money.

Years later, in 1917, a World War I battery was built on the only remaining Sea Grove property to protect the cape from enemy invasion. During World War II a coastal defense post was built on the grounds, including the familiar

bunker, Battery 223. Complementing the large bunker were a group of four Panama Mounts, with 155mm guns and an additional battery charged with protecting the coast from torpedoes.

In 1962 all the lands of the former coastal defense base were officially turned over to the state and Cape May Point State Park was created. The same lands that were once reserved for soldiers scouring the horizon for German warships and U-boats are now being explored by millions of people each year.

Unlike the soldiers, however, these individuals are searching the horizon for assorted varieties of shorebirds and hawks. Cape May Point State Park is considered one of the country's best locations for viewing migratory birds.

The old WWII bunker that once housed the shells and logistics for twin six-inch gun mounts now lies empty and eerily quiet. The crumbling structure stands as a monument to the passing of time, like the ancestral watch in William Faulkner's *The Sound and the Fury...*

When Father gave it to me he said I give you the mausoleum of all hope and desire... I give it to you not that you may remember time, but that you might forget it now and then for a moment and not spend all your breath trying to conquer it. Because no battle is ever won he said. They are not even fought. The field only reveals to man his own folly and despair, and victory is an illusion of philosophers and fools.

View at Lily Lake, Cape May, N. J.

AND BEACH, CAPE MAY POINT, N. J.

View at Sea Grove, Cape May Point.

Sea Side Home.   CAPE MAY POINT, N. J.

View at Lily Lake, Cape May, N. J.

Rustic Gate, Entrance to Sea Grove now Cape May Point.

Pavilion by Lily Lake, Cape May, N. J.

Lake Lily.   CAPE MAY POINT, N. J.

RUSTIC GATEWAY TO SEA GROVE. LOOKING SOUTH.

U S LIFE SAVING STATION

PUBLIC BATH-HOUSE, SEA GROVE.

S LIFE SAVING STATION

Gunboats And Steamships

A NEW DAY had dawned on Cape Island. The town slowly grew from a small colonial settlement into a self-sustaining town. Farmers and fishermen saw great prosperity with the influx of new residents to purchase their goods, while the increasing number of summer visitors fostered a new industry on the island — hospitality.

Cape Island saw its first post office in 1804. The man chosen to be the postmaster was the proprietor of the Atlantic Hotel, Ellis Hughes. He shared his time between the inn and the post office with relative ease since the small amount of mail that did arrive came only once a week by stagecoach.

The business of vacationing at Cape Island continued to grow and by the turn of the century travelers had a new option for making the trip. Stagecoaches ran regularly from Philadelphia to the island and a ticket could be purchased for $2.

Hughes's Atlantic Hotel was the most basic of structures. There were no finished walls, no insulation of any kind and the exterior was neither painted nor stained. It was a true utilitarian structure and served as the only large inn on Cape Island for many years.

As people became more interested in visiting the burgeoning seaside retreat of Cape Island and Hughes received more requests for lodging, he added on to the original building. Large bays were constructed, similar to a rudimentary barracks. People slept on cots or directly on the floor, with blankets and sheets acting as privacy curtains.

The second hotel was constructed in 1812, and it was the predecessor of today's Congress Hall. It was built by a colonial hotelier named Jonas Miller, who moved to Cape Island from Port Republic, about 50 miles to the north.

Miller had heard tales of the seaside resort and knew that the Atlantic House was the only hotel in town. Seeking to secure some of those tourist dollars for himself, he built his inn on the corner of what is now Perry and Lafayette streets.

Meanwhile, hard feelings from the Revolutionary War were leading to minor confrontations all over the new American Union. In the region of Cape May, British ships routinely interfered with merchant vessels, sometimes even refusing them entry into the Delaware Bay.

These skirmishes, along with British trade restrictions, caused the United States to once again declare war in 1812.

Cape May reassembled its military battalions in May of 1814, while a small militia was

DELIVERING THE GOODS
This page: A horse and carriage brings local produce to hotels in Sea Grove (later known as Cape May Point), with the Hotel Sea Grove in the background in this early, undated, photograph
Cape May County Museum

WHERE IT ALL BEGAN
Opposite page: Cape May's first hotel, the Atlantic, sits next to its predecessor, the New Atlantic
Don Pocher

maintained on Cape Island, led by Captain Humphrey Hughes.

Colonial newspapers reported on a series of encounters with British frigates and tenders in 1813, just off Cape Island. The situation culminated in a full British blockade of the Delaware Bay in 1814, which was soon ended thanks to the efforts of Cape Island sailors who refused to acquiesce to the British.

The Cape Island militia faced its biggest challenge in 1814 when *HMS Ponticiers* anchored off the island, with many of its 74 guns aimed at the village. The crew were in search of fresh water and sent an envoy to the island to speak to Captain Hughes.

The British representatives approached the island, waving a white flag that signified their desire for a truce. They told Captain Hughes that they were in need of fresh water and wanted to replenish their stores on Cape Island. Hughes adamantly refused and sent the envoy back.

Almost immediately, the representatives returned to the island with the message that either Captain Hughes allow them to secure fresh water or they were going to open fire on the village. Hughes decided to capitulate to the threat, fearing what the guns could do to Cape Island and he ordered his forces to stand aside as the sailors filled their water tanks.

Captain Hughes was later arrested for his decision and charged with aiding and abetting the enemy. The crime was considered treasonable and Hughes could have been executed for his actions. Time was on his side, however, as the war soon ended and America claimed victory. His superiors chose to belay the charges and Hughes was released from prison.

With the second war over, Cape Island residents again turned to their new tourism business. Jonas Miller's new inn began to thrive, along with the competing Atlantic House.

That success paved the way for Ellis Hughes's son, Thomas, to purchase Jonas Miller's lodge in 1816. Thomas promptly demolished Miller's inn and replaced it with a colossal three-story hotel that offered 100 guest rooms.

The Big House, as Thomas Hughes called it, was the biggest inn to be built near the ocean up to that point. In fact, it was one of the biggest in the American Union, a fact not lost on the locals of Cape Island. People in the area felt the hotel was a ludicrous endeavor, far too large to ever turn a profit. They questioned Hughes's intelligence in building such a behemoth and not-so-affectionately renamed his hotel Tommy's Folly.

The odds seemed stacked against Hughes when he opened for business, but he was a determined and headstrong man and he knew it was the will of the travelers that would decide his fate, not the snarky comments of local townspeople.

It didn't take too long for Hughes to be vindicated — the Big House was a huge hit. Guests clamored to visit the new Cape May hostelry that had raised such a commotion. His extraordinary gamble paid off in spades and the only folly was in the minds of those who doubted him.

Foreshadowing events to come, the Big House burned to the ground only two years later. Undaunted, Hughes hired a team of builders and had the hotel rebuilt for the following season. The new version was even larger than the original and offered more rooms.

After Thomas Hughes was elected to the United States House of Representatives in 1828 the name of his hotel was changed to Congress Hall, a designation that lasts to this day. The new name came from a suggestion of one of the hotel's guests and after it was widely discussed one evening over dinner a ceremony was planned to rechristen the hotel.

In 1815, a tall ship began making regular rounds between Philadelphia and Cape Island, joining the stagecoach in bringing summer vacationers to the island. More and more visitors traveled to Cape Island each season and the resort earned a reputation as the fashionable place to be among society folks.

The city faced a sad day in April of 1817, when the father of Cape May hospitality, Ellis Hughes, passed away at the Atlantic House. His son, William Hughes, inherited the property but kept it for only three years. In 1820, he sold it to Dr Roger Wales, who then sold it the next year. The new owner, Alexander McKenzie, made a number of improvements to the vintage hotel and greatly expanded the capacity. He also made improvements to the existing sleeping bays and enlarged the dining hall, which was used for dancing and live drama in the evenings.

Meanwhile, another landmark was emerging on the tip of the island. Cape May's first lighthouse was built in 1823, rising 68 feet from the sands on the beach of what would later become Cape May Point. The beacon was lit with burning whale oil and unlike today's lighthouses it did not blink.

Unfortunately, the tower was built far too close to the ocean and the land was pulled out from underneath it within 25 years, due to erosion.

In 1824, a third mode of transportation was

New Resort Gets Rave Reviews

Bathers enjoy Cape May's beach and surf in the early 1800s, with nary a swimsuit in sight *Greater Cape May Historical Society*

Excerpt from a letter in *The Richmond Enquirer*, **July 31, 1829**

TO A lady in our party, who had been here before and who has more tact than I have, we are indebted for being most comfortably fixed at Hughes', receiving every attention that the most fastidious could require from the landlord, his wife, the bar-keeper, and every domestic about the establishment. My visit has been but a flying one, and each day I have been more and more pleased, refreshed and invigorated; and, what is far more gratifying and apt to my purpose, my better half, as you know every man's wife is, in countries where the law allows him but one, she was so much debilitated when we arrived at Newcastle, that she could with difficulty walk to the steam-boat; already she is incredibly re-animated and strengthened, no longer fearing to expose her delicate frame to the buffetings of the stoutest wave; and when "the soft hour of walking comes" at noon, she can tread, with elastic step, the firm and beautiful sea-shore for miles, and then at night, as is the custom here, when music sounds, she can trip it lightly through the "mazy dance," leaving me, who, you know, am of sober turn, and not given to the lighter amusements of the world, either to talk sentiment aside with some fair lady, or to play in silence le role d' observateur.

The good landlord is ready to instruct you in all the modes, and to see that you are supplied with all the various means of amusements. And here I ought to describe some of them.

You breakfast at half past seven; for which you are prepared even though it may be against your lazy city habits, after the profound sleep which is so happily promoted by the murmur of the waves that roll so majestically and break in eternal succession on the shore. After breakfast, you amuse yourself in various ways according to your inclination, whether it be to walk, or to ride, to read or pitch quoits, or go shooting, to make love, or to philosophize, or to bowl at ten pins; nine pins being positively against the statute in such eases made and provided by the wise Legislature of New Jersey, that decided Mr Southard was no citizen of his own state, because he had sojourned for a time in Washington, where there are no citizens at all. Some make up parties, and ride in their Jersey-wagons, peculiar for their lightness and strength of structure and materials; one party going to the "cool spring," a pure, copious and delightful fountain that rises in the midst of a salt lake or pond, whist another rides by a shaded road to the lighthouse, three miles distant; and after climbing up, by one hundred steps, to the top, and looking out over the country and the ocean, presently comes flying home again on a shore so firm, that horses and vehicle scarcely leave an impression as you pass along.

The Baltimore Patriot, **August 11, 1828**

CAPE MAY – Among the different places of resort for health and recreation during the summer season, there is no one that offers more inducements than Cape May. The shore is generally admitted to be safer than any now used for bathing and other advantages peculiar to this place may be enumerated. On the Cape Island, as it is termed, there are at least twenty or thirty houses, of various sizes, for the accommodation of visitors, the most distant of which is sufficiently contiguous to the shore to be convenient. Of the houses, four or five are public establishments, calculated to accommodate a large number of persons, from fifty to two hundred. The principal establishment kept by Mr Hughes, has heretofore been known by the name of the "Big House," and is one of the largest houses of the kind in the United States. During the present season it has been named by the visitors "Congress Hall," and its new nomenclature was sealed with the ceremonies usually performed on such occasions. Besides this establishment, the houses kept by McKenzie, Bennet, and others, possess their peculiar advantages, and are worthy of public patronage.

THE WHALE HUNTERS

This page: A small whaling boat sits ready to be launched into the ocean, as the working men in this early 1800s picture take a short break.

Cape May County Museum

THE FIRST LIGHT

Opposite page: An artist's depiction of the original Cape May lighthouse, which was replaced in 1847

Cape May Point State Park

FROM THE ARCHIVES

Protecting The Harbor

The New England Palladium, **March 26, 1813**
Extract of a letter from Cape Island to the Editor *of the Freeman's Journal, dated March 17, 1813*

ON SUNDAY last a 74 came into the Capes of the Delaware, about five or six miles inside of the lighthouse, and anchored with her top gallant masts housed, and on Monday a frigate came and anchored two or three miles about the 74, where they still remain.

On Monday, the ship John Dickenson, Captain Baush, from Lisbon, came under Cape Island, got a pilot (William Eldridge), proceeded up the Bay, until bro't to by the ship's tenders, detained two or three hours, and then put her to sea again. The same day the barg Concord, of Philadelphia, came under Cape Island, and got a pilot (Joseph Way). She then proceeded up the Cape May channel, was cut off by the tender of the British ships, and is now lying at anchor about ten miles from the point of Cape May, up the Delaware, along with a fore-topsail such supposed to be from the northward, and a pilot boat, supposed to be the Joseph Sime, both prizes.

An Egg Harbour sloop was also taken inside of the Capes by the tenders, and is now with the 74, in Cape Henlopen road.

The people on Cape May are of opinion, that a few gun boats and small privateers might keep the Eastern channel clear of the British (as the force the now have, or can have, is small) owing to the shoalness of the water.

The tenders have been sounding the shores and attempted landing on Cape May, but were prevented by the militia.

added to the list of options for visitors wanting to sample this new resort. Wilmon Willdin, Sr, a Delaware River captain, bought a steamship and began making regular rounds between Philadelphia and Cape Island. Willdin's ship, *The Delaware*, quickly became the most popular mode of conveyance for travelers.

One ship turned into three and Captain Willdin grew his steamship business into a rousing success. He later expanded beyond Cape Island and began providing service to Virginia, Delaware and points on the Chesapeake Bay. When he retired from sailing he passed the reigns on to his son, Wilmon Willdin, Jr, who continued to run the steamships until the late 1800s.

The 1830s brought another major improvement to Cape Island, with the first schoolhouse built on the island. It was little more than a bare room with benches and tables, but it provided local children a place they could go to escape their daily work and focus on education. In the early 1800s, children were used for labor on their fathers' farms or fishing boats. The boys were expected to help with the manual labor, while the girls would work with their mothers in the kitchens.

Prior to the new schoolhouse, teachers made rounds throughout the county, stopping in different villages at specific times of year. They rarely made it to Cape Island and when they did most children were unable to attend classes because of their chores at home. With the new school, regular classes were established and parents could allow their children to attend classes in the morning, then return home to work in the afternoons.

ORIGINAL LIGHTHOUSE AT CAPE MAY.   REMOVED IN 1847.

CAPE CURIOSITY

African Americans On The Island

ONE OF the often-overlooked aspects of Cape May's history is the city's rich African-American heritage. Dating back to the early 1880s, the city has been a welcome retreat for people of all colors and home to a thriving black community. Even during the tumultuous Civil War days, Cape May remained free, even though there were some locals who favored secession from the union.

As the city grew during the Victorian years so, too, did the African-American neighborhood, which was primarily situated along Lafayette Street from Jefferson to Jackson streets. Segregation was the norm in America up until the 1950s and Cape May's black community had their own stores, restaurants and a separate school.

From the early years until 1928 the city's African-American children were primarily taught at home or in groups at the local church. In 1928 the Franklin Street School opened to serve the growing community and it continued as a segregated school for 20 years until New Jersey abolished the notion of "separate but equal" in 1948.

Along with the local population, Cape May also welcomed hundreds of African-American vacationers each season. Joining them were civil rights visionaries like Booker T. Washington and W. E. B. Dubois, both of whom stayed at the Hotel Dale.

The Hotel Dale was the largest and most prominent of the local hotels that catered to blacks, followed by the New Cape May Hotel, on the corner of Jackson and Broad. The Hotel Dale building was built in 1850 by Samuel S. Marcy and for the first 60 years of its life it was known as White Hall.

In 1911, a local African American entrepreneur named E. W. Dale purchased White Hall and opened for business later that season under the new name. Just prior to the reopening, Dale completed a number of additions on the old structure, including a new bar and entertainment hall, laundry facilities, a poolroom and tennis courts.

The Hotel Dale remained in business until 1935, when Dale made the decision to sell all his Cape May properties and move

The Hotel Dale was a favorite spot for African Americans in Cape May
Opposite page: Cape May had a thriving black community *Don Pocher*

away from the area. By the end of the following year, the hotel was razed by the city and the land was cleared.

In 1963 the land that once held the hotel's tennis courts was purchased by a family friend of E. W. Dale, John Nash. For Nash, the land held a sentimental value because he was born in a private home about one block away and he grew up in the shadow of the Hotel Dale.

Nash built a motel on the property and he ran it with his wife for 16 years. The motel is still standing today and goes by the name of Cape Winds. Next door, where the Hotel Dale had stood, two large homes were built, though Dale's old brick house is still standing on the corner.

Much of Cape May's original African-American community was bulldozed during the city's Urban Renewal initiative. To make way for a planned 'Victorian Village', an entire city block was leveled in was what once the heart of the black community. Today that land is home to Rotary Park and Lyle Lane, just north of the Washington Street Mall.

A Hotel Building Boom

B Y THE YEAR 1832 Cape Island had grown into a fully-fledged resort town. The island's population had risen to nearly 5,000 people, with a number of small guest houses and three hotels. Visitors had their choice of Atlantic Hall, Congress Hall or the new Mansion House.

The Mansion House was constructed in 1832, between Jackson and Perry streets, along the north side of Washington Street. It was the talk of the town due to its large stature and the modern accoutrements it offered, mainly separate rooms for all guests, along with plastered and lathed walls. Like its predecessors the Mansion House did not include exterior paint, though it did offer finished interior walls.

The hotel was built by Richard Smith Ludlam, who also had the distinction of establishing Washington Street. When Ludlam constructed the hotel he planned the street to create a new commercial district and connect his hotel with what was the commercial town center of Jackson Street. The first Washington Street ran approximately six blocks, at a width of 50 feet.

Cape Island continued to garner attention through Thomas Hughes, a United States Assemblyman and the owner of Congress Hall. Hughes took office in 1829 and served until 1833. While in office, he was present when the notion of a state seceding from the union was first brought forth by Robert Y. Hayne, a senator from South Carolina.

The debate between Hayne and Senator Daniel Webster from Massachusetts caught the attention of the country. The two senators argued over the merits of protectionist tariffs that were enacted after the war of 1812, during the presidency of John Quincy Adams. The tariffs were designed to promote American products over those made by the British.

The arguments were of particular interest to Hughes because Cape Island sailors were being accused of circumventing the tariffs by smuggling in foreign goods. In addition, Hughes had become friends with President Adams, who was elected to congress following his presidential term. Hughes and Adams listened intently as Hayne and Webster argued over the tariffs and the right of a state to leave the union.

It was only after the situation took a turn for the worse, when South Carolina passed a law to ignore the federal tariff law, that Hughes was forced to publicly take a side. South Carolina not only defied the federal rule, they authorized a state militia to stop federal troops from enforcing the tariffs.

Their actions created a constitutional crisis that required the immediate response of the federal government. Hughes voted to side with the American Union, a position that was widely supported in Cape May. Congress then passed a bill that authorized the president to use the US military as a means of enforcing the tariffs in South Carolina.

Luckily, the South Carolina legislature repealed its rebellious law against the tariff in 1833 and a crisis was averted. Congressman Hughes was able to return to Cape Island at the end of his term and spread the news that a civil war had been averted and that the American

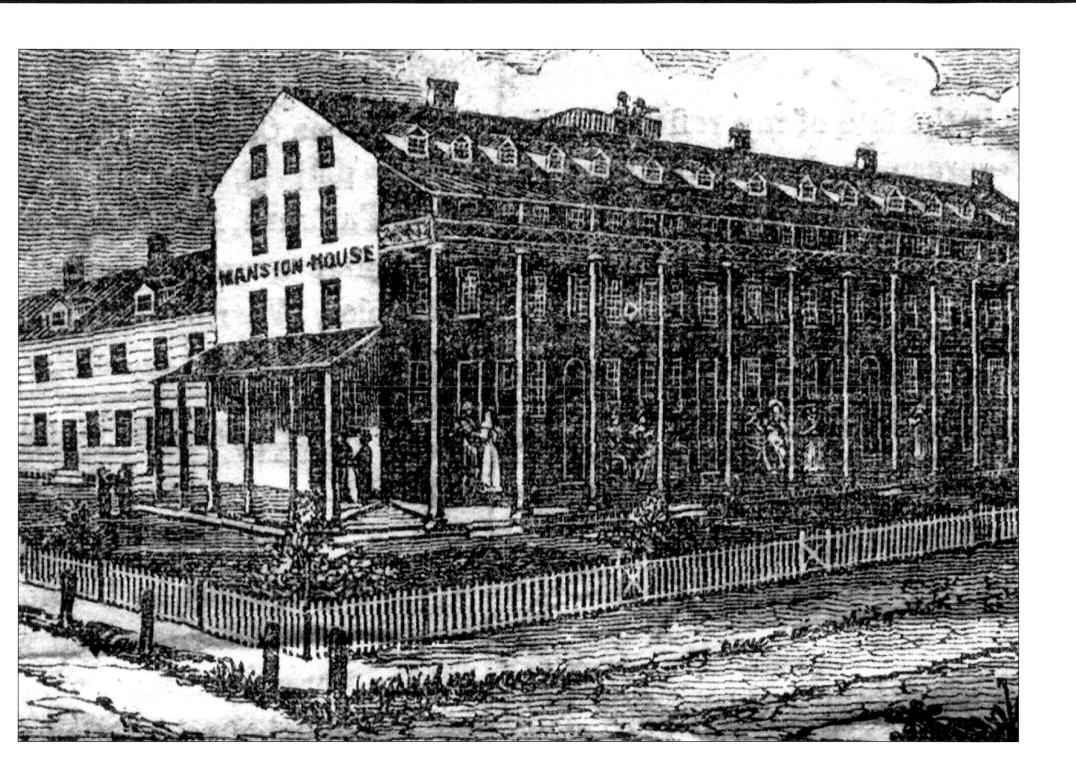

**CENTRE
OF FUN**
This page, top: The
Centre House was
a local hotspot for
live entertainment
in the late 1800s.
Like many other
great Cape May
hotels, it was
destroyed in the
inferno of 1878.
Don Pocher

**A NEW QUEEN
ON THE THRONE**
This page, below:
Princess Victoria
hears the news of
her ascension to
the throne in 1837
*The Letters Of
Queen Victoria*

**BEFORE
THE FIRE**
Opposite page:
The Ocean House
in 1876... two years
later, it was no
more
Don Pocher

Union remained strong.

Meanwhile, on Cape Island, summer tourism continued to grow and the official season for vacationers began on July 1 and ran through September 1. An increase in visitors called for the construction of new hotels and, in 1832, the Ocean House was built.

Situated along the eastern side of Perry Street, the Ocean House was conceived by Israel Leaming. Some history books have mistakenly claimed that the Ocean House was built in 1856, but period accounts of the hotel and vintage news articles have proven that to be incorrect. The confusion most likely stems from a substantial renovation and enlargement of the Ocean House that was completed in the mid-1850s.

The Ocean House was three-and-a-half stories tall, with a wraparound balcony on the third floor, a handful of attic rooms and another balcony on the roof. Its location across from Congress Hall's expansive front lawn meant that visitors to the Ocean House would be treated to panoramic views of the Atlantic Ocean.

In 1837 the death of England's King William IV paved the way for a new era in Great Britain and a change in the empire's stature around the globe. Since King William had no surviving children, his 18-year-old niece, Princess Victoria, was chosen to succeed him.

Princess Victoria became Queen Victoria and her ascension to the throne marked the beginning of the Victorian Era in Cape May and all around the world. Much has been said about Queen Victoria's rule, but history records that for the first half of her 64-year reign she lived a life of seclusion and relative unpopularity.

On Cape Island, residents welcomed the construction of another large hotel in 1840. The Centre House was built on Washington Street, opposite the popular Mansion House, and next to the Ocean House. By that time, Washington

Centre House. CAPE MAY, N. J.
Destroyed by Fire 1878.

Street had blossomed as the city's commercial district and other small businesses had been established near the hotels.

The Centre House was designed to merge the early-American style of architecture with the Second Empire look of Congress Hall. It was also the first boarding house on Cape Island to be painted — the owner chose an earth tone shade of brownish-yellow.

The Centre House was the largest of Cape Island's hotels, with the ability to accommodate 400 guests. The building spanned the whole block from Perry to Jackson streets with immense three-story columns adorning the hotel along Washington Street.

A GIANT OF THE SHORE
This page: Bath houses and a pavilion dot the grand Columbia House hotel's enormous front lawn in this 1850 picture
Don Pocher

A BUSY RESORT
Opposite page: The New Atlantic Hotel sits across the street from Cape May's first hostelry, the original Atlantic Hotel
Don Pocher

The next boarding house to be constructed in the budding seaside resort was the New Atlantic. The original Atlantic Hall had been purchased in March of 1839 by two brothers from Philadelphia. When Captain Benjamin McMakin and Captain Joseph McMakin bought it, they also purchased land across Jackson Street with the intention of expanding their business.

In 1842 the McMakin brothers had the New Atlantic built on that parcel of land and increased their lodging capacity by 300 beds. Their new hotel spanned 100 feet along what would later become Beach Drive and rose four stories tall. It featured large porches in front and a third floor balcony that wrapped around the building.

One of the most prominent features of the New Atlantic was its dining chamber. Patrons were welcomed into a gigantic hall that encompassed the full first floor of the hotel. Rather than occupying separate tables, as today's diners would expect, guests of the New Atlantic were seated at one of four long tables that ran the length of the hall.

The Cape Island hotel surge continued with the construction of the Columbia House in 1846. The Columbia House was built by a Delaware River captain named George Hildreth on a large plot of land between Decatur and Ocean streets. The parcel was nothing more than swampland when Hildreth bought it, so he hired laborers to fill in the bog with dirt and sand from the northern section of the island.

Hildreth's Columbia House was four stories tall and was considered the most elegant of the Cape Island hotels. Both interior and exterior walls were plastered and painted, with elaborate piazzas that followed the 180-foot length of the hotel. The Columbia House was later expanded into an L-shape, similar to Congress Hall, which doubled the number of rooms and made it the largest boarding house on the island.

The year 1851 brought the construction of yet another boarding house, the United States Hotel. Built by A. W. Tompkins the hotel was a huge four-story structure that sat on 10 acres spanning from Decatur to Ocean streets, along Washington Street. The United States quickly became one of the most popular hostelries in town, with its wide, sweeping verandas, panoramic ocean views and evening entertainment that amused guests and locals.

Cape Island was presented with the grandest spectacle of all in 1852 when construction began on the Mount Vernon Hotel, designed to be the largest in the world and including features that no Cape Island hotel had ever offered before or,

N.J. — Cape May
(50 yrs ago)

A GRAND SPACE
This page: A rarely-seen picture of the original Congress Hall dining room and ballroom shows the magnificent space decorated to the nines for a Fourth Of July ball
Don Pocher

for that matter, ANY hotel. The Mount Vernon, according to the *London Illustrated News*, was the first in the world to offer en suite bathrooms.

The building was purported to accommodate up to 3,500 people, a number that was unheard of in the early Victorian period. Plans for the hotel were elaborate and called for running hot and cold water, a pistol-firing range, bowling alleys and gas lighting in every room.

The hotel was funded by a number of investors in Philadelphia and New Jersey who teamed with a gentleman named John West and founded the Mount Vernon Hotel Company. The amount of work required to build their fantastic hotel was so great that it had to be undertaken in phases. This was done to allow the completed portions of the hotel to accommodate guests while the rest was still under construction.

Four years after building started, the Mount Vernon was able to accommodate a little more than 2,000 people. But, as the craftsmen were finishing up work on the last section of the hotel in September of 1856, tragedy struck. The hotel was empty, with the exception of the innkeeper, Phillip Cain, his four children, Anderson (20), Phillip Jr (18), Martha (16) and Sarah (13), along with a housekeeper, Anna Albertson. All were asleep on the second floor, when an unknown person broke in to the building and set it the fire.

Only Phillip Jr escaped, though he suffered severe burns and died the following afternoon in the United States Hotel. Before he passed, he was able to describe the scene in his family's apartment, as they realized they were trapped by the flames and tried to escape by jumping off the balcony or running through the flames.

Phillip's story was confirmed the following day, with the discovery of his older brother Anderson's charred body, curled on the ground in front of where the hotel once stood. Authorities suspected the fire to be arson almost immediately and one of the family's former house-

keepers was arrested for the murders. It was surmised that her reason for setting the fire was a money dispute with Phillip Cain. The housekeeper was also accused of stealing money from the hotel before she ignited the deadly fire.

The early Victorian period was especially important for the infrastructure of Cape Island, with the first local government being established in 1848. On March 8 of that year, the New Jersey General Assembly passed an act that officially incorporated Cape Island.

A temporary leadership chain was created with James Mecray named Chief Burgess and a small staff selected to help him run the new borough. Two years later, the General Assembly amended their previous designation and incor-

porated The City of Cape Island.

A new government structure was established with a mayor and six councilmen, along with an alderman and recorder. Isaac M. Church was the City of Cape Island's first mayor and the council comprised James Mecray, John G. W. Ware, Joseph Ware, Aaron Garretson, James S. Kennedy and David Pierson.

The city's alderman was Walter B. Miller, and Joseph S. Leach was the recorder. Cape Island's new leadership team met for the first time on March 15, 1851 in the Cape Island schoolhouse on the corner of Lafayette and Franklin Streets. Relatively little was done that evening in the way of legislation, but the foundation was laid for a strong city government.

The Legend Of The Blue Pig

From *A Book of Cape May, New Jersey*

GAMBLING in the country had reached a place of importance and by 1840 numerous gambling clubs had been formed in all resorts and were patronized extensively. The wealthy Southern planters, statesmen and many other prominent men of the day were devotees of the games of chance, and while the fact was generally known, it appeared to detract none from their social standing.

Some of the proprietors of these notorious clubs were widely known and achieved national prominence. Cape Island's most noted member of this fraternity was Henry Cleveland who conducted the club known as the Blue Pig, which was situated on Perry Street and Beach Avenue at the ocean end of Congress Hall's six-acre lawn. The Blue Pig was known throughout the North and South and its proprietor was as prominent as the famous Canfield of Saratoga Springs. Cleveland was notoriously lucky and amassed a tidy fortune; withal he had the reputation of being a sportsman and "square".

The noted Tennessee gambler, Pettibone, spent several summer seasons at the Cape.

Pettibone was said to have been one of the wealthiest gamblers, and his marital affairs created some interest, he having married three times and then completed the cycle by remarrying his first wife. One of the popular stories of the Blue Pig is that of a dashing New York widow who won upwards of $50,000 one evening and was never again seen in the club. The Blue Pig, a two-story building of the cottage type, was afterwards moved to North and Congress Streets and is today a private dwelling.

There were at least two other gambling clubs much patronized, and both buildings are still standing. The larger of the two is located at Howard Street and Columbia Avenue, and the third is now occupied by the Christian Science reading rooms at Ocean Street and Columbia Avenue. This club had a room without windows or a visible door which has often been visited by the curious.

[Author's note: The Blue Pig building is still standing today and it has remained a private residence. The location of Ocean Street that was referenced is now known as The House of Royals and it is part of the Queen Victoria Bed and Breakfast. The third gambling house that was mentioned as being on the corner of Columbia Avenue and Howard Street is now the Mainstay Bed and Breakfast.

It's interesting to note the Mainstay is actually on the corner of Columbia Avenue and Stockton Place, but at the time this narrative was written, Stockton Place did not yet exist. The single block that ran alongside the Mainstay building was considered an extension of Howard Street.]

Above: The old Blue Pig casino, where it now sits on the corner of Windsor and North *Greater Cape May Historical Society* **Top left: The gambling hall on Ocean Street is now part of the Queen Victoria B&B** *National Archives* **Top: The Mainstay Inn was formerly an infamous gambling club** *National Archives*

CAPE CURIOSITY

The Keeper Of The Light

ILLUMINATING the night up to 24 miles out to sea the Cape May lighthouse has guided sailors for more than 180 years. The present structure that can be seen towering over the State Park at Cape May Point has only been in place since 1859. Prior to that, two other lighthouses helped ships navigate in the Delaware Bay and Atlantic Ocean.

What is believed to be the first lighthouse was built in 1823 and rose to a height of 68 feet. For the sake of comparison, the present one is 157 feet tall.

There's been some debate on whether or not the 1823 tower was, in fact, the first. Public records show a land purchase in 1785, with a notation that the land was to be used for a beacon. An advertisement that appeared in a Philadelphia newspaper in 1801 also spoke of the "... confluence of Delaware Bay with the ocean, in sight of the lighthouse..."

Supporters of the notion of an earlier lighthouse have also claimed that President George Washington spoke to congress about the issue in 1790. Fortunately, President Washington's entire speech was recounted in a 1791 edition of *Clay Poole's Daily Advertiser* and it debunks the idea.

While it's true the president did mention the erecting of a lighthouse on Cape Island in 1800,

he was referencing a message he had received from the governor of North Carolina. It seems the General Assembly of that state enacted a plan to build two lighthouses, including one on 'Cape Island.' Further research has revealed that the first Cape Hatteras lighthouse in North Carolina was constructed between 1799 and 1802.

The US government officially recognizes Cape May's 1823 lighthouse as the first and has pointed to a 1790 report by former Secretary of the Treasury, Alexander Hamilton, to back up that claim. Hamilton noted in his report that there was no lighthouse in Cape May.

With hindsight, the 1823 lighthouse was unfortunately constructed a little too close to the water. Due to a series of brutal storms, the land was eroded out from underneath it by the Atlantic Ocean.

A second beacon was built as a replacement in 1847. In what would prove to be a bad decision, it was hastily constructed so that it could be placed into service as quickly as possible. The newer tower was placed further inland and the height was increased to 78 feet tall. The additional elevation made it much more visible to the sailors, who relied on the light for navigation.

TAKEN BY THE SEA
Cape May Point's second lighthouse was almost completely demolished when its replacement was built in 1859, save for a one-story section that was covered over and used for storage. That last piece of the old beacon was crushed in the 1962 nor'easter and eventually succumbed to the encroaching sea.
Cape May Point State Park

The builders employed a certain level of urgency, which meant that corners were cut in the construction. Mainly, the tower walls were not as thick as they should have been and the entire structure soon became unstable. As a result, the United States Lighthouse Service was forced to build a third tower, only 12 years later.

This third building is the one that stands at Cape May Point today. Construction began in 1857 and was completed in 1859. It was built much differently than the previous two. The third lighthouse was erected with two separate walls to increase the stability and longevity of the structure.

It was also designed to endure winds more powerful than those of a major hurricane, thanks to a design that called for the outside wall to taper as the height increased. It measures almost four feet thick at the bottom and 18 inches thick at the top. The inside wall is just under nine inches thick from top to bottom and supports the spiral staircase.

The lighthouse holds the distinction of being built by a man who would go on to shape the course of American history. Long before he was leading the Union Army to victory at Gettysburg, Major General George Meade managed the construction of the Cape May project. Meade also helped construct similar structures in Absecon and Barnegat while he worked with the Army Corps of Engineers.

The third lighthouse originally featured an original Fresnel lens with 16 flash panels. Its lamps were first lit on Halloween night, 1859, sending a white beam of light out into the

GETTING TO THE POINT
This page, top:
The electric trolley travels between Cape May and the Point in this early 1900s picture, which shows the lighthouse in the background
Cape May Point State Park

THE LAST REMNANTS
This page, below:
An amateur photographer snaps a shot of the remains of the second lighthouse in 1963, before it was washed away completely
Cape May Point State Park

A CELEBRITY SIGHTING
Opposite page:
Statesman Henry Clay paid a visit to Cape May in 1847 and the local women were enthralled
National Archives

darkness every 30 seconds. The lanterns were kept burning by whale oil and tended by professional keepers. The men who kept the Cape May light going were employed by the government and lived with their families in the adjacent quarters.

In 1938 a change was made in the lighthouse operation that made the keeper virtually obsolete. The beacon was converted to electric, with a 250-watt bulb installed that had the ability of casting a beam up to 19 miles at sea. One year later, in 1939, the coast guard assumed control of the nation's lighthouses and the United States Lighthouse Service was dissolved.

The electric bulbs burned in the tower until 1941, when it was purposely extinguished on account of World War II. The entire coast was ordered to go dark in an effort to confuse enemy ships and prevent a surprise night landing by invading armies.

In 1946, operations resumed in the lighthouse and the lamp began flashing once again. The original Fresnel lens was removed and replaced with a more modern, rotating lens. The 250-watt bulb was also replaced with a powerful 1000-watt light. The coast guard completely automated the lighthouse and with the new system in place, the beacon flashed in a continuous 15-second pattern.

The lighthouse sat solitary for more than 40 years, until an arrangement was made to restore the structure and open it to the public. Visitors and residents who enjoy seeing the Cape May lighthouse in all it present glory we a debt of gratitude to the Mid-Atlantic Center for the Arts. The non-profit organization began leasing the structure from the Coast Guard in 1986 and petitioned the government for financial grants to aid in the restoration.

More than two million dollars in grant money was received for the overhaul, with MAC largely to thank. The organization has worked with a

number of agencies to acquire the money and has overseen all restoration work at the lighthouse.

To make the process even smoother, the coast guard officially sold the beacon to the State of New Jersey in 1992.

Now that the lighthouse is once again in great shape and looking beautiful in the original daymark (the red-and-beige color pattern on the outside), MAC offers daily tours to the general public. Visitors are able to climb 199 steps of the old spiral staircase to the top and catch the same inspiring views of the Cape May coastline that greeted lighthouse keepers 150 years ago.

FROM THE ARCHIVES

The Arrival Of Henry Clay

From *The History of Cape May County*

IT WAS in 1847 that Henry Clay, the great Kentuckian, came to Cape May, and Mr Ludlam years afterward said: "The big time was when Harry Clay came. He had been at the White Sulphurs, and said he had notion to go to some of the Northern watering places: that was in 1857. So I sent him an invitation and he accepted, and stopped at the Mansion House for a week. It was in the latter part of August, and the people had before that thinned out. When, however, it was announced that Harry Clay was to be here, the place filled up to overflowing. Two steamboat loads came on from New York. They wanted him there. Horace Greeley came down to see him, and the people from Salem and Bridgeton and all the country around flocked in their carry-alls to Cape May to see Harry of the West."

As soon as it was known that Clay was to become a visitor the people began to arrive from all over the Middle and Southern states. United States Senator James A. Bayard, of Wilmington, accompanied by Charles C. Gordon, of Georgia, was among the first to arrive. On the Saturday previous there came a large party from Philadelphia. Clay had come by stage and rail, so far as there was any, to Philadelphia, being greeted on his route by hosts of friends who had, and by others who had not, cast their ballots for him three years previous, when he ran for the presidency against Polk. Clay came for rest, and to wear away sorrow which had come upon him by the killing of his son in the Mexican War.

On the morning of Monday, August 16, 1847, the great statesman, with his party, left Philadelphia on the steamboat then plying between that place and Cape Island, and arrived at the landing about one o'clock in the afternoon.

The party was driven over the turnpike to the Mansion House, where a big dinner was in waiting for the distinguished guests. The band engagement having expired before this event, Beck's Philadelphia band was brought down on the boat with Mr Clay. The old hotel register, which is still preserved, has upon it the names of the Kentuckians who came that day.

Mr Clay was given a rest on his arrival, but on the following was his busiest while on Cape May's grand beach. During the day many more arrived, and the Island was filled with country folks anxious to see the great man. Rev Moses Williamson made the address of welcome, to which Mr Clay fittingly responded in words that electrified his listeners. Among other things he remarked to a friend that Mr Williamson made one of the best addresses of the kind he ever heard, and made many inquiries about the good and well-known divine. Mr Clay's magnificent language, says one who heard him, held the crowds spellbound. After the speech-making there was hand-shaking and a grand feast. The speech-making took place in the old "Kersal," the music pavilion and ballroom of the hotel, which had been built in the spring of that year.

Mr Clay was received on the part of the county of Cape May by Dr Maurice Beesley. During his visit there were more arrivals each day than there had been for any previous day of that summer. While at Cape May Mr Clay loved bathing and went in as often as twice a day, and it was while enjoying it that he lost a great deal of his hair. The ladies would catch him and with a pair of scissors, carried for just that purpose, clip locks from his head to remember him by. When he returned to Washington his hair was very short, indeed.

Tragedy At The World's Biggest Hotel

From *The Maryland Sun*, September 8, 1856

TERRIBLE DISASTER AT CAPE ISLAND
Destruction of the Mt Vernon Hotel
Five Persons Burned to Death
Only One Survivor of the Family of Mr Cain

THE mammoth Mount Vernon Hotel, at Cape Island, NJ, took fire on Friday night, at a quarter to 11 o'clock, and was entirely consumed.

The other hotels escaped uninjured. The origin of the fire is unknown. Mr Cain, the lessee of the house, was residing in the building, and had retired previous to the alarm of fire. His son, Phillip Cain, Jr, escaped from the building by leaping from the second story window, but was badly burned, and lies at the point of death.

With the exception of the son, the whole of Mr Cain's family perished in the flames. The following is a list of those lost:

Phillip Cain, Sr, the lessee; Andrew Cain, Martha Cain, Sarah Cain and Mrs Albertson.

The charred remains of Mr Cain were found on Saturday morning. *The Philadelphia Bulletin* says:

Mr Phillip Cain, Sr, with Colonel Frank T. Foster, of this city, were the proprietors of the ill-fated hotel. Mr Cain resided at Vincentown, NJ, and went to Cape Island the present season for the purpose of opening the hotel. He was 65 years of age.

Andrew Cain, his son, was about 20 years of age. Martha was in her seventeenth year, and Mary was but 13.

Mrs Albertson was 35 years of age. She was a widow. She had gone to the island to act as housekeeper of the hotel.

The elder Mr Cain leaves a wife and several children in Vincentown. Mrs Albertson also resided there. Young Phillip Cain is about 19 years of age.

The Mount Vernon was built by a company of gentlemen at a cost of $125,000, upon which there is not one cent of insurance.

People often assume that the picture of the Mount Vernon Hotel on the opposite page shows the view from the beach. In fact, this is looking from the north, toward the ocean. Note the sailboat in the left of the picture *Don Pocher*

The building was first occupied in 1853, but Messrs Cain & Foster did not become the lessees until the past season. The hotel was celebrated for its immense size and for the superior accommodations the building afforded to guests. The interior was well finished, and the apartments were larger and more comfortable than usual at watering-place hotels.

Although the hotel, in its late condition, was capable of accommodating 2100 visitors, it was not finished at the time of destruction. It was designed to have the buildings occupy three sides of a hollow square, or courtyard, and the front range and one wing were up.

One wing had never been commenced. The building was constructed entirely of wood; it was four stories in height in the main, with four towers each five stories in height. Three of these towers occupied the corners of the building, and one stood midway of the only wing.

In addition to these towers, there was an immense tower six stories in height in the centre of the front. The entire structure, both outside and upon the court-yard, was surrounded with wooden piazzas that extended from the ground to the roof, with floors at each story. The wing was a quarter of a mile in length, and the front covered nearly an equal extent of ground. The dining room, which was 425 feet long, and 60 feet in width, was capable of accommodating 3000 persons. There were 432 rooms in the building. It was claimed that the Mount Vernon was the largest hotel in the world.

In addition to the main building there was a stabling for fifty horses, carriage houses, ten-pin alleys, &c, &c.

Melancholy as the disaster is, it is a most fortunate circumstance that the fire did not occur during the bathing season. There were no guests in the house at the time, and Colonel Foster, the surviving proprietor, was in this city.

The Mount Vernon stood at a considerable distance from the other houses on the Island, or the destruction of the property would have been still greater. Had the flames communicated to the more densely built portions of the town, Cape Island would probably have been laid in ruins, as the hotels and other buildings are all of the most combustible description, and there is no fire apparatus in the place.

There was a tank in the centre tower of the wing of the Mount Vernon capable of holding twenty thousand gallons of water. The water was forced into it by a steam engine. The furniture of the hotel belonged to Messrs Cain & Foster. It was valued at $21,000, upon which there was no insurance. The total pecuniary loss by the conflagration will not fall short of $150,000.

Latest by Telegraph
PHILADELPHIA, September 6 – The passengers from Cape May report that nine persons were burned by the fire at Mount Vernon Hotel. Mrs Cain was not among the victims. Most of the furniture had been previously removed by the proprietors.

An Irish woman had been arrested for setting fire to the building.

MOUNT VERNON HOTEL.

CHAPTER SIX
Good Times, Bad Times

**PRIMITIVE
EQUIPMENT**
**This page: Cape
May's first fire
apparatus is
shown in this
1860 photograph**
*Cape May County
Museum*

**READ ALL
ABOUT IT!**
**Previous page: A
vintage photograph
shows the Cape
May Daily Star
newspaper being
delivered by horse-
drawn wagon.**
*Cape May County
Museum*

**A JEWEL IN
THE CROWN**
**Opposite page:
The United States
Hotel was located
on the corner of
Washington and
Ocean streets
and is beautifully
represented in
this late 1800s
illustration**
National Archives

THE 1860s were tumultuous years for the new city of Cape Island, filled with both great prosperity and suffering. While the hotels continued to welcome large numbers of visitors each season, the southern travelers abruptly stopped coming to the Cape.

The state of affairs with South Carolina that Congressman Hughes was party to years earlier had escalated to a grave level. Even with South Carolina's capitulation to the federal government over the issue of tariffs the southern countrymen remained uneasy about the national government.

Even in remote Cape Island, which had been secluded from most of the nation's previous hostilities, villagers and visitors anticipated the impending confrontation. Joseph S. Leach, editor of the *Cape May Ocean Wave*, discussed the situation in a December 13, 1860 editorial...

DISSOLUTION OF THE UNION

We have not much space to say much... Suffice it to say, that the peril is imminent; and those who have hitherto clung to the anchor of hope, now nearly despair of success; and we greatly fear the worst, while we faintly hope for the best. The succession feeling in the South is deepening and widening, and there is no use in attempting to disguise the fearful aspect of the present dreary and beclouded political skies.

Cape Island remained an ardent supporter of the union and two weeks after Leach's editorial, Mayor Joseph Ware called a meeting to discuss the situation. A resolution was drafted that demonstrated the town's support and pledged to take any necessary actions to help preserve the union.

Even with the backing of the city and most of its citizens there was still a small group

who dissented and favored secession from the union. The faction tried to assemble but they were unable to muster any real support.

There were two attempts at publicizing their feelings by flying South Carolina flags from city flagpoles, in reference to the state's recent declaration of secession from the union on December 20 of that year. Both displays were met with stiff resistance and the flags were burned at an impromptu union rally.

The secessionist movement escalated dramatically on April 12, 1861 when confederate forces began firing on Fort Sumter in South Carolina. By the end of the next day, the union forces had surrendered the fort to the confederates and the American Civil War had begun.

On April 27, Cape May County leadership held a convention at the courthouse to garner

support for President Lincoln and the American Union. The meeting was well attended by residents of Cape Island, who were concerned of a possible confederate attack on the Cape.

City delegates pledged that Cape Island would create a military unit to join others from the county and fight the confederacy. Local resident Henry Sawyer was the first to sign up for the unit and his enthusiastic backing of the group persuaded others to follow his lead.

In addition, another company would be mustered to remain in the area and defend the cape from any attacks. The Cape Island Home Guards, as they were called, were led by Captain John West.

The home guards were initially supplied with arms and ammunition, then later a large cannon affectionately known as "Long Tom."

FROM THE ARCHIVES

The Miracles Of Salt Water

From *The Weekly Patriot and Union*, August 8, 1867

I HAVE been down here for the past few days "looking around," and although the weather has not been very pleasant, I have had a very pleasant time of it "floundering" (flounders cost six cents a pound) around the sounds, with a "bluefish wriggling on a line."

This is the season here for the fishing rod and dog and gun, for there are so many inlets, and outlets, and house lets, that if you have any "music in your soul" you can get along quite comfortably, particularly if you are centered at the cottage of ye Mecray Jerry.

The poets have sung all kinds of songs about "the sea, in the open sea," and although they have not wasted much sentiment, it is a great waste of water, which is very beneficial to health during the "dog days." There is nothing so exhilarating and invigorating as a healthy rouse into the inviting breakers when the thermometer gets above ninety and is rapidly running up to a hundred. Then the ladies, the dear creatures, how they enjoy an ocean bath. They envelope their precious little bodies into a bloomer dress of many bright colors, and trustingly lean on the arm of their "dear Charles, "dear Henry," or "dear Augustus," and submissively kiss the cool cheek of old Neptune, with a slight scream, so that their dears can press them more closely to the bosom of old ocean.

The ladies, for without them we would not have any mothers or sisters, have a great

The old Columbia House was the first of the early hotels to include trees and landscaping
Opposite page: Cape May's famed Columbia Avenue in the 1890s *Both illustrations courtesy of Don Pocher*

weakness for sea bathing, and I do not wonder at it, for it brings the roses to their cheeks, elasticity to their steps, and wonderfully improves their appetites.

Now a man who had a beloved mother, a charming wife, a beautiful sister, that does not take them down to Cape May, should be voted a deuced mean fellow. Don't you think so, ladies? Or if he, unfortunately, has neither mother, wife, nor sister, let him take somebody else's sister, for Cape Island is one of the most lovingest places you ever did see. Salt water is a great healer of the heart disease, and puts many an odd greenback into the pockets of the clerical profession.

Cape Island as a bathing resort has many advantages over any place on this continent, or any other continent. Nature, in her kindness to the sandy soil of New Jersey, picked out the spot as a paradise for seekers after health and pleasure.

You would be astonished at the many improvements which have taken place on the Island during the past few years. Cottages are springing up everywhere. Some of them are very beautiful indeed, costing from ten to thirty thousand dollars each. The taste displayed

speaks well for the liberality of the owners of them.

The coming season promises to be a brilliant one. All the large hotels are preparing for it. The noise of the hammer, saw and plane, almost drowns the incessant roar of the ocean.

By-the-by, speaking of the Hotels, reminds me that I met one of your townsmen here last week, Mr George J. Bolton, of the Bolton House. He was here for the purpose of putting to rights the Columbia House, which he has kept (and he knows "how to keep a hotel") for the past three or four years. The "Columbia" is the acknowledged fashionable resort, and is certainly the most comfortable and eligibly situated Hotel on the Island. I need scarcely say to you that Mr Bolton is the Prince of Hotel keepers, and that by his courteous and affable manners, he had "won golden opinions" from all sorts of people. The "natives" here say (and they ought to know everything) that he is the most popular gentleman that ever conducted a Hotel on the Island. And then he has a faculty of securing the services of good men about him.

Mr Bolton is one of those straightforward, indefatigable practical businessmen that is

bound to succeed in everything he undertakes. A large number of rooms have already been engaged at the Columbia, and I presume the same may be said of the American, as well as some of the other first class hotels.

A new enterprise has been undertaken by some public spirited gentlemen in establishing a driving park and hotel association on "Diamond Beach." It is situated about five miles from the Island, and the drive to it during the season will be most delightful.

The hotel, with double porticos all around, is being rapidly pushed to completion. The driving track will be one mile in length, and it is thought will be one of the finest in the country. The grounds are situated on a bluff, overlooking the bay, and comprise one hundred and twenty-three acres, with an abundance of shade trees. The stock of the company is held by twenty gentlemen, and at no time will any of it be put upon the public market for sale. No gambling of any kind will be allowed on the premises.

"Diamond Beach" has always been a favorite resort of the ladies in quest of the brilliant Cape May pebbles, and its attractions will now be greatly enhanced.

It is expected that the park will be open for visitors about the first of July. Another improvement worthy of note is the filling, grading and laying out of lots and streets upon a vacant piece of land opposite the Columbia House. This property belongs to Messrs John C. Bullitt and Frederick Fairthorne, of Philadelphia, and the improvements are under their management.

Through these improvements, Ocean Street, upon which stands the Columbia House, will be extended in width and otherwise much improved, and thereby rendered the finest avenue to the beach on the Island. Mr Bullitt has for some years taken an active interest in the welfare of Cape May and many of its attractions and advantages have been secured through his personal efforts.

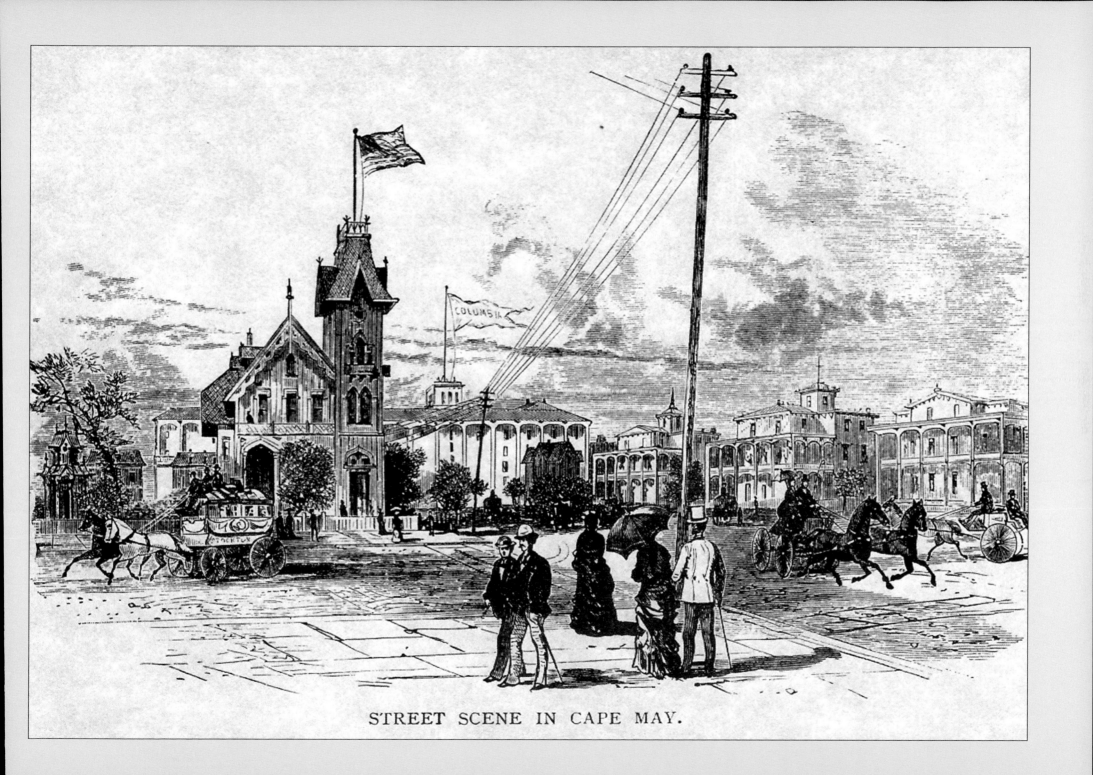

STREET SCENE IN CAPE MAY.

A GLASSY
OPERATION
This page, left:
Workmen load sand
from the beach
into carriages in
this late 1800s
photo. Cape May
Point was the home
of a glass-making
factory that used
large quantities of
local sands in their
products
*Cape May County
Museum*

FAMILY
OUTING
This page, right:
A horse-drawn
carriages carries
a load of children
alongside the
boardwalk in this
early photograph
*Cape May County
Museum*

PLAYING AT
THE POINT
Opposite page: A
couple of young
Victorian ladies flirt
with the camera
in front of Villa
Lankenau in Cape
May Point around
the turn of the
century
*Cape May County
Museum*

*Digging Sand
Cape May*

The cannon was received by the county after the war of 1812, but it was inoperable. When county leadership was initially approached by the home guards, who requested their help in having the artillery piece repaired, they refused. However, after the hostilities moved northward and the cape was proven vulnerable to an invasion, the necessary funds were quickly appropriated and the cannon was placed back into service.

As the war raged on against the Confederate States of America, Cape Island residents remained vigilant and ardent supporters of the union. One of the greatest symbols of the city's commitment to its country was Henry Sawyer himself.

Sawyer returned to Cape Island in the end of 1861, having been commissioned a second lieutenant and served his first enlistment. He immediately reenlisted a second and then a third time. In October of 1862 he was promoted to the rank of captain and given command of Company K in the First New Jersey Cavalry.

Sawyer's fortunes took a turn for the worse in the following year when he was wounded and taken prisoner by confederate forces at the battle of Brandy Station. He was subsequently transported to Libby Prison in the confederate capital of Richmond, Virginia.

Conditions in the prison were harsh and many prisoners lost their lives through neglect and maltreatment. Sawyer was forced to confront a different fate after he was selected for execution through a lottery amongst the prisoners. The confederacy was upset with the execution of two of their soldiers at union hands, so they planned to put to death Sawyer and another soldier in retaliation.

After the intervention of President Lincoln himself, Sawyer's life was spared. A trade of prisoners was arranged between the warring sides and Sawyer was exchanged for the son of confederate leader Robert E. Lee. By the end of the Civil War, Sawyer had received a total of four wounds and risen through the ranks to become a lieutenant colonel.

Thanks to the vigilance and protection of the Cape Island Home Guards, no attack on Cape May was ever attempted.

After General Lee surrendered to the union's General Grant in April of 1865 the victorious soldiers returned to Cape Island and it was, once again, business as usual.

Just prior to the end of the war, Cape Islanders witnessed another event that would prove to be integral to the continued growth and success of the resort. In the summer of 1863 the final track was laid in the railroad between Philadelphia and Cape Island. With the driving of those final rail nails the resort suddenly became accessible to thousands of potential vacationers.

Farming and fishing continued to be popular on the island and the hospitality industry grew stronger than ever before. It has been estimated that the total of summer visitors in 1865

surpassed 50,000 as the war's end brought the return of southern vacationers.

That jump in prosperity also led to a new round of construction for hotels and cottages. The two biggest were the New Lincoln and the Sherman House, which were both constructed on Jackson Street.

The city government also made significant capital improvements to the town's infrastructure. Drainage lines were dug to facilitate the removal of rain or flood waters, roads were rebuilt, a city water system was established and Beach Avenue was created.

Contrary to popular belief, the name of the road was originally Beach Drive. This is documented in both historical documents and 19th-century maps. It was not until the 20th century that the name was inexplicably changed to Beach Avenue.

The year 1867 marked the takeover of the Cape May and Millville railroads by the West Jersey Railroad, which quickly began work on

a new hotel of their own. The Sea Breeze, as it was known, was completed the following year on the former Mount Vernon Hotel property.

The Sea Breeze was more of an excursion house than a hotel, meaning it catered to both day-trippers and people staying overnight. There was a large dining room that could seat around 1,500 people, a tavern, billiards room, bowling alleys and two upper floors of sleeping quarters for those who did choose extended stays.

That same year the name Cape Island was tossed aside when the New Jersey Legislature re-chartered the town as the City of Cape May. The newly-renamed city welcomed a boom in construction, with the building of 68 new cottages in and around the city limits.

In December the West Jersey Railroad began work on a new hotel project that promised to be the biggest of its kind on the island. The railroad chose a location between Columbia Avenue and the beach, from Gurney and How-

ard streets. There was little more than sand on the lot when it was purchased, and part of the land parcel was actually under water.

During particularly high tides the water was known to come as far inland as Columbia Avenue. To remedy the situation the railroad hired laborers to bring fill from East Cape May to level off the land and make it suitable for their new hotel. It took the workers months to complete, but their hard work paid off.

The railroad's new hotel, the Stockton, opened for business at the beginning of the 1869 season. Much like the Mount Vernon developers promised years earlier, the Stockton was considered to be the largest hotel in the United States. With 475 guest rooms, two very large dining rooms, a theatre and numerous other amenities, the Stockton was the biggest and best that Cape May had ever seen.

With the publicity caused by the opening of the new Stockton Hotel, Cape May had the best season the city had ever experienced. Unfor-

tunately, the year's good fortune took a devastating and unexpected turn at around three o'clock in the morning, on August 31.

In a small Washington Street shop known as the Japanese Store an unknown arsonist started a fire. Almost immediately the Japanese Store was engulfed in flames, which spread to the nearby Post Office and then to the United States Hotel, which was almost completely occupied with guests.

Within hours the fire grew into a monstrous inferno that devoured a quarter of the city and left nothing but ashes in its wake.

A *New York Times* article dated September 1, 1869 noted, "Almost in a moment this last was but a huge ball of fire, and as it shot out 'forked tongues of flames,' it was seen that the great United States Hotel nearby was doomed. The guests hurriedly poured out in a great crowd, men, women and children, scarcely clothed, and unnerved by fright... The great hotel, in a

few moments, was like the Post Office, enveloped in flames, which cast its lurid light far out upon the ocean."

A *Cape May Wave* article later explained the reason the fire spread so rapidly from the Japanese Store to the rest of the city: "A few men had assembled... but without a leader each set to work to break in windows, knock down doors, and create a vent for the fire to reach the adjoining two-story building on the west, which was soon enveloped in flames... through misdirected energy, the Post Office building was broken open on the eastern side so as to provide a vent for the flames to reach the United States Hotel."

When the fire was finally extinguished and the damage could be tallied, residents of Cape May finally learned the toll flames had taken on their city. The United States Hotel, the New Atlantic and the American Hotel were also lost, along with 20 other homes and businesses. In

addition, the post office and other city offices were destroyed.

The culprit was never determined, though many in town blamed the fire on the proprietor of the Japanese Shop, Peter Paul Boynton. Boynton was well-known around Cape May as The Pearl Diver and had made a career as a sort of lifeguard for hire. Boynton knew the ocean well and was credited with saving a total of 75 people who were in danger of drowning.

After the accusations against Boynton were made public he was forced to appear in court and face the charges that he set the fire. He vehemently denied the accusations and explained that, along with all his wares, he also kept his life's savings in the store and lost everything in the fire.

Taking into consideration Boynton's personal losses and the lack of any credible evidence against him, he was found not guilty and released. The 1869 fire remains unsolved.

FROM THE ARCHIVES

Memories Of A Pupil

An excerpt from *The Inkwell*, detailing 1868 schooling in Cape May

THE city of Cape May is proud, and justly so, of the educational advantages it affords, of the ability and capability of its teaching force, and more than anything else of the enduring character of the instruction given and the high standing of the graduates, many of whom have attained eminence in other fields.

The writer, who was born in Cold Spring, moved to Cape Island in 1867, and from there to Jersey City in 1872, spending 52 years in and around New York City, and returning to Cape May in 1924, has been asked to give a few reminiscences of the early days, and offers these as far as memory serves him.

Cape Island, as the town was named in 1867, but changed January 15, 1869, to the City of Cape May, had about half the population it has today and one school, at Washington and Queen Streets, familiarly called The Indian Queen. My father, who taught various schools in the Lower Township, had been supplementing the public school instruction by taking private scholars, to whom he taught higher branches and prepared for college, for even in those days the people wanted the best obtainable. His rates were from $3 to $6 a term, according to the character of the instruction and the age of the pupil. We note that a few of those private scholars are still alive and more or less active, also that in 1866 he had a school of about 40 students, but received only $154.10 for their tuition.

The old schoolhouse proving inadequate for

The old Cape May High School, now the site of an ACME, in Washington Commons Mall *Don Pocher*

the needs of the growing population, in 1868 the present building on Franklin Street was erected and opened in the fall and the Indian Queen was abandoned. And there on the opening day I entered as a pupil. The one incident that remains most firmly fixed in my mind is that when we were dismissed in the middle of the morning for a short recess, but which I thought was for dinner, I hied me home, only to be "warmed," as mother called it, and sent back.

The structures now used as City Hall and Fire House were not yet built, but the jail had just been constructed, and there was nothing between it and Washington Street. One of the children's sources of diversion was looking at and talking to such of the prisoners as looked out from behind the bars. Another was testing the new coal tar pavement which the town had laid in front of the school and seeing how far they could sink their feet in it on very hot days without being caught altogether. Needless to say, that pavement didn't last long.

There was no Fire Department; in fact, the town had no fire apparatus at all and on august 31, 1869, a fire occurred that destroyed all that portion between Washington Street and the ocean, between Ocean and Jackson Streets, including three large hotels: the United States, American House and the Atlantic. This led to the eventual organization of a Fire Department, the nucleus of which was a Babcock fire extinguisher.

Joseph Q. Williams was mayor; George B. Cake, Wm S. Schellenger, Samuel R. Ludlam, John W. Blake, James Mecray, Jr, Samuel R. Magonagle, Councilmen; Samuel R. Stites, City Clerk; Eldredge Johnson, Treasurer; Thomas B. Hughes, Recorder; and my father, John W. Lycett, Alderman, and the sponsor of the resolution changing the name of the town to Cape May. I cannot recall and Board of Education, although there was one. The Town Hall was on the opposite side of Franklin Street.

Nicholas Corson was the Principal, or main teacher, with one lady assistant, Miss Johns.

Everybody knew him as Nick, "Old Nick," we children disrespectfully called him behind his back. Before we moved away he was displaced by A. L. Haynes. At that time the Principal had, in a way, more extended duties and responsibilities than at present, and the position was taken on contract to supply other teachers necessary and janitor service also, the town supplying, I think the books and stationary required. A bill from J. Swain Garrison, who furnished the text books on the list, and one set of Cube Root Blocks. The quantities supplied were small, but the books were all standard, such as *Wilson's Readers*, *Greenleaf's Arithmetics*, *Warren's Geographys*, *Spencer's Copy Books*, etc. I still have my old Reader, as a cherished memento.

As today, the instruction given was thorough, and what we learned in the old Franklin Street School formed the foundation, and a perfect one, for future requirements. I remember that my older sister in her first term in Jersey City took the honors of the class, and the Jersey City Evening Journal, commenting on it, praised the excellence of the instruction apparently being given in Cape May, as demonstrated by the acquired knowledge of Miss Lizzie Lycett, who recently came from there. The local papers here published the note.

And there are numerous others who can bear the same testimony. We believe that the foundation laid to our education in Franklin Street is responsible for much of the success that attended us in New York, and that today, rounding out sixty years of educational activity, we can be truly thankful for the early opportunities of Cape May, and we congratulate the High School students here on their exceptional advantages and on the fact that they have a school and faculty the peers of any in the State.

Be not neglectful thereof.

"'Tis education forms the common mind: Just as the twig is bent the tree's inclined."

- William Lycett

CENTER OF ATTENTION

Various pictures show Cape May's bustling commercial district on Washington Street, long before it was paved over and turned into a pedestrian mall. The top picture on this page shows the 300 block, looking from Perry Street. Below left is now Lace Silhouettes and Cotton Company. Below right, the old *Daily Wave* building, which is long gone, was opposite the spot now occupied by the Whale's Tale. The opposite page shows the 400 block of Washington Street, looking east from Jackson, on the Fourth Of July (year unknown). The building on the right-hand corner was demolished and is now the site of Jackson Mountain Café.

Don Pocher

CAPE CURIOSITY

The Evolution Of Washington Street

FROM its creation in 1832, Washington Street has been Cape May's commercial district. Rather than the boutiques and restaurants that line today's pedestrian walk, Washington Street was populated with traditional businesses like a mechanic's garage, beauty salon and a furniture store. It was also the place to find other small-town staples like the town bank, pharmacy and a movie theatre.

All that changed in 1970 when city leaders conceived of the Washington Street Mall as the economic hub of their planned Victorian Village. The new walkway would extend along the three busiest blocks, from Perry Street to Ocean Street. The project was created to help revitalize downtown Cape May and a federal Housing and Urban Development grant was utilized.

The city leaders were trying to attract new vacationers to the city and they believed that a Victorian-themed outdoor mall would fit well in Cape May. Merchants who owned stores along the affected blocks of Washington Street were not so sure. They fought the development initially, believing that the mall would take away customers and drive them out of business.

By the time the project was completed, in June of 1971, costs topped $3.8 million and three blocks of the busy street were turned into a thriving pedestrian mall. The storekeepers soon found that their businesses were actually benefiting.

AT YOUR SERVICE
This page: This 1917 picture shows Freihofer's market at the corner of Washington and Union streets
Cape May County Museum

SIGNS THEY ARE A CHANGING
Opposite page: The north side of the 400 block of Washington Street looks much different today than it did in this early 1900s photograph – none of these buildings remain.
Cape May County Museum

**DIRT
ROAD**
This page, top:
The intersection
of Washington and
Decatur is shown
in this 1865 picture
– the Commercial
House hotel is on
the left
*Cape May County
Museum*

**A QUIET
DAY IN TOWN**
This page, below:
This early 1900s
photo shows
Washington Street
looking west from
the site of today's
city hall.
*Cape May County
Museum*

The Washington Street Mall was hailed as a huge success and in the years following its construction the idea was emulated in cities all around the country. In Cape May, the flowers and trees, open walkways and plentiful park benches were well appreciated by visitors and locals.

For 36 years, the mall served the city of Cape May well, though it had begun to look a little worn with time. The trees had grown tall and full, cracking their decorative concrete planters and blotting out the sun in spots. The walkways that were constructed with a concrete mixture had broken apart and shifted.

In 2007 the city unveiled a revamp for the mall. Designs called for the excavation of all three blocks, virtually wiping the slate clean. After the underground public works lines were replaced, the mall would be reconstructed, better than before.

Once all the plans were finalized, work began in November of 2007. The renovation was done in phases to allow the businesses to stay open throughout the six-month project. By the end of February all underground work was completed and the concrete foundation was laid.

Red brick pavers were positioned over the concrete, oversized bench planters were constructed on all three blocks, two fountains were erected, and recessed lighting systems were installed.

The only real setback occurred with regard to the three electrical transformers that were incorporated into the mall in 1971. Officials hoped to be able to relocate them away from the main walkway, but the plan was too expensive and, instead, wooden pergolas were built to hide them.

By the time the renovations were completed, in May of 2008, the Washington Street Mall featured a new exterior, but retained the same congenial atmosphere. Merchants interacted with customers, diners enjoyed eating in a beautiful outdoor setting and countless pedestrians were offered samples of fudge.

T. MONT. SMITH,
MANUFACTURING CONFECTIONER,
No. 9 WASHINGTON STREET,
CAPE MAY, N. J.

SWISS STORE.
E. MISSON,
No. 26 Washington Street,
CAPE MAY,

SWISS CARVINGS,
FANCY PORCELAINS,
FISH SCALE JEWELRY,
FRENCH PAINTINGS ON WOOD,
SEA BEANS,
SEA SHELLS, etc.

T. MONT. SMITH,
MANUFACTURING CONFECTIONER,
No. 9 WASHINGTON STREET,
CAPE MAY, N. J.

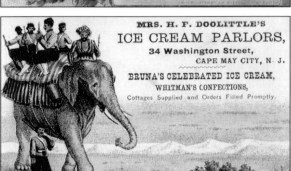

MRS. H. F. DOOLITTLE'S
ICE CREAM PARLORS,
34 Washington Street,
CAPE MAY CITY, N. J.
BRUNA'S CELEBRATED ICE CREAM,
WHITMAN'S CONFECTIONS,
Cottages Supplied and Orders Filled Promptly.

H. A. KENNEDY, M. D.,
RESIDENT PHYSICIAN & DRUGGIST
Toilet Articles
Perfumery, Family Medicines, Fine Cigars &c.,
United States Pharmacy
East Corner of Washington & Decatur Sts.,
CAPE MAY CITY, N. J.

F. VIETRI
DEALER IN
FOREIGN & DOMESTIC FRUITS
AND CONFECTIONS
40 Washington Street
Cape May, N. J.

260 N. EIGHTH ST.
AND
341 & 343 S. THIRTEENTH ST.,
PHILADELPHIA.
Henry R. Hallowell,
CHOICE
FRUITS and CONFECTIONS

MILLAR'S BAZAAR, 30 Washington Street, Cape May City,
DRY GOODS, TRIMMINGS, NOTIONS,
NOVELTIES IN FANCY GOODS FOR SOUVENIRS.
Fine China and Bisque Ware, Japanese Vases and Bowls, greatly reduced.

WALTER S. CARROLL'S
Popular Shaving Saloon,
No 23 WASHINGTON STREET,
CAPE MAY CITY, N. J.

COMFORT COTTAGE,
STEAMBOAT LANDING,
CAPE MAY, N. J.,
C. HAGGERTY, Proprietor.

ISAAC H. SMITH'S
Clothing Emporium
47 Washington Street,
CAPE MAY CITY, N. J.

OLD STEAMBOAT HOTEL, Cape May Point, N. J.

PEDDLING THEIR WARES
This page: Assorted advertising cards for Cape May businesses in the mid to late 1800s. They were vividly colorful and often fancifully exotic – the only elephant in Cape May was a wooden one at the southern end of the beach.
Don Pocher

FROM THE ARCHIVES

The Henry Sawyer Lottery

From *The History of Cape May County, New Jersey from Aboriginal Times to the Present Day*

HENRY Washington Sawyer, a native of Pennsylvania, at the age of nineteen years came in 1848 to Cape Island, where he engaged in his trade as a carpenter. He was among the first to respond to President Lincoln's call for the first army of seventy-five thousand men, in April, 1861. As there was no probability of a company being organized in Cape May, he went to Trenton and saw Governor Olden, who gave him important letters to Secretary of War Cameron.

There were then (April 19) but a handful of soldiers in the national capital, and Sawyer was detailed as one of a company of guards organized to protect the government buildings. Later he became a private in a Pennsylvania regiment, and soon afterward he was appointed Sergeant, and a month later he was commissioned as Second Lieutenant. The term of service of the regiment having expired, he was discharged. February 19, 1862, he was commissioned Second Lieutenant in Company D, First Cavalry Regiment, and he was promoted to First Lieutenant April 7, and to Captain of Company K on October 8.

June 9, 1863, Captain Sawyer commanded his company in the battle of Brandy Station,

one of the most desperate cavalry engagements of the war. Well toward its close, he received two pistol bullets — one passed through his thigh, and the other struck his right cheek, passing out at the back of his neck near the spinal column. Despite his wounds, he kept his saddle until his horse was shot under him and fell with him to the ground, his senses leaving him with the concussion. On recovering consciousness, he found himself a prisoner. His wounds were pronounced very dangerous, if not mortal. Recovering sufficiently to his removal, he was convened to Richmond, where he was committed to the famous Libby Prison.

July 6th, without preparation, he was called to face an ordeal which might well real the stoutest heart. With the captives of the rank of captain, he was called into the presence of General Winder, commander of the Prison.

They entered with hope, anticipating a release by exchange, but to their horror were informed that two of their number were to be selected to be shot in retaliation for the execution by General Burnside of two Confederate officers who had been taken while engaged in recruiting within the federal lines.

The little company were formed in a hollow square to witness the lottery of death. The name of each was written on a separate slip of paper, and these slips were placed in a box; the commander giving notice that the first two slips drawn would designate the men to be executed. To those from whom the victims were to be taken was granted permission to select those who should conduct the drawing.

At the suggestion of Captain Sawyer, who maintained a marvelous self-possession, the pitiful task was committed to Chaplain Brown, of the Sixth Maryland Regiment. Amid the most awesome silence the chaplain drew a slip, that bearing the name of Captain Sawyer, and another, bearing that of Captain Flynn, of the Fifty-first Indiana Regiment. Testimony to the splendid fortitude of Captain Sawyer is afforded by one of the first rebel journals of the day, the *Richmond Dispatch*, which said, "Sawyer heard it with, no apparent emotion, remarking that some one had to be drawn, and he could stand it as well as any one else."

The doomed men were at once placed under special guard, and were notified by General Winder that they need not delude themselves with any hope of escape, and that their execution would take place July 14th, eight days hence. Sawyer, however, did not abandon hope, and he asked and received permission to write a letter to his wife, conditioned upon its reading by the prison authorities. This epistle is at once remarkable for its display of cool deliberation in planning for the preservation of

BIRTH OF THE CHALFONTE
Opposite page: Henry Sawyer's beloved Chalfonte Hotel as it looked after the first addition was added to extend the building to Sewell Avenue. The original building on the left was simply mirrored in the addition. Although the sign says "Sawyers", the hotel was always known as the Chalfonte.
Don Pocher

his life, courageous resignation in the event of death, unflinching- patriotic devotion, and the infinite pathos of his farewell to his loved ones. It is well worthy of preservation to the remotest days of history as illustrative of one of the noblest of the American soldier:

Provost Marshal-General's Office.
Richmond, Va, July 6th, 1863.
"My Dear Wife—I am under the necessity of informing you that my prospects look dark."

"This morning all the captains now prisoners at the Libby Military Prison drew lots for two to be executed. It fell to my lot. Myself and Captain Flynn, of the fifty-first Indiana Infantry, will be executed for two captains executed by Burnside."

"The Provost Marshal-General, J. Winder, assures me that the Secretary of War of the Southern Confederacy will permit yourself and my dear children to visit me before I am executed. You will be permitted to bring an attendant. Captain Whilldin, or Uncle W. W. Ware, or Dan, had better come with you. My situation is hard to be borne, and I cannot think of dying without seeing you and the children.

You will be allowed to return without molestation to your home. 1 am resigned to whatever is in store for me with the consolation that I die without having committed any crime. I have no trial, no jury, nor am I charged with any crime, but it fell to my lot. You will proceed to Washington. My government will give you transportation for Fortress Monroe, and you will get here by flag of truce, and return in the same way. Bring with you a shirt for me."

"It will be necessary for you to preserve this letter to bring evidence at Washington of my condition. My pay is due me from the first of March, which you are entitled to. Captain B. owes me fifty dollars, money lent to him when he went on a furlough. You will write to him at once, and he will send it to you."

"My dear wife, the fortune of war has put me in this position. If I must die a sacrifice to my country, with God's will I must submit only let me see you once more, and I will die becoming a man and an officer, but for God's sake, do not disappoint me. Write to me as soon as you get this, and go to Captain Whilldin, he will advise you what to do.

"I have done nothing to deserve this penalty. But you must submit to your fate. It will be no disgrace to myself, you or the children, but you may point with pride and say, I gave my husband, my children will have the consolation to say, I was made an orphan for my country."

"God will provide for you, never fear. Oh, it is hard to leave you thus. I wish the ball that passed through my head in the last battle would have done its work, but it was not to be so.

My mind is somewhat influenced, for it has come so suddenly on me. Write to me as soon as you get this, leave your letter open, and I will get it. Direct my name and rank, by way of Fortress Monroe.

"Farewell, farewell. And I hope it is all for the best. I remain yours until death,
"H. W. SAWYER,
"Captain First New Jersey Cavalry"

Sawyer and Flynn were now placed in close confinement in an underground dungeon so damp that their clothing mildewed. Feeble light and foulest air were admitted by a six inch square hole in the door, outside of which stood a sentinel, who every half-hour, day and night, challenged the prisoners, who were obliged to respond.

Owing to these ceaseless calls, and the presence of a multitude of great rats, the miserable men were well nigh totally deprived of sleep.

But, although they were unaware of it, deliverance for the captives was at hand. Saw-

yer's faithful wife hastened to Washington and laid before the President the message that had been received. She needed to make no plea when she gazed into the pitying, careworn face of the tender-hearted Lincoln.

Bidding her take courage, he set to work every agency to save the condemned men and also procured for the poor woman a safe-conduct which enabled her to visit her husband, who, with his companion, was granted a fifteen-day respite.

Under the direction of the President and the Secretary of War, a son of General Robert E. Lee and a son of General Winder, the Libby Prison commandant, then prisoners in the hands of the federal authorities, were ordered into close confinement, and General Benjamin F. Butler was directed to notify the Confederate government that these men would be executed immediately upon receipt of information of the death of Sawyer and Flynn.

The notice was sufficient in terms, but its forcefulness was augmented by the naming of General Butler as the agent of retribution, for his determination in the use of heroic measures was proverbial. The executions were postponed from time to time.

After a three weeks incarceration in the noisome dungeon, Sawyer and Flynn were removed to the same quarters with the other prisoners. Meantime the Richmond newspapers clamored for their execution, and they never once felt that their lives were really saved until in March, 1864, nine months after their capture, and eight months after their condemnation to death, when they walked out to freedom, through exchange for the Confederate officers held as hostages for them, and under similar sentence.

Captain Sawyer was honorably mustered out of service, with the rank of Lieutenant Colonel, in September 1865.

CHAPTER SEVEN

Summer Cottages And Victorian Mansions

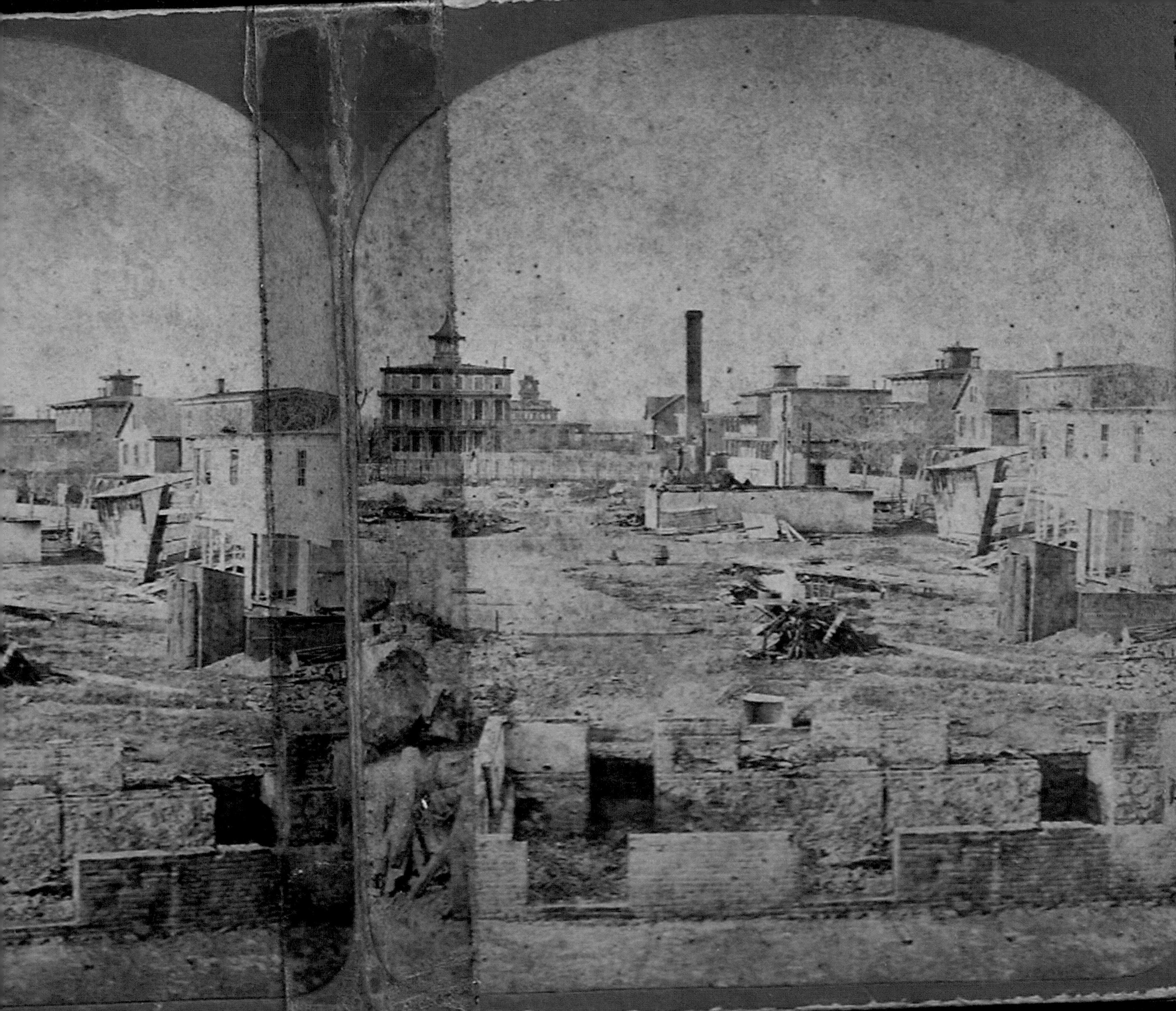

VIEWS OF CAPE MAY AFTER THE FIRE, NOV. 9, 1878.

**NEW NAME,
SAME PLACE**
This page: The
Hotel Arlington
is shown in this
early 1900s picture
and, although the
name has been
changed to Hotel
Alcott, very little
of this view, of
Grant Street, looks
different today
Don Pocher

**A LOCAL
LANDMARK**
Opposite page: The
Shoreham Hotel is
shown in this 1890s
photograph – the
building survives
today and is known
as St Mary's By the
Sea, a nuns' retreat.
Don Pocher

**BURNED TO
THE GROUND**
Previous page:
This stereoscope
picture of the fire
damage from 1878
shows the charred
foundation of
the once-mighty
Congress Hall. It
was quickly rebuilt,
but at only half
the size of its
predecessor.
Don Pocher

SOON AFTER the 1869 fire, the people of Cape May cleared away the rubble and began to rebuild. John B. Lycett and Robert Swain led the way by constructing large homes along Ocean Street, each with a private office.

Taking advantage of the post-fire situation, both Swain and Lycett used their offices for practical purposes. Swain offered real estate from his, including parcels of land where the previous structures had been lost to flames. Lycett used his office to sell home insurance.

The biggest property cleared in the fire was the site of the United States Hotel. The owner of the hotel, Charles Conway, had just purchased the United States only a week before

the fire for $80,000. Without any money and no source of income, rebuilding the hostelry was not a possibility.

Instead, the acreage was subdivided and sold as individual parcels of land. Storefronts and businesses were built along Washington Street, cementing the area as Cape May's commercial district. On the southern portion of the old United States property cottages were built, facing Decatur and Ocean Streets.

Cape May also ordered its first fire-fighting equipment, from Philadelphia in March of 1870. The horse-drawn fire engine cost the city around $3,000 and its arrival coincided with the beginning of the Cape May Fire Association, led by James Mecray. The city pledged to never again be left without fire protection.

Even with the devastation from the previous year's fire the 1870 season was very profitable for the local innkeepers and hotel proprietors. John McMakin's newly-rebuilt Atlantic Hotel opened for business and a large, $20,000 addition was added to Congress Hall.

Sailing became especially popular in 1870 and although Cape May had no organized sailing or yacht club many of the hotels worked together to host Cape May's first Grand Regatta. An invitation was sent to the New York Yacht Club and to sailing clubs in Philadelphia, many of which responded by sending a number of vessels to the cape.

Cape May ship captains and Delaware River pilots volunteered their time to ensure that each of the ships involved in the regatta had

SLEEPING BEAUTY

This page: Jackson's Clubhouse (now the Mainstay Inn) is shown in this 1879 photograph of Columbia Avenue. The shutters have been closed and the building appears to sit empty.

Don Pocher

MANSION BY THE SEA

Opposite page: A remarkable view of the Emlen Physick Estate as it looked when it was first built, with nothing separating the backyard from the beach but rolling meadows

Mid-Atlantic Center for the Arts

a seaman onboard who was familiar with the often-treacherous Cape May waters. There were two races held, one for schooners or larger ships and another for sloops and smaller vessels.

History records the schooner prize was awarded to the crew of the *Sappho* and the sloop winner was a boat named *Gracie*. Both vessels were from New York and they each won a $1,000 prize for their respective victories.

The regatta was considered a grand success, bringing droves of people to Cape May and establishing the region as a prime location for yachting. Arising from the triumph of those first races, the Cape May Yacht Club was formed in 1872 and yearly races were organized.

The year 1873 saw the creation of Cape May's first sewage system, which was organized by the city's Board of Health and B. Swain. There were no treatment plants or other means of sequestering the raw sewage, which was pumped directly into the Cape Island Creek and the Atlantic Ocean.

Summer seasons continued to improve year after year and, in 1874, the city received a huge honor when President Ulysses S. Grant chose Cape May for an important meeting among government and Republican Party leaders. He stayed at Congress Hall and was so impressed with Cape May that he returned the following year. Again he stayed at Congress Hall and was accompanied by his entire cabinet of advisors. The president was given a private office for his use in the hotel and it has been said that cabinet meetings were held in the first-floor parlor.

The president's selection of Cape May naturally increased the popularity of what was already considered to be the grandest seaside resort in the country. Steamships continued to make the rounds from southern ports to the

island, along with the original Philadelphia run.

Meanwhile, cottages continued to be built all over Cape May, with new hotels and boarding houses popping up regularly. Henry Sawyer constructed his famous boarding house on Howard Street in 1875. He chose to name his house Chalfonte, which meant cool fountain in French.

A number of reasons have been speculated over the years for the name choice, ranging from a book Sawyer read to an individual he met while in Libby Prison during the Civil War. Unfortunately, Sawyer never documented his reasoning and the true origins of the Chalfonte name are unknown.

Once construction was completed on the original part of the Chalfonte, in 1876, Sawyer purchased all the properties around his hotel.

He owned the whole block, with the exception of a parcel on the corner of Howard Street and Columbia Avenue that he was unable to buy.

In 1878, John J. Kromer built the Hotel Arlington (now called the Alcott) on the other side of Cape May at Grant and North streets. It was considered to be the fanciest of all the Cape's hotels, although not on the same scale as larger hostelries like Congress Hall or the Stockton.

That same year marked the beginning of construction of one of Cape May's most widely-recognized mansions, the Emlen Physick Estate. The home was built by Dr Emlen Physick, who purchased an area of swampland on the eastern end of Washington Street, with sweeping views of the Atlantic Ocean.

At the time the home was built, that entire area of the island was nearly barren and when

**ALL ROUTES
LEAD TO HERE**
This page: Some
travelled by
steamboat and
other by rail but,
either way, Cape
May was the
nation's premier
seashore resort
just prior to the
fire of 1878 that
demolished much
of the city
Don Pocher

powerful storms brought particularly high tides the ocean was known to come all the way to the edge of Dr Physick's property.

The main house was fully constructed by the next year and, upon its completion, Dr Physick moved down to Cape May with his mother, Francis Ralston, and his aunt, Emilie Parmentier.

The year 1878 saw Cape May's seasonal businesses flourish, with more steamship passengers disembarking at Denizot's Decatur Street Pier than ever before. The famous steamship *Republic* also began making bringing visitors to Cape May, primarily disembarking at the Delaware Bay landing.

The *Republic* was the largest of all the steamships, capable of transporting 3,000 travelers in one trip. The boat offered amenities uncommon in those days, including three passenger decks with plenty of comfortable seats, a dining room that served four-course meals, and a full band that played throughout the voyages.

Meanwhile, construction was completed on the precursor to today's Sunset Boulevard, which ran across the island from east to west, connecting Sea Grove with Sewell's Point. It was a stellar year in the history of Cape May, right up until the morning of November 9.

At approximately 10:45 in the morning, an unknown individual entered the Ocean House hotel, which had been closed for the season. The person was able to evade the watchman who had been hired to keep the building secure, then quietly climb the stairs to an attic room. He or she then lit a match and set the room's furnishings ablaze, before hurriedly rushing down the stairs and out of the hotel.

It all happened in a matter of minutes — the small attic fire quickly grew into a raging inferno. A workman on the roof of the Stockton Hotel, four blocks away from the Ocean House,

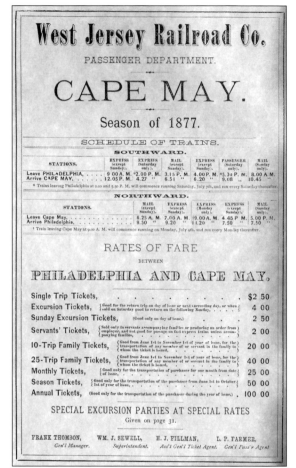

spotted the fire and alerted local authorities. The city's volunteer firemen immediately brought their antiquated fire apparatus into service and worked valiantly to avert a disaster like the fire that leveled much of the city nine years earlier.

Unfortunately, the fire association was ill-equipped to handle the blaze and with the benefit of especially strong coastal winds the fire soon spread to neighboring properties. Local citizens did their best to assist the fire team and they instituted water brigades to

help drive back the fire.

Their efforts did little to stop the flames, however, as the fire burned its way through the city for more than 18 hours. After it became obvious that the Cape May Fire Association would not be able to contain the blaze, they wired other cities for assistance. Modern fire engines from Philadelphia and Vineland eventually made their way to Cape May, equipped with the latest in fire-suppression gear and seasoned fire-fighters.

Thanks to those fire engines and their

faithful operators, along with the perseverance of the Cape May volunteers and local citizens who never gave up the fight, the flames were eventually vanquished before they consumed the entire city. Even so, the damage was extensive — nearly 40 acres in the heart of Cape May were leveled.

Many of Cape May's most popular hotels, boarding houses, bathhouses and storefronts were burned to the foundations. The city's hospitality industry was the hardest hit, with the loss of Congress Hall, Ocean House, Centre House, Columbia House, Atlantic Hotel, Merchants, Centennial and the Wyoming.

A number of private cottages were also destroyed, including some of the oldest in town, along Jackson Street. Three of the eight identical Stockton Row cottages on Gurney Street were badly damaged and Mr Ware's drug store on the corner of Ocean Street and Columbia Avenue (now the House of Royals) was repeatedly ignited by flying embers. Luckily, there were dedicated volunteers on hand to douse the flames before they had an opportunity to take hold of the building. The citizens knew that if the pharmacy was lost, the fire would have continued to spread along Columbia Street through the closely-built cottages. That would also have put the fire north of the Stockton Hotel, with the powerful winds pushing the flames directly into it.

Though the fire was stopped and the Stockton Hotel saved, it still appeared that all was lost for the Summer City by the Sea and many questioned if Cape May would be able to come back from such a devastating blow.

People worried because the insurance money did not entirely cover the losses. Even if the owners could rebuild their properties, it would still take years to recover.

RUNNING ON HORSEPOWER
This page, top: Horse-drawn trolleys were a popular means of conveyance between Sewell's Point and Cape May Point in the days before the electric trolley
Cape May Point State Park

HARD WORK AT THE BEACH
This page, below: Construction workers are digging sand from in front of the Stockton Hotel, most likely to use as landfill in the swampy areas of the city that were being developed
Cape May County Museum

FROM THE ARCHIVES

Glorious Days For Cape May

The Philadelphia Inquirer, **August 8, 1870**

EVENTFUL TIME ON THE ISLAND

SINCE my last the Island has been one buzz of excitement, and "from the grave to gay, from lively to severe," has been the order of the day. Death by day, a ball at night! Only a woman crushed into the next world, on with the dance! Cape May has no patent for this; it is with us every day, and everywhere, but only here is it, where the space is so circumscribed, that it shows in strongest colors. The old hotel story, "Brandy and water for one hundred and twenty-six," can be realized every hour, but without it what would life be at a fashionable watering place? If it were all sugar the taste would pall, and the savor of life would be gone. So it is that a death a day, as we have had it the last week, only kept up the excitement, and gave the lovers of the horrible—and we all have more of less of it in our compositions—something to talk of.

Speaking of this makes me accord to the management of the West Jersey Railroad a praise that they really deserve. When it is taken into consideration that this road has a peculiar public to transport, a public out of the usual calm, business traveling style, but a reckless pleasure-seeking crowd, it seems wonderful that they have managed to carry them with so few accidents. Their customers are of all classes, but all with the same intents and purpose. They are bent on enjoyment, and it is a singular fact no matter how quiet and methodical a man may be at home or in business, or how deserved and precise a woman, once set them traveling for pleasure, and the

Above: **Gathering on Congress Hall's veranda**
Opposite page: **The railroad's popular Grant Street Summer Station** *Don Pocher*

first seems to think it necessary that he should assume something of the "Hurrah, boys! Come on" style, and the second to be in a hurry and lose presence of mind. It is this public that the Cape May road has to contend with.

There has been no lack of pleasure during the week, providing it is allowed that such as I designate are pleasures. First, among these was the children's ball at the Columbia, which certainly carried out the intention of the proprietor, Mr Bolton, to make it the affair of the season. There can be nothing more charming than a child's party, and the only fault I have to find with those already given is that too many grown persons are admitted. There is something delightfully exciting in looking on at the abandon of the little ones to their pleasures, and their carelessness of comment upon their enjoyments.

But to the ball. It opened at 9 o'clock, under the personal management of Harry Risley, the music by Dodworth. At 11, with a precision and rapidity that was marvelous, the ball-room was

transformed into a supper-room, and the little ones were instantaneously reveling in a profusion of ice cream, cakes, lemonade and sundry other 'nicies,' to say nothing of candies to carry home, which they did on its conclusion, and left the floor to the elder youngsters, who hopped it up until 12:00, when a second supper mysteriously appeared and disappeared. This time the viands comprised solids as well as fluids, and chicken salads, oysters, Roman and other punches, found delighted consumers, who, being every way satisfied, went home happy.

The next day we had a sack race in front of the Stockton, eligible for any member of the Fifteenth Amendment, and engineered by a committee of gentlemen comprising the names of judges, merchants, theatrical nobs, and other eminent persons, whose names, were I to write them for the benefit of your readers, would astonish them to see how democratic Cape May is becoming, and how all social distinction is dropped when once the revel commences. I am happy to be able to inform you that Philadelphia is still ahead, the first prize, $50, having been won by a gentleman from thence, a waiter at the Columbia House, whose name I am only induced to withhold from fame at his own request.

The same evening we had a serenade upon the plaza of the Stockton, given by Hassler's band to Mrs John Drew, who is stopping there. Some one said that Mark, seeing that he is to be that lady's leader next season, wanted to show her what he could do, and that he had a soul above the frivolous. If that was the intention, none can say but what he succeeded and come off with unbounded applause.

Speaking of this puts me in mind of one or two little abuses which I would like to see corrected. The first is on the sale of tickets for a complimentary hop. The price charged, no matter what, should include the admission of ladies, and not be so arranged that a gentleman on providing himself with a ticket, finds, on presenting himself at the door, that he has the annoyance of being turned back to duplicate or triplicate his ticket,

as the case may be, children being calculated the same as adults. A second annoyance is the practice of allowing the waiters at hops or other entertainments to control the chairs, and I may say sell them to guests, for it is, in some cases, impossible to obtain them without a bribe. If the larger hotels would have a superintendent of chairs he would be a useful officer.

The Stockton has now about a thousand guests, and the other hotels in proportion.

I am glad to see that my proposition for a line of street cars from the depot to the inlet is attracting attention. It would pay if only to accommodate the fishing parties, which just now abound, as do the fish. Weak fish and blue fish do there much congregate, and are confiding. I speak knowingly, having tried it, though I don't mention a word about the army of crabs, which will eat off your bait, or of the unlucky fisherman, who, not catching anything himself, will put other people's fish on his hooks and catch them again when nobody watches him, so that when the party comes to count fish they find themselves mysteriously short. If the road cannot be accomplished, at least let us have a line of omnibuses.

It seems almost useless to speak of this or that hop when there are so many of them; but on Wednesday there was a very brilliant one in honor of Charles Dodsworth, at which, I think, the ladies dressed more than usual, though I must pronounce that Cape May does not dress as does Newport and Saratoga. A seaside watering place is not provocative of high end in dressing, for many reasons. One, because bathing in itself is productive of carelessness of toilet, and, second, because sea air is destructive of the perfection of dress, it having a bad effect upon starches and stiff fabrics, to say nothing of its being a disarranger of hair and a discolorer of high colors.

For this reason it may be that Cape May dressing does not touch Saratoga, and, unpleasant as the truth is, my duty as a journalist compels me to record it.

FROM THE ARCHIVES

The Great Fire Of 1878

The Philadelphia Inquirer, **November 11, 1878**

I**T WAS A SAD** sight which presented itself this morning to the people of Cape May when they gazed upon the destruction caused by the flames yesterday. It was a bad day for Cape May, and the people who had not yet got over the excitement felt as if they would not care about having another such a day dawn upon them. The view was, indeed, a gloomy one; there lay a desolate tract of some thirty five or forty acres of land burned over in the choicest section of the town. Hotels, cottages, boarding houses, bath houses, trees and everything within the track of the devouring element had disappeared with the exception of the foundation bricks and a few charred trunks of trees.

The flames even attacked the board walk, and last night I saw portions of it burning right merrily, fanned by the brisk wind which still continued. Next to the fire the wind did the damage. It blew strongly all day, first from the northwest, and then from the west, and to day it is blowing as heavily as ever from the latter quarter. It there had been but little wind the fire would have only burned the Ocean House, Centre House and Congress Hall. If there had been a good fire department here it would not have extended beyond the Ocean House, in which it originated, and probably nearly all of that building even would have been saved. But fate decreed otherwise, and now the

finest portion of Cape May is nothing but a pile of ashes. The light from the burning buildings could be seen far out in the ocean and for nearly thirty miles up the railroad. It was, indeed, a big blaze, which will not be forgotten for a long time by those who saw it.

The fire broke out in the attic of the Ocean House, on Perry street, below Washington, and directly opposite Congress Hall. It was first discovered by a man from the roof of the Stockton Hotel, who at once rushed down to terra firma and gave the alarm. The few people who were around about this time (eleven o'clock) were immediately around to action, and brought into service the entire fire department of the city, which, of course, proved inadequate.

Strange to say, the fire burned slowly, and if a

good steam engine had been on hand with proper hose, the flames would have been quenched right here. The individuals who took charge of the fire, assisted by a number of busy bodies who hold official business, knew no more about putting out a fire then they do of running a newspaper. Then the hose which they brought into use was of the most miserable kind, and section after section burst as soon as water was forced through it.

Fortunately there was an excellent supply of water, and, even with the bad management, it is thought the fire could have been subdued had it not been for the miserable hose; but it burst and kept on bursting, and the fire spread. The cause of the fire is still a mystery, and it looks now as if it would remain so for some time, or, perhaps, for all time. It is believed, however, to have been

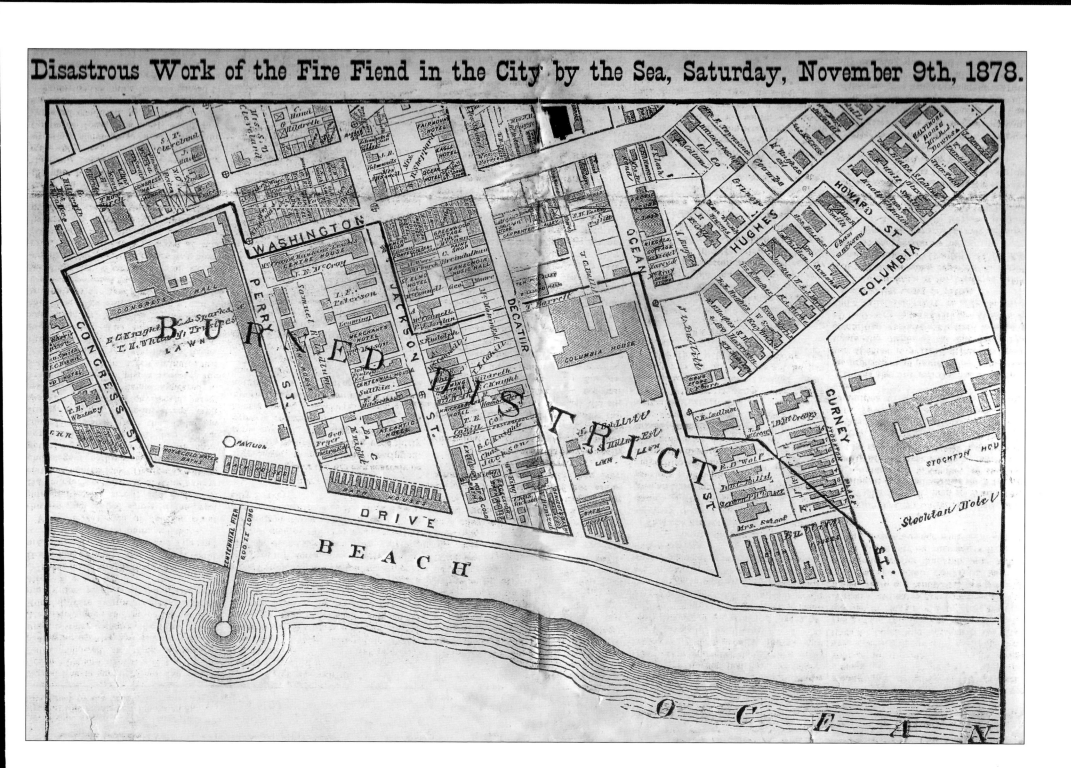

Disastrous Work of the Fire Fiend in the City by the Sea, Saturday, November 9th, 1878.

the work of an incendiary, and last night and this morning there were many conjectures as to the motive of the wicked individual who caused so much trouble.

What object was to be gained by the destruction of even one hotel cannot be understood. It could hardly have been for gain, because there was nothing in the building which could have been safely stolen. Nobody could very readily get away with furniture, carpets and bedding without being detected, and none of the burned buildings contained small articles of any value which could be hidden about the person.

Whoever applied the match yesterday morning must have a very poor opinion of himself today. There had been no fires in the Ocean House for several weeks, and nobody had any business there except the watchman. The attic was a queer place to start a fire, too. It is strange that the incendiary fellow did not light this his fire on the second or third floor and then give it the necessary draught by opening doors and windows. But it seems he did not. What a good thing that he chose to start his fire in November instead of in July or August. But a man who would do it in the month first named would hardly hesitate to start a blaze in either of the last named months.

Well, the fire having started, burned slowly at first, as previously stated, but as the efforts for its subjugation were so futile, of course it soon began to spread from one room to another, and then from story to story, and in a short time the beautiful, but frail hotel building was a mass of flames, and, fanned by the strong wind, raging furiously. Perry street, which separated the Ocean House from Congress Hall, is a narrow thoroughfare, and, of course, there was but little to prevent the flames from communicating to the latter hotel. In fact, the heat was so intense that it caught fire even before the flames touched it. Nothing could be done to save the building, and the fire gradually gathered it wholly into its embrace, and soon it was noth-

THE OCEAN HOUSE.
PROPRIETOR, SAMUEL R. LUDLAM, CAPE MAY CITY, N.J.

ing but a lot of smouldering, burning embers in a field of hot ashes. The flames first attacked Whisky Row, which was the nearest point to the Ocean House, and then the new wing soon followed. It was a sad sight to see this fine property being destroyed, and no one able to save it. About this time the wind forced the flames towards the Merchants', southeast from the Ocean House, and which fronted on Jackson street.

The fire appeared to attack it from all quarters about the same time, and in a very few minutes it was burning wickedly. But there was no help, and, like the Ocean House and Congress Hall, it went down under the fierce onslaught, and nothing is now to be seen of it except its brick supports. As soon as the main wing of Congress Hall, on Washington street, caught fire, the flames were forced across the street to the Centre House. This fine

hotel fronted on Washington street, and occupied the space between Perry and Jackson streets. Strong efforts were made to fight the flames here, as it was feared that the heat, which was no intense, would set fire to the stores and other buildings on the upper side of Washington street. But the wind blowing from the west kept the flames from the north, and drove them south and southeast. When this was burning at its full height the old wing of the Ocean house was also ablaze.

The fire now communicated to the centre House Cottage, just back of the Centre House, which fronted on Jackson street, and soon it was too burned to the ground. Peterson's cottage, just below the Centre House cottage, naturally followed, and in a very short time it was level with the ground upon which it had been built. The fire had then burned about two hours and a half, or

Photo. by GILBERT & BACON, 40 N. 8th St. Phila^a.

VIEWS OF CAPE MAY AFTER THE FIRE NOV. 9, 1878.

ALL THAT REMAINED
This page: The destruction caused by the 1878 fire is vividly apparent in this stereoscope, which shows the burnt remains of the Stockton Hotel bath houses
Don Pocher

perhaps a little more. Just below Peterson's cottage was John Filton's tenpin alley, shuffleboard hall and this, too, was soon consumed.

The people, who had gathered in great numbers at various points, no began to be considerably frightened, as it really looked as if the whole town would before night be laid in ashes. Everything that could be suggested was done, but all their efforts were futile. Telegrams had by this time been sent to Camden and Philadelphia seeking that steamers be sent down, as, without the aid of improved fire apparatus, there was no hope of safety. The Camden Fire at once responded, and Chief Engineer Bradshaw, with one of his steam engines and the necessary men, left at once on a special train, and, the road being clear, came down to the scene of the conflagration in but little over an hour. As soon as they arrived Chief Bradshaw at once took charge of the fire ground, and, under his instructions, soon had things in a very good working order. It is a pity that he did not get here several hours sooner. By the time the chief had got the bearings of the fire it had forced its way down to the beach, consuming everything within its reach. Fenton's cottage by the sea was soon wrapped in the devouring element, and it took but a few minutes to start the Centennial House, which was last summer kept by Charles Sullkie. Of course, it wasn't long before there was little or nothing left of those buildings. Mrs Miller's cottage, on Jackson Street, was the next to go, and then the old Atlantic, fronting on the ocean, followed in its wake. The bath houses along the beach were then visited and soon they were nothing but ashes. The wind at this time was so strong that it forced the flames almost to the water, and actually set the boardwalk on fire in several places, and it smouldered and burnt nearly all night.

The fire at this time was burning furiously on Jackson, and at this point the gallant Camden firemen worked energetically. But almost unaided as they were except of the old hand engine of the Cape May folks what could they do in the lieu of such stubborn resistance — almost nothing. And yet they worked nobly, and the Cape May residents and cottage owners, and everybody else who has a pecuniary interest in the place, can thank them for saving the valuable property which I see standing around me this beautiful November afternoon. Having taken in the whole block on the west side of Jackson Street the fire row crossed the street and attacked the Wyoming House. It took but a few minutes to thoroughly envelope this building. The cottage owned by the estate of Thomas E. Cahill, president of the Knickerbocker Ice Company, recently deceased, adjoined to the north, and the flames, of course, communicated to it, and what was a handsome structure yesterday morning is now gone.

The Knickerbocker, south of the Wyoming, caught fire about the same time that the Cahill cottage was struck. It is now a thing of the past. William E. King's hot bath establishment, to the south of the Knickerbocker, soon shared the same fate, and George Fryer's cottage, which was between the Ocean House and the bluff, fronting on Perry Street, then gave up the ghost. This pretty cottage stood alone and everybody thought it would be saved. It had a slate roof, and this, with

the fact of its being isolated, led strongly to the opinion that it would not be touched. But it was fated. The flames seemed to break out all over it at once, although no one seemed to see the flames touch the building. The heat, however, was so intense that nothing like a frame building could resist it. Even a brick structure would have gone and a granite edifice would have crumbled. Next to Mr Fryer's cottage was the Avenue House. This Stood on the Bluff At the foot of Perry Street. Last summer it was run by George T. Doughty. It was owned by the Bierns estate. Nothing scarcely is left to tell the take today. Then S. A. Rudolph's cottage, on Jackson Street, above Cahill's, was

attacked by the flames, and was more than half destroyed. It was not after twelve o'clock, and the Camden fire boys having arrived, they succeeded in checking the flames at this point, although Alex McConnell's two cottages, adjoining to the north, were somewhat damaged, the price, however, is not heavy. Back of Cahill's cottage, and fronting on Decatur Street, was the cottage of Judge Hamburger. This was destroyed, as was also three of King's cottages. Denezott's bath houses and cottages met the same fate. While the fire was progressing at this point things continued to be very animated on Washington Street in the efforts to save the blocks on the north side of the street.

---

24   *CAPE MAY.*

LIST OF PRINCIPAL HOTELS AND BOARDING-HOUSES.

SEASON 1878.

STOCKTON HOTEL,	Foot of Gurney street.	CHARLES DUFFY.
CONGRESS HALL,	Foot of Perry street.	J. F. KINGSLEY & Co.
COLUMBIA HOUSE,	Foot of Ocean street.	GEORGE C. WARD.
OCEAN HOUSE,	Foot of Perry street.	SAMUEL R. LUDLAM.
ATLANTIC HOTEL,	Foot of Jackson street.	LEVI E. JOHNSON.
SEA-BREEZE HOTEL (EXCURSION HOUSE,)	Beach avenue.	J. C. GRAY.
NATIONAL HALL,	Franklin and Corgis streets.	A. GARRETTSON.
CENTRE HOUSE,	Jackson and Washington streets.	J. E. MECRAY.
MERCHANTS' HOTEL,	Jackson street.	WILLIAM MASON.
WHITE HALL,	Lafayette street, above Franklin.	S. S. MARCY.
UNITED STATES HOTEL,	Jackson and Lafayette streets.	T. F. HARKINS.
MILLER'S COTTAGE,	No. 4 Perry street.	MRS. MARY W. HOFFMAN.
WEST END HOUSE,	Nos. 13 Wood street and 21 Congress streets.	WALTER W. GREEN.
MINERAL SPRING HOTEL,	Foot of Madison avenue.	
FRANKLIN HOUSE,	Lafayette street, below Franklin.	
ARCTIC HOUSE,	Ocean street, below Washington.	H. H. POWERS.
CAPE MAY HOUSE,	Jackson street, above Lafayette.	A. F. W. LEHMAN.
AMERICAN HOUSE,	Nos. 11 and 13 Washington street.	J. L. MOORE.
GREENWOOD COTTAGE,	Decatur street, below Washington.	JOHN McCANN.
EAGLE HOTEL,	Decatur street, above Washington.	MRS. HALPIN.
YOUNG'S COTTAGE,	Jackson street, above Lafayette.	CHARLES YOUNG.
JONES' COTTAGE,	Howard street, opposite Stockton Hotel.	MRS. H. E. JONES.
AVENUE HOUSE,	Foot of Perry street.	GEORGE T. DOUGHTY.
FAIRMOUNT HOUSE,	Decatur street, above Washington.	MRS. SHIELDS.
SEA VIEW COTTAGE,	Seagrove, below Columbia avenue.	J. W. JOHNSON.
CHALFONTE,	Howard street, below Columbia avenue.	H. W. SAWYER.

CAPE MAY.   25

KOENIG'S HOTEL,	No. 8 Washington street.	PHILIP KOENIG.
DELAWARE HOUSE,	Lafayette street, below Franklin.	JAMES MECRAY.
TREMONT HOUSE,	Washington and Franklin streets.	H. H. HUGHES.
BALTIMORE HOUSE,	Hughes street, below Franklin.	MRS. M. L. DOWNS & SON.
CLARENDON HOUSE,	Wood street.	
COTTAGE BY THE SEA,	Jackson street, below Washington.	T. MUELLEN.
WYOMING COTTAGE,	Jackson street, opposite Atlantic Hotel.	MRS. S. M. HILDRETH.
KNICKERBOCKER COTTAGE,	Foot of Jackson street.	GEORGE W. SHOEMAKER.
RIEGEL'S HOTEL,	Ocean street, below Washington.	MRS. RIEGEL.
LANSING COTTAGE,	Washington street.	JOHN L. LANSING.
HUGHES' COTTAGE,	No. 35 Lafayette street.	MRS. F. H. WILLIAMSON.
BANNAKER HOUSE (COLORED),	Lafayette street.	MRS. E. A. PALMER.
WEST JERSEY HOUSE,	Jackson street.	MRS. J. MERGEM.
SHAW'S COTTAGE,	Jackson street.	J. SHAW.
GRAND CENTRAL (COLORED),	Lafayette street.	H. F. DOOLITTLE.
WASHINGTON HOUSE,	Washington street, between Jackson and Perry.	MRS. CARMAN.
CARMAN COTTAGE,	Franklin street.	WILLIAM M. GREEN.
OCEAN BREEZE HOTEL,	31 Washington street.	MRS. HALLENBECK.
MARINE VILLA,	Howard, opposite Stockton Hotel.	MRS. W. H. MILLER.
COTTAGE GREEN,	Broadway.	MRS. W. H. MILLER
REEVES' COTTAGE,	20 Wood street.	H. N. REEVES.
SCHELLINGER'S COTTAGE,	Washington street.	MRS. W. SCHELLINGER.
MECHANICS' HOUSE,	Decatur street, above Washington.	JOHN STEWARD.
ST. ELMO HOUSE,	Jackson, below Washington.	CHARLES P. SUHLER.
CENTENNIAL HOUSE,	No. 9 Jackson street.	W. H. BURROUGHS.
SEA GROVE HOUSE,	Cape May Point.	MRS. M. C. STEWARDSON.
CAPE HOUSE,	Cape May Point.	MRS. C. B. REEVES.
CENTENNIAL HOUSE,	Cape May Point.	GEORGE W. SMITH.
SMITH'S COTTAGE,	Washington street.	MRS. E. GRIFFITH.
BOUCER'S COTTAGE,	South Lafayette street.	MRS. M. A. CAMP.
CHESTER COTTAGE,	South Lafayette street.	J. J. KRONER.
ARLINGTON HOUSE,	Corner Grant and North streets.	MRS. E. GRIFFITH.
GRIFFITH COTTAGES,	13 and 18 South Lafayette Street.	

The Camden steamer was stationed at Jackson and Washington streets, playing two streams, one to the east and the other to the west. With plenty of water at their command, the flames were prevented from crossing the principal thoroughfare of Cape May. If they had once got a foothold on the north side, it is hard to tell where the fire would have stopped. The alarm then came that the Columbia House was on fire. Nobody had thought of this well-known house, as it was thought to be comparatively safe, fronting as it did on Ocean Street. The flames appeared to take it from several quarters, and in a very few minutes it was burning briskly, the well-seasoned lumber making excellent fuel for the demon.

In an hours time this large building was almost leveled with the ground. The heat was so intense that it could not be approached except from the west, and, therefore, after it had started there was not the slightest chance of saving it. The fire then extended to the north of the Columbia House, and attacking Tom Barrett's bowling alley, soon settled it. A number of outbuildings attached to the Columbia House also went under. The fire was now directly in the rear of the *Cape May Daily Wave* office, and Editor McGrath, who had before this taken simply a journalistic view of the conflagration, now began to look out for his own safety.

He began hauling his things into the street, and many of his neighbors prepared to do the same, but finally the fire in this direction was got pretty well under control, and the minds of the Washington street folks became a little easier. The Columbia House, which had formed a sort of bulwark between the fire and the point to the east, having gone, endangered another locality which up to this time had been thought to be safe. This part of the town, to the east of Ocean Street and to the south of Columbia Avenue, was filled with many fine properties, and great efforts were made to check the flames. Among the properties were Beaver's cottage, Thomas T. Tasker's cottage. Colonel S. S.

Smoot's cottage and Wolf's cottage. These were all burned, as well as the bath houses connected with the Stockton Hotel, on the beach immediately below. There were upwards of a thousand of them, so I'm told.

This was getting to be pretty hot work. The fire being on Ocean Street, and almost on the beach fears were expressed that the Stockton, which loomed up grandly and as yet untouched, would surely go. This was about half-past four o'clock, and another steamer had arrived. This time Vineland was the sender, and this steamer was sent down to look after matters near the Ocean. The fire was now separated from the Stockton only by Warne's cottages in Stockton Row. Several of them were on fire at different times, but the flames were extinguished. Sparks and cinders at intervals lodged upon the roof of the Stockton, but by the vigilance of the fire men and citizens there were not allowed to do any damage. The fire really

terminated at Wolf's cottage about half-past four, at which time three engines were playing upon it.

Only a few sticks of Wolf's cottage remain. MeCray's cottage, on Jackson Street, between the Centre House and Merchants' was destroyed after the Merchants' went under. On the lawn of the Columbia House two cottages belonging to the hotel were consumed. The fire having spent its force, now lay smouldering, and burned off and on through the entire night. The engine, however, remained on duty, and the people felt comparatively safe. As before stated, the fire ground probably covers an area of about forty acres, and extends from Congress street on the west, Lafayette Street on the north, the ocean on the south and a point halfway between Ocean and Gurney streets on the east and southeast. The fire was forced into a southeast direction by the wind and it seems almost a miracle that the Stockton was saved, as the wind was very high when the fire was checked.

CAPE CURIOSITY

The Physick Family

THE Physick family roots go back to the earliest days of America, when the men we know as our Founding Fathers were preparing to revolt against Great Britain. Dr Emlen Physick's great-great grandfather, Philip Syng, was the silversmith for the American revolutionaries. When the time came to draft the Declaration of Independence it was Philip Syng who was called upon to design the inkstand that would be used for the document. Later, it was used in the writing of the United States Constitution.

Dr Physick's great grandfather, Edmund Physick, was a counselor and personal friend of the Penn family. He held the official title of Keeper of the Great Seal and his primary job was to manage all the Penn holdings in America during the Revolutionary War. Once the fighting was over, Edmund Physick assumed additional duties as an agent of the Penn family. He oversaw all the family's properties and acted on their behalf in legal matters. That included negotiations with the newly-created American government and its leader, President George Washington.

Next in line was the most famous member of the family, Dr Physick's grandfather, Dr Phillip Syng Physick, a prominent Philadelphia physician who changed the course of modern medicine. He studied medicine at the University of Pennsylvania before traveling to Scotland, where he furthered his education at the University of Edinburgh.

Within a few years of returning to Philadelphia he accepted a position with the nation's first hospital, Pennsylvania Hospital. Rather than becoming one of the jack-of-all-trades physicians who were typical of his time, Dr Physick

Left: Dr Physick with his mother and aunt and in later years with his beloved dog
Top right: Famed surgeon Dr Phillip Syng *Mid-Atlantic Center for the Arts*

specialized in performing complex surgeries and quickly built a reputation for being the most skillful surgeon in the country. Patients included Chief Justice of the US Supreme Court, John Marshall, and Dolly Madison, wife of President Madison. He was also the Attending Physician for President Jackson.

A story that is still talked about in medical schools involves Dr Physick's performance during the devastating yellow fever epidemic that hit Philadelphia in the late 1790s. He worked long hours in a clinic for yellow fever patients, helping those he could and trying to make things comfortable for those he could not. He chose to spend much of his free time performing dissections of those who succumbed to the illness, hoping to find a cure. What makes his story

particularly inspiring is the fact that on top of all the hours Dr Physick spent seeing patients and conducting research, he himself was suffering from fever.

Later in his career, Dr Physick continued his research and developed surgical innovations that are still in use, most notably the technique for pumping a stomach. He also invented a number of instruments and tools that revolutionized the medical field.

Because of his tremendous prowess as a surgeon, his extensive research and his dedication to the field, Dr Phillip Syng Physick is honored as "the Father of American Surgery."

As for Dr Emlen Physick, his story is a little different from his predecessors. He attended medical school and appeared to be preparing to

become a physician like his famous grandfather. Upon graduation, however, he surprised his family and chose a completely different lifestyle. Instead of treating patients and performing surgeries, he decided to become a tenant farmer and animal breeder.

After his father passed away, he moved into his Cape May mansion with his mother and her sister, an interesting living arrangement that was only made more curious by the fact that Dr Physick never chose to marry.

He devoted his time to the many animals he housed on the Physick estate and stayed active in local civic affairs. He was well known in Cape May circles for both his gregarious and philanthropic nature. He had many friends in town and was credited with funding a number of local organizations, like the Cape May Yacht Club.

Dr Physick was the first Cape May resident to own an automobile, a Ford Model T that he purchased in 1915. And while the original is gone, a replica of the vehicle is on display at the Emlen Physick Estate. The MAC organization also renovated the house and turned it into a Victorian museum that is open to the public.

CHAPTER EIGHT
Ashes To Affluence

AFTER TWO disastrous fires ravaged Cape May, leveling nearly all the hotels and cottages in the heart of the city, naysayers proclaimed America's Original Seaside Resort as dead and buried. They were very much mistaken.

In fact, Cape May returned the following season, 1879, stronger than ever. Residents and city leaders assembled almost immediately after the fire, in November of 1878, to discuss how to rebuild. The first order of business was agreeing on the purchase of a new, state-of-the-art steam fire engine.

The following January saw Cape May take possession of a horse-drawn Selsby fire engine. Citizens were proud of their new fire apparatus, which had the power to propel two one-inch streams of water more than 200 feet. They were confident that the town would finally be protected from fire disasters like that of 1869 and 1878.

One of the first hotels to be rebuilt was the venerable Congress Hall. Rather than constructing the new hotel on the same footprint as its predecessor, the decision was made to rebuild on a smaller scale and subdivide the northern area of the property. A new street was created, Congress Place, running along the foundation of the original building.

On the northern side of the street, individual lots were sold to private investors. On the south side the new Congress Hall was constructed of brick and mortar, albeit half the size of its predecessor.

Across Congress Street, Thomas H. Whitney saw the opportunity presented by the fire and took the opportunity to expand his cottage into a hotel. The Windsor, as Whitney called it, was constructed in the same L-shape design as Congress Hall and was also three stories tall

CONGRESS HALL

Brick Building.

Cape May, New Jersey.

SEASON, JUNE 15 TO SEPT. 15.

LOCATION. Congress Hall stands in an enclosed lawn of three acres, fifteen feet above the ocean beach drive, thus commanding an uninterrupted view of the ocean. It is reached by the Reading and Pennsylvania railroads by 90-minute trains.

ADVANTAGES. Only brick hotel at the Cape. All rooms are outside ones. Pure water from the famous Cold Spring. Passenger Elevator, Electric Bells, Bath Rooms on each floor. Perfect sanitary arrangements. Fire escapes from every room.

AMUSEMENTS. It is the social and musical centre of attraction. *Offers the finest and safest beach on the Atlantic Coast* Golf, Tennis, Shuffle Boards, Billiards, and fine roads for Riding, Driving and Cycling. Hops three nights each week. Orchestra concerts every morning and evening.

For terms, etc., address,

R. HALPIN, Proprietor,

the breakers, so that the smallest children may take the water with the same freedom as the larger ones, who find their depth further beyond. The beach is singularly free from holes as well as from undertow and peril of any kind, and the pleasure of the bath is enhanced to the average bather by its security.

The wide strand is a natural playground for children. They camp on it in the daylight hours and there is nothing to harm nor make them afraid, but they do acquire the bronze of wind and sun and store up a stock of health and strength which vitalizes the weak and makes stalwart the robust. Some marvellous transformations of weaklings into sturdy youngsters have been wrought in one season in

THE BATHING HOUR

the out-of-door sanitarium of the Cape May sands. There are seven miles of beach front. Walking on it is a pleasure; driving a delight. For the automobile it is an ideal roadway, and at the automobile speed trials last summer held under the auspices of the Cape May Automobile Club the record

Principal Hotels at Cape May, N. J.

	No. Guests Accommodated.
Aldine	125
Baltimore Inn	150
Brexton Villa	200
Carroll Villa	80
Chalfonte	250
Colonial	125
Columbia	300
Congress Hall	750
Deven	100
Ebbett	100
Elberon	100
Lafayette	300
Marine Villa	250
Mt. Vernon House	75
Star Villa	200
Stockton Hotel	1000
Windsor Hotel	250
Wyoming	75
Twenty others	1250

with a Mansard roof.

In front of the two hotels the Congress Hall Hotel Company built a new pier that extended 580 feet over the ocean. There were no amusements built on to the pier, although it was attached to the newly-rebuilt boardwalk. The ocean end was intended to accommodate steam ships and other vessels, allowing the hotels to bring visitors to their doorsteps.

The Columbia House land was also subdivided and Columbia Avenue was extended to Decatur Street, effectively cutting the old hotel's large property in half. The expansive front lawn was split into separate parcels that were used for both new homes and for the relocation of one very special cottage.

The William Weightman cottage was originally constructed on the corner of Washington and Franklin streets. In 1881, the building's namesake, Mr Weightman, decided to purchase one of the Columbia Hotel lots and have his large cottage moved to it. He chose the front parcel on the corner of Ocean Street and Beach Drive, which would give his family the best ocean views available. Since he lived in Philadelphia during the off-season he hired local workers to accomplish the feat.

Unfortunately for Mr Weightman the move hit a bit of a snag. It seems the technology existed for laborers to split his cottage into two pieces and pull them the five-and-a half blocks to the new lot, but nobody could figure how to put the pieces back together again. The workers decided to build new walls to enclose each side

of the house. When Mr Weightman returned to Cape May the next season, he found his cottage had been converted into two.

Across Decatur Street, on the site of Victor Denizott's bath houses, a new hotel was constructed. The new inn was called The Ocean View and, like others around the city, it was built on a much smaller scale than the older hostelries.

The Ocean View was designed to provide hotel rooms on the second, third and fourth floors, with a large restaurant on the first. Almost immediately the Ocean View's restaurant established a strong reputation as the best eatery in town, with the freshest seafood available.

Directly in front of the Ocean View, the Denizott pier extended into the ocean with small

CAPE MAY PANORAMA Most of the buildings are still standing, like Congress Hall, the Sea Villa and the Denizot Hotel, now Cabanas and Martini Beach *Don Pocher*

amusements on the beach end. Like the Congress Hall pier, the Denizott pier was able to accommodate both steam ships and sailing vessels.

The Columbia name was resurrected in 1879, with the building of the New Columbia Hotel on a one-block parcel between Perry and Jackson streets. It was constructed of brick, like Congress Hall, with the belief that this would protect the hotel against subsequent fires. That notion was proved wrong when the New Columbia burned

to the ground in September of 1889.

The years immediately after the fire saw the largest construction movement in the history of Cape May. In addition to the many cottages built throughout the burned district the western side of the city was developed.

In 1882 the land that formerly housed the ill-fated Mount Vernon Hotel was purchased by a group calling itself the Cape May Beach Improvement Company. They established a series of new

roads to divide the land and sold off individual properties for the construction of new cottages.

The company was later bought out in 1887 by a new organization, The Mount Vernon Land Company. This new group further developed the western area of the city and founded the borough of South Cape May in the vicinity of the current Cove beach, with an extensive series of streets and individual properties. Although it ultimately succumbed to the ocean in 1944 after a series of

powerful storms, South Cape May was once a thriving, desirable district.

The years between 1882 and 1884 were especially momentous for Cape May, with the construction of the Carroll Villa and the new Atlantic Hotel on Jackson Street, the Lafayette Hotel on the corner of Beach Drive and Decatur Street, the Star Villa on Ocean Street and the famous iron picr. Additionally, electrical lines were run throughout the city, along with gas lines.

The iron pier was finished in 1884, extending the boardwalk 1000 feet over the ocean. The length of the pier was 30 feet wide and underneath the main deck a second pier was constructed for public fishing. The structure included more than 21,000 square feet of space for amusements, shops, and an 8,000-square-foot dancing pavilion on the ocean end.

In 1886 the dancing pavilion was enclosed so that it could be also be used for opera and theatre.

The iron pier was much more than a simple jetty or boardwalk. It was the place for local gatherings, social events, dances and weekly concerts. The citizens of Cape May took great pride in the iron pier and believed it to be a symbol of the modern resort into which the city was evolving.

Cape May saw the third incarnation of the Columbia Hotel when Colonel Henry Sawyer leased the old Arctic Hotel on Ocean Street in 1890 and renamed it. This time the moniker

BEHEMOTH ON THE BEACH This early picture of the iron pier, which began at Decatur Street, was taken before the entryway and the end of the pier were built up with commercial interests. Even at this early stage in the pier's life, beachgoers had already begun seeking shade underneath it in the hot afternoon sun
Don Pocher

proved to be lucky and the third Columbia Hotel was very successful for Sawyer and subsequent managers.

The city saw increased expansion in 1892 after the completion of an electric railroad linked Sewell's Point with Cape May Point. The rail lines ran parallel with the boardwalk, on the beach side, and the new service proved very popular with seasonal visitors.

The next large hotel to be built in Cape May was the Baltimore Inn, which was constructed on Jackson Street and spanned almost the entire block to Decatur. And in 1895 the Colonial Inn opened for business on Ocean Street.

The following year, Cape May widened the boardwalk and raised it two feet off the beach. Shops were constructed on Beach Drive alongside the many bath houses, the entrance to the iron pier was expanded with additional shops, and a new entertainment hall was built on Jackson Street.

In 1898 Cape May was again forced to face the specter of war with the threat of hostilities against Spain. After the US government officially declared war in April, volunteers from the city assembled to form a light artillery unit to protect the coast. Off the shore, navy vessels patrolled both the Atlantic Ocean and the Delaware Bay, alleviating worries that the ships from the Spanish Armada would shell the Cape. The Spanish-American war continued only four months, ending with a peace treaty signed in Washington.

Cape May was preparing to enter the 20th century and as citizens reflected on the past 100 years they were hit with the largest snowstorm that had ever been recorded in the region. The 1899 blizzard brought heavy winds that accompanied the snow for four days. By the time the storm ended, on February 14, nearly four feet had been dumped on the city.

FROM THE ARCHIVES

A Truly Great Seaside Resort

From *The Baltimore Sun*, June 20, 1885

THE CUSTOM of visiting coast resorts during the summer months has become almost universal both in this and European countries, and the fashion which originated in Europe of visiting such resorts in winter has also taken a firm hold upon the people of this country.

The question now is not so much as to whether you will go to the seaside in summer as to where you will go. Every place has its attractions and its warm admirers. Cape May, one of the best known and most popular of the "cities by the sea," has many distinctive characteristics. The magnificent beach is acknowledged to be one of the finest in the world, the temperature is delightful, the ocean view grand and the surf all that can be desired by bathers.

Another characteristic of the place is the refined society found here, besides summer life is made brilliant by the many social events following each other in rapid succession at the various large hotels. Germans, concerts, fishing, parties, yachting go to make up a diversified programme, suited to the tastes of even the most fastidious.

There is to be what may be called a "grand opening day" here on Saturday next, though quite a number of the hotels and boarding cottages

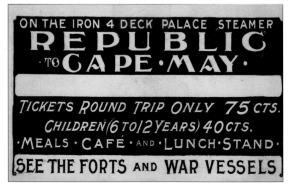

ON THE IRON 4 DECK PALACE STEAMER
REPUBLIC
·TO·**CAPE·MAY**·

TICKETS ROUND TRIP ONLY 75 CTS.
CHILDREN (6 TO 12 YEARS) 40 CTS.
·MEALS·CAFÉ·AND·LUNCH·STAND·
SEE THE FORTS AND WAR VESSELS

are already open. On Saturday the celebrated Weccacoe Band of Philadelphia, which had taken such a prominent part in the musical festivals held here the past few years, and which is engaged for the summer from July 4, is to give a concert on the grand pavilion of the new iron pier. There is also to be a hop given in the pavilion, which has been enclosed with glass, and can be closed up if the weather should prove unfavorable. On Sunday the band is to give a sacred concert in the pavilion. Prof Gosche is to have charge of this as well as the musical festivals during the summer at the Cape.

As a general thing there is not much of a crowd here until about the Fourth of July, but the arrivals last Saturday and this week have been quite numerous, and everything indicates a lively and prosperous season. The weather seems not to be getting down to business and the hot spells which are expected to follow make the bosom of the summer resort hotel men swell with delight, as they are also expected to make his pocket swell

Hotel Stockton Baths, Cape May, N. J.

Life Saving Boat, Cape May, N. J.

Cape May, N.J. from the Lighthouse.

at the end of the season. There has not been much bathing yet, except by excursionists, but the water is becoming pleasant, and soon a dip in the surf will be the order of the day.

There are but few places along the coast which can rival Cape May for well-regulated and commodious hotels. The Stockton, so well and popularly known, will be in charge this season of Mr A. L. Mellen, of the St James Hotel, Baltimore. Mr Mellen has secured the services of Mr D. Pinknew West, the well-known Baltimore detective, who will have charge of the police arrangements of the house. He also engaged Andrew Nevtis, well known as "Andy," formerly of Guy's Hotel, Baltimore, and now of the Colonnade, Philadelphia, to take charge of the bar connected with the Stockton.

Congress Hall, a popular house for Baltimoreans, is again in charge of Colonel Duffy, who is well and favorably known to visitors generally to Cape May. He has made a number of improvements to the house, which is now in first-class order.

The New Columbia is conducted by Mr James D. McClellan, formerly of the Logan House, Altoona, PA, and who kept the Stockton, Cape May, last summer. It is a fine brick structure, and one of the most substantial along the coast.

The Windsor, of which Mr Walter W. Green is proprietor, is located directly on the beach, and is one of the coziest and most home-like hotels found anywhere.

The Arlington, the well-known Baltimore house, continues under the popular manage-

ment of Mr John J. Kromer, who is a former well-known Baltimorean. The Arlington has undergone a number of improvements.

The Arctic House, also popular with Baltimore people, is under new management this year. Mr A. E. Lyons, the present proprietor, was formerly proprietor of Cresson Springs Hotel, PA, and kept the New Columbia, Cape May, last winter. He has had eighteen years experience in the hotel business.

The West End Hotel, kept by Mr L. E. Johnson, is pleasantly located, and is largely patronized by Baltimoreans.

The many friends of ex-Mayor F. J. Melvin will find him in a new role this year. Mr Melvin has made a good mayor, and thinks he can keep a hotel. He will be found at the Sea Breeze hotel.

CAPE MAY

1890

SCALE

1 MILE

1 LAKE LILY, CAPE MAY PT.
2 LIGHTHOUSE POND
3 SHALLOW POND
4 LIGHTHOUSE
5 COAST GUARD STATION
6 OLD BOAT LANDING
7 POND CREEK MEADOWS
8 PONDS BACK OF S. CAPE MAY
9 HIGBEE'S BEACH
10 NEW ENGLAND MEADOW
11 PRICE'S SALT POND
12 TOWN BANK
13 POND NEAR BROADWAY
14 RACE TRACK POND
15 W. CAPE MAY PONDS
16 CAPE ISLAND CREEK
17 SCHELLENGER'S LANDING
18 GOLF LINKS
19 PHYSICK PLACE
20 BRIER ISLAND
21 MILL LANE
22 WEEKS' LANDING

A TEAM OF WINNERS
"A Fine Record Made By the Collegians" proclaimed the newspapers, as the Cape May baseball team ended the 1893 season with a record of 21 wins, five losses and a tie. The local athletes claimed their victories against a diverse collection of teams, including the renowned New York Athletic Club. The Cape May Collegians boasted two players with a batting average over .400, another at .394 and the team's three pitchers struck out 223 batters.
Tom Dvorschak

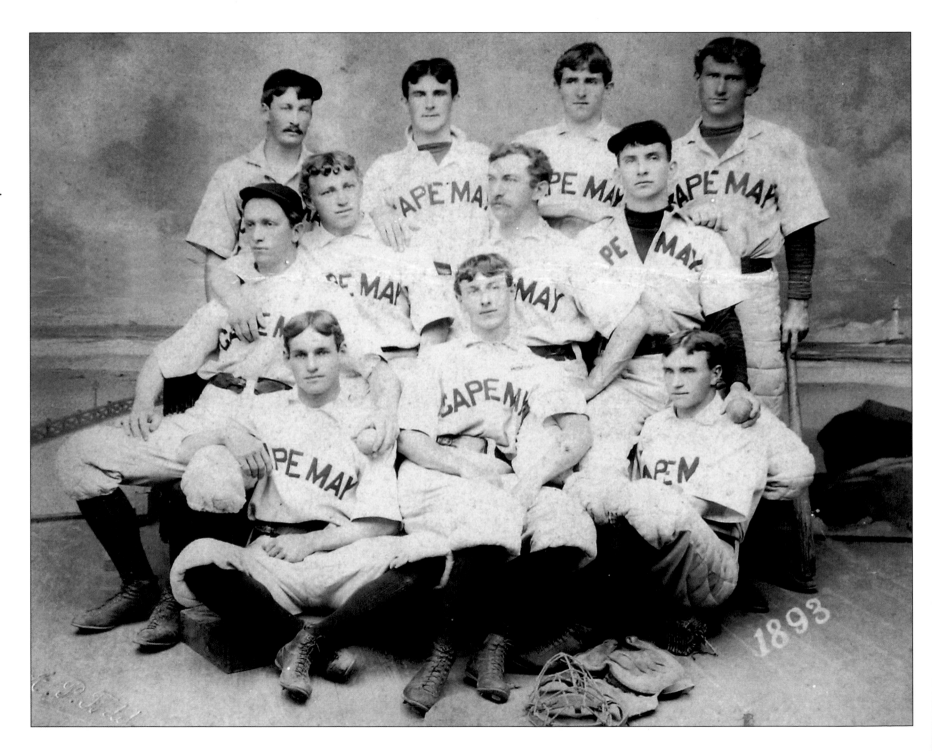

BUILDINGS ON THE MOVE
At the time this picture was taken, both the Morning Star Villa, on the left, and Evening Star Villa, on the right, were operated in conjunction with the Colonial Hotel. The Morning Star and Evening Star were moved to a new property on the eastern part of Beach Avenue by Reverend Carl McIntire in the 1960s, after they were slated for demolition by the owners of the Lafayette Hotel, who sought to use the land for a parking lot. The Weightman Cottages, visible on the far left of the picture, were also moved by Reverend McIntire and are now operated as the Angel of the Sea bed and breakfast. The Evening Star has since been demolished and the Colonial Hotel is now known as The Inn of Cape May.
Tom Dvorschak

A BEAUTIFUL COLLECTION This page: The Stockton Row cottages are still standing today along Gurney Street, although some have been modified significantly *Cape May County Museum)*

FAMILY PORTRAIT Opposite page: Local developer Humphrey Hughes is shown in the center (with a white beard and moustache) with his family in this late 1800s portrait. *Don Pocher*

The house has been greatly improved and completely renovated. It is the only excursion house at Cape May proper.

The Star Villa is a new and attractive house built since last season. It is located on Ocean street, near Beach avenue and has a frontage of 80 feet and depth of 135 feet, containing 50 rooms. It has all the modern conveniences and is first-class in its appointments. Mr J. C. Garwood, late of the Baltimore House, is lessee.

The Brexton Villa is one of the coziest houses — or rather series of houses, for it combines five villas joined in one — on the island. It is eligibly located and has a fine ocean view. Mrs J. A. Myers, the proprietress, is a well-known Baltimore lady, and formerly kept the Brexton in that city. Mr Hanway, president of the first branch city council, has secured quarters at the Brexton Villa for his family during the season.

The Marine Villa, one of the best-known houses at Cape May, is in charge of Miss Harrison, of Baltimore, this year, and has a large Baltimore patronage. The location (near the beach) is delightful and the appointments first-class.

The Hotel Lafayette, located opposite the iron pier, continues under the management of Mr F. H. Hildreth. It is located on Beach Avenue, and is one of the finest houses on the coast.

Cottage life is a feature of Cape May, and board can be obtained at the various boarding cottages at moderate rates, with as good fare as at the hotels. The cottages are generally large and roomy, well located and well kept. Mrs M. J. Hubball, of Washington, and who formerly kept the Highland Park Hotel, near Baltimore, this year is proprietress of the McCollum House, on Hughes street. Mrs F. L. Richardson continues at the head of Carroll Villa, one of the coziest houses on the island. The Williamson cottage, on Lafayette avenue, kept by Mrs E. H. Williamson, is a favorite house.

The Light of Asia, as the large building

ALL ABOARD THE EXPRESS
This page, left: The West Jersey Railroad put out this advertisement for their express trains to Cape May in the 1890s
Don Pocher

GOODBYE, JUMBO
This page, right: The Light of Asia wooden elephant was constructed on the beach of South Cape May as part of a real estate venture. It was designed by the same gentleman who created the famous Lucy the Elephant that remains a big attraction in Margate, NJ. The Cape May elephant only lasted until 1900, six years after it was built.
Cape May County Museum

SOAKING UP THE SURF
Opposite page: 1885 beachgoers revel along the Cape May strand in front of the Windsor Hotel. Note the Light of Asia, circled in the background.
Don Pocher

erected in the shape of a big elephant, along the beach midway between Cape May and Cape May Point, is called, though begun about eighteen months ago is not yet completed. It is so near completion, however, that when approaching it has the appearance of a genuine elephant, and attracts much attention from visitors.

Mr F. C. Fossett, a well-known merchant and property-owner of Baltimore, and Mr P. T. Dawson, a well-known real estate broker and agent, have been spending a week at Cape May, enjoying an early visit to the seaside, stopping at the Windsor. Both have been visitors to Cape May for many years, and speak highly of the advantages of the place as a healthful resort. They have inspected the Light of Asia since their arrival here, and are discussing the feasibility of buying the elephant as a matter of speculation.

The National Flint and Glass Association hold their meeting here this week at Congress Hall.

Mr Donald R. Collier, a well-known Baltimore merchant, and Mr Wm F. McKewen, clerk of the City Court, have again secured quarters for the season at Congress Hall. Mr Collier is known to almost everybody at Cape May, and will receive a hearty welcome on his arrival.

Cape May has two good seaside papers, the *Wave* and the *Star*, both of which issue daily editions during July and August. Mr Williamson, proprietor of the *Wave*, will erect a fine cottage this year at the corner of Washington and Decatur streets.

Mr Samuel C. Little, of Guy's, Baltimore, who has been summering at Cape May for many years, has tried Atlantic City this year, and is occupying a cottage there.

The Pennsylvania Railroad Company, alive to the requirements of a seaside city, furnishes the best kind of rapid transportation to Cape May, as well as all the resorts along the coast. The cars are of modern design, comfortable, light and airy, and the time made is not surpassed by any of the railroads in the country.

FROM THE ARCHIVES

Cape May Re-Awakens

The Philadelphia Inquirer, April 19, 1896

CAPE MAY HAS A BOOM
Special to the Inquirer

THE residents and authorities of this resort are waking up from their long sleep of inactivity, and Cape May has taken on a boom.

When the local residents began to move on lines of enterprise the non-residents began to help, and the Cape May Cottagers' Association was organized, with some of Philadelphia's most prominent residents as its executive board. John F. Craig is its president; John H. Sloan, vice-president; George Gluyas Mercer, secretary, and Thomas Robb, treasurer. Those on the Executive Committee are Frank Willing Leach, William King, A. J. Gillingham, Robert H. Beattie, John J. McConnell, United States Senator Sewell, of Camden, and others of as equal prominence. Several meetings of this association, in conjunction with residents and the City Council, were held, and they at last agreed upon a plan to spend this spring $50,000 in beachfront improvements.

A few days ago the City Council adopted plans for a big oceanfront pavilion, to be erected on the Strand, just south of the Stockton Hotel, between the foot of Ocean and Stockton Row.

The ground on which it will stand has been donated by John C. Bullitt, of Philadelphia. It is intended to have musical concerts given there three times daily during the season- morning, afternoon and evening. The subscription for this is large. The contract for building it will be given out within a week.

Beach Avenue is being raised to correspond with Madison Avenue, on the east end of the place, and Stockton Avenue is being carried out to Madison Avenue. These two make about 4,000 feet of new drive. Madison Avenue will probably be extended to the water works at Cold Spring, and when this is done there will be a nine-mile circuit around the place, including the beach drive on the front and turnpike from Cape May to Cape May Point through the woods on the north end of the place. The water works' plant is being extended by the addition of extra mains and the taking in of new territory.

The work the city is doing will cost $90,000 altogether. Besides this much money is being expended on the improvements at hotels and cottages; $10,000 is being spent on Congress Hall. The Windsor, Stockton, Chalfonte, Marine Villa, Star Villa, Aldine and other hotels are being renovated and improved. Several new cottages have been built.

The pile of black bricks which were left by the fire of the New Columbia Hotel in October, 1889, and which have been an eyesore and barrier to progress, are at last being cleared away. For three weeks workmen have been clearing the three million brick and piling them up for future use. The Columbia was probably the handsomest house on the shore. The site will change hands when cleared up, and upon it are to be built some large boarding cottages.

Since last summer the Pennsylvania Railroad has built a handsome winter brick station, which equals any upon its lines outside of the big cities. The company has spent about $10,000 on its various improvements on this end of the line.

This page, top: Grant Street Summer Station in 1885 *Don Pocher*

This page, right: Victorian sunbathers used beach tents very similar to what we have today *Cape May County Museum*

Opposite page: A busy beach scene with the iron pier in the background *Don Pocher*

FROM THE ARCHIVES

Cape May Of The Early 1900s

From *South Jersey, A History, 1664-1923*

O
LD CAPE MAY practically began at the Summer Station, at the foot of Grant Street. Here stood net-covered horses drawing busses in every stage of repair or dilapidation, awaiting passengers and the dimes that were the fare "to any part of town."

A small street car started its peregrinations beside the boardwalk and wandered along the other end of town. For several years the cars have not run at all, and today jitneys and the old-time busses, the "Alpha" and "Omega" of transportation, offer the only means of conveyance to those who do not own automobiles.

In this vicinity a dozen or more commodious cottages had been erected on large plots of ground. They were frame and built in the southern style, with double porches, painted white and vine embowered. Well kept lawns with gardens and ornamental trees surrounded them, enclosed in turn by hedges of a bush much like the tropical tamarisk.

Among the bushes the white marble statuary gleamed, and the calls of many birds that have made of these secluded spots a feathered sanctuary, carried one far from the sea that broke at the end of the walk. Hydrangeas, that reached perfection here, meet one's eye at

every turn. In this delightful group of seaside homes were those of General William J. Sewell; of the Sellers of Millbourne, and the Knight family.

The first hotel beyond the station is the Windsor, a three-story clapboard building with a long wing parallel with the sea. A porch runs inside the angle and across the end, while verandas hang from the upper story. Sheltered by the building there used to be a pebbled terrace with an ornate fence an "a fountain in the center." Broad wooden steps lead down to the street level and gave the hotel an air at once

imposing and unique. Now the pebbles have gone, the fountain is dry, and where once the water sparkled "in its gleaming marble rim," green paint has transformed the basin that is filled with soil in which geraniums (not lilies) grow.

Grass plots separated by sandy walks replace the pebbles, and the only touch of its vanished beauty is in the groups of the lovely hydrangeas that still grow upon the terrace. The solid wooden fence with its wide flat top, that guarded the ocean side of the boardwalk, has been replaced by modern gas pipe. In the

past it was a convenient resting place, available at any moment when fatigue threatened, when one cared to linger, or felt that consuming desiring that comes to the young, to commune, a deux, with sea and sky.

Far back from the ocean stands Congress Hall. The large brick buildings were for many years neglected. The porch roof hung in scallops between the tall square columns, one of which rested against a wall. Part of the roof lay, a mass of debris, on the floor. Broken window panes looked out like sad blind eyes, and even birds hesitated to build amid such evidence

of decay. The hotel register contains many names that have made history. Statesmen, artists, travelers and the great of many lands sought hospitality there, left their marks upon these "sands of time," and went again into the unknown. Recently the house has been renovated and is now open to the public. The tragic atmosphere of decay that so long pervaded the building has been dispelled.

Visitors passing old Columbia, near the corner of Washington Street and Ocean Avenue, lingered to hear colored waiters sing. The crooning musical voices of the negroes in their

own weird melodies have a strong appeal. They seem to reach out and set a heart-string quivering with vague longing for something yet unknown.

In 1878 a fire, which has been an active enemy of Cape May, destroyed the then Columbia House and made a place for its successor, the New Columbia. Of all the old hotels the Columbia House showed most plainly the prevalent influence of the South. It might have been a huge plantation home transported from some far off southern scene and set down by the sea.

The New Columbia was a brick structure, moderate in size and of commonplace type. It, too, was burned, and the place of the two Columbias is filled with small cottages built in a Close, surrounded by grass and hedges and hydrangeas, with a common entrance and exit to the sea.

Baltimore Inn is near. Shining in white paint, with shaded awnings and flower boxes on the porch, it looks inviting.

Above the old bath houses are the same names as in years gone by. Maguire's and further on Shield's. From under one of them a huge rat scampered and ran across the drive. There was a peculiar fetid odor of old wood rotting in salt water.

A second generation of Japanese conduct the "Art Store," but a touch of modernity is given by "Arnold's Hotel" where before the era of prohibition good dinners and 'good times: were to be had. Still in the window rests the frame of scarlet lobsters, an enticement still, but inside the gayety is subdued to the level of the refreshment now offered. "near beer."

On Decatur Street, a little way back from Arnold's is Zillinger's Café. Beside the house a garden invites the hungry, and between the large leaves of the vine that clings to the latticed roof with its spiral tendrils, are pendant bunches of green and purple grapes.

The remains of the pier voice the old question: "If I am so soon done for, I wonder what I was begun for?" Cut off abruptly in mid-air a few feet from the entrance, it juts into space. At low tide jagged rusty supports stick up from the sand, but at high tide the water covers them and hides the danger they have become.

The pier was built in 1885, at the foot of Decatur Street, and for many years the only amusement place in town. Now it houses a shop where ice cream cones and salt water taffy are sold; a moving picture theatre; a Japa-

nese rolling ball game; a shop where commonplace embroidered kimonos are shown.

At the entrance years ago a giant sword hung, its long serrated sword striking terror into young hearts. Beyond the merry-go-round, and further out a theatre, and then a fishing platform with a lower deck where boats landed. Light opera and musical comedies were given on the pier by stars like Jennie Prince, who shed their historic light on Cape May in the summer time.

Across from the pier is the Lafayette, a relic of Cape May's gay old days. Theatrical people frequented it and it was thought a "lively" place.

On the next corner are cottages originally owned by the late William Weightman, of Philadelphia. They were considered the finest and most modern houses at the Cape. Now painted a dull battleship grey and overshadowed by the

Just ran across an old friend on the boardwalk. Cape May, N. J.

BOARDWALK PRANK
This fun late 1800s postcard shows a minor accident on the pier when a carriage driver strikes a pedestrian
Don Pocher

newer residences, they are unremarkable.

On Ocean Avenue, near the beach and over-looking the Stockton Baths, is the colonial, a medium sized house of "middle age"; and "run" on unpretentious fashion. Opposite is Star Villa, a house of the same type.

The Stockton Hotel was the hub of Cape May, but the Stockton Baths were surely the most important spokes. They cover one end of the block between Ocean Avenue and Stockton

/row, and are the last remnant of the Cape May property of the late John C Bullitt, of Philadel-phia, the framer of the Bullitt Bill.

Always painted yellow with brown trim-mings and red tin roofs, they are today just as they were years ago. In the center is a small house, its porch surmounted by a clock, in which are office and store rooms.

The bath houses extend in rows on either side. This was the daily meeting place for all

socially inclined. At eleven o'clock on any summer morning the porch was filled with daintily dressed women and men in flannels. In those days girls were mermaids and went into the sea with flowing locks, regardless of the damage of Father Neptune might do.

The popularity of the girls was measured by the number of men who asked to dry her hair. A very popular one had to "cut" the drying, as her modern sister does her dances.

VERY IMPORTANT
VISITOR
This page, left:
President Andrew
Jackson was one of
the first American
heads of state to
visit the resort
National Archives

OVAL OFFICE
TO THE SHORE
This page, right:
Franklin Pierce
was another
presidential visitor
who travelled to
Cape May during
his term in the
White House
National Archives

CAPE CURIOSITY

Visits From The Presidents

NO FEWER than 11 American presidents visited Cape May, including Andrew Jackson, Benjamin Harrison, Franklin Pierce, James Buchanan, Woodrow Wilson, Gerald Ford, George Bush and Ronald Reagan.

What sets President Harrison apart from the others is not simply that he decided to stay in Cape May while in office. Presidents Franklin Pierce, Ulysses S. Grant and Chester Arthur also made the sojourn from Washington DC to America's Original Seaside Resort.

In 1890 President Harrison decided that a few days of vacation in Cape May was not enough and he planned to spend the entire summer on the island. Personal friend and Postmaster General in the president's cabinet, John Wanamaker, had invited President Harrison to summer in Cape May and Congress Hall was chosen to be the Summer White House.

The honor was repeated in 1891 when the 23rd president of the United States again transformed Congress Hall into his Summer White House. But President Harrison did not take the summer months off or spend his days sunning himself on the beach in front of Congress Hall. Instead, he continued to do his job as chief executive of the United States, managing the government from his offices in the hotel.

In actuality, President Harrison presided over a number of important matters and landmark decisions in American history. Two of his most notable decisions were made during that 1890 stay, changing the face of America indelibly.

On July 3, 1890 President Harrison signed a bill admitting Idaho into the union and officially recognizing the territory as a state. A week later, the president repeated the action, creating a second new state. By the president's hand, on July 10, the Wyoming Territory was admitted into the union and Wyoming was officially recognized as a state.

It was during that same summer that President Harrison made another crucial decision, with the ramifications still being felt today. The Sherman Antitrust Act was passed by Con-

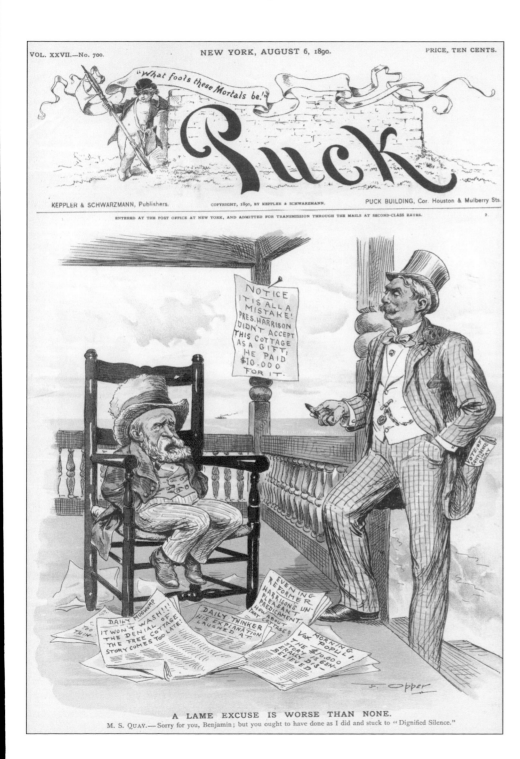

FRONT-PAGE NEWS
This page, left: The satirical magazine *Puck* took a shot at President Harrison after he was gifted a cottage in Cape May Point by renowned Philadelphia businessman John Wanamaker
Don Pocher

FAMILY MAN
This page, right: President Benjamin Harrison pictured with his wife and children
National Archives

TROUBLE IN THE HOUSE
This page, below: President Harrison finally paid $10,000 for this cottage in the Point, but he had already been damaged by the political scandal
Don Pocher

gress and forwarded to the president on July 2 of 1890. The bill, which was authored by the man he defeated for the Republican nomination, Senator John Sherman, prevented American businesses from restricting trade and creating monopolies.

President Harrison's monumental act of signing the Sherman Antitrust Act into law has been revisited many times throughout history. The same bill signed by the president as he began summering in Cape May has been used by the government in famous court cases against the Northern Securities Company, AT&T and Microsoft. Last June, President George W. Bush added to the act by signing into law a bill that increases corporate and individual penalties.

Another major issue facing the president while working from his summer White House in 1890 was the tremendous influx of foreign products being imported into the country and sold at cheaper rates than American goods. He began working with Republican senator and future president, William McKinley, to create a new tariff that would address the problem.

Later that year, while back in Washington, President Harrison signed into law the McKinley Tariff, which raised the average import tax to 48%. Unfortunately, the exorbitant taxes greatly raised the prices of goods for average Americans, who were not too appreciative. Presidential historians believe it is this issue, along with his strained ties to the party bosses, which cost Harrison reelection in 1892.

Although President Harrison returned to his Cape May White House in 1891 things were much different. In the November election the previous year, Democrats had taken control of Congress, with many of the president's political allies being defeated at the polls. Primarily, Harrison was kept busy with the day-to-day operations of the government, as opposed to the landmark bills of the previous summer.

It's not widely known that in 1890 President Harrison became a Cape May landowner. He was presented with a fully-furnished, new summer cottage in Cape May Point. The gift was made by Wanamaker, who had been a primary investor in the defunct Sea Grove Association, which tried to develop Cape May Point into a Christian resort. Actually, the cottage was officially given to the president's wife, Carrie. President Harrison refused to accept it himself for fear of being accused of bribery.

However, President Harrison failed to anticipate the public's reaction to his wife taking ownership of such an extravagant gift, and he found himself mired in controversy.

As much as the president wanted to relieve himself of the stigma associated with the bribery allegation, he also wanted to keep the house. His solution was to pay $10,000 to Wanamaker for the property and make the sale public.

President Harrison continued to spend time at the cottage, using it as a retreat after

PRESIDENTS IN
THE MAKING
Both Woodrow
Wilson, left, and
Ronald Reagan,
right, visited Cape
May prior to taking
their seats in the
Oval Office
National Archives

his wife's death and his defeat in the election of 1892.

It wasn't until he made the decision to remarry in 1896 that Harrison chose to sell the Cape May Point cottage and build a new home in New York.

History remembers this famous Cape May visitor as a fair man and influential president who endured a number of hardships and stood by his principles, despite political backlash. Regardless of political affiliations or leanings it is clear that President Harrison elevated Cape May to a new level with his decision to relocate the executive office here during the summer months.

The Fun Factory, Sewell's Point.   CAPE MAY, N. J.

CHAPTER NINE
The Rise And Fall Of East Cape May

4/17

HOTEL CAPE MAY

9 *Weather fine* J.

**PIER
PLEASURE**
This page, top: The
Cape May beach
was a popular place
in the early 1900s
and, as the picture
shows, the iron pier
had been adorned
with multiple
amusements at the
ocean end
*Cape May County
Museum*

**A DAY ON
THE WATER**
This page, below:
A rare picture of
people posing in
front of the iron
pier on the beach
at Decatur Street.
Note the beach
patrol members in
the front and the
number of people
on the pier – it's
packed!
Lynn Zettlemoyer

**AN ILL-FATED
VENTURE**
Previous page: This
postcard of the
Hotel Cape May
under construction
is dated 1909, one
year after the
hotel was actually
completed, and
within months of
it being reopened
under new
management. The
ambitious hotel
project seemed
doomed to fail
from the start.
Don Pocher

B Y THE year 1900 the luster of Victorian Cape May had begun to fade and the resort was starting to show its age. Once-proud cottages had fallen into disrepair, many of them sitting empty and abandoned. The city's older hotels were saddled with an alarming number of empty rooms and even the new ones were having trouble making ends meet.

Cape May was developing a reputation as an old-fashioned town, too steeped in the past to appeal to modern visitors. At the same time, one of the chief factors blamed for the decline in summer visitors was the loss of Cape May's most recognizable hotels to fire. The Columbia House, United States Hotel, Centre House, Atlantic Hotel, Mansion House and Ocean House were gone and many of their loyal guests left the city in search of a new summer resort.

Summer visitors to Cape May had always fallen into two categories — regular citizens of average means who came to the resort for a good time, and the upper echelon of society who came to Cape May because it was fashionable to do so. As the city's reputation weakened, two main competitors rose to prominence.

The first was Atlantic City, which also offered contemporary hotels, a long boardwalk and the typical seaside amusements that pleased tourists. Atlantic City hotels were built on a much bigger scale than those in Cape May. The best example of this was the famous Traymore, which offered 450 guest rooms and by 1915 had grown into a 16-story behemoth.

The second competitor was Newport, Rhode Island, which appealed to the many in the upper class. Some of the country's most influential and affluent families chose to summer in Newport, and those that wished to stay in society's graces soon followed. Wealthy

A VIEW OF THE ROOFTOPS
This page, top: An early 1900s aerial view of South Lafayette Street, with the Grant Street Summer Station in the background. Many of the homes in the picture are still standing today, including the one on the corner of South Lafayette and Congress Streets, with the witch's hat turret.
Don Pocher

A DAY ON THE WATER
This page, below: Boat houses and small row boats at Schellenger's Landing, now the location of the Lobster House, in 1903
Cape May County Museum

THE McCREARY

Americans clamored for an invitation to the Vanderbilt family's mansion, The Breakers, or the Astors' house, Beechwood.

While many in Cape May felt the increased competition would spell disaster for the resort, some looked at the situation differently and felt it could be just the catalyst the city needed. The latter was a group of citizens and summer visitors who had a grand design for the city's future and pushed to see their vision realized.

The Cape May Real Estate Company was formed and plans were distributed to the local papers that detailed a massive development on the eastern side of the island. The company hoped to turn Cape May into an upscale playground for the rich.

The cornerstone of their proposal rested on the dredging of a harbor and using the sand and silt to fill in the swampy, eastern section of Cape Island. The harbor would cover more than 500 acres, with an average depth of approximately 40 feet, allowing it to accommodate even the largest ships afloat at the time.

The dirt and sand that was dredged from the ocean floor would be used to level and grade the 3600 acres of swampy lands adjacent to the new harbor. The crown jewel of the plan, and one of the major selling points for the city of Cape May, was the proposed construction of an enormous, million-dollar hotel on the property.

Behind this tremendous real estate endeavor was a man by the name of William Flinn, president of Beechwood Improvement Company, Limited. He was initially approached by two Philadelphia businessmen, Anthony Zane and Frank G. Edwards. Flinn, a power broker from Pittsburgh, was known as a very controversial figure in turn-of-the-century politics.

Flinn and his partner, Christopher Magee, had held a tight control over local politicians and made millions through what many people considered to be underhanded manipulations of various public works projects. Their Beechwood Improvement Company had been successful in a number of other real estate development projects, like their sizeable industrial development in the coal region of Sharon, PA.

By 1903, however, Flinn's political rivals had gained control of Pittsburgh and he lost much of his clout. His partner, Magee, had passed away recently and there was little left for him to do in Pittsburgh, so he turned his focus to Cape May. With his newly-incorporated Cape May Real Estate Company, work began on the harbor dredging in July of 1903.

Building commenced on the Hotel Cape May in 1906, with its completion coming two years later. The hotel was slated to be ready much earlier but plans had to be changed after

**PORTRAIT OF
A TYCOON**
This page, left:
Henry Ford bought
land in Cape May
and planned to
build an automobile
plant. It never
happened, and the
site later became
Camp Wissahickon.
National Archives

**A WINNER
LOSES OUT**
This page, right:
Ford is shown
racing on the
beaches of Cape
May against Louis
Chevrolet, among
others. Ford lost
the race but did
not, as local legend
states, have to sell
his car to pay his
bill at the Stockton
Hotel.
*Cape May County
Museum*

**A BIG DAY AT
THE BEACH**
The rarely-seen
official program for
the auto races –
the names of Ford
and Chevrolet are
underlined in red
Lynn Zettlemoyer

**RACING ON THE
BOARDWALK**
Opposite page:
Local children got
caught up in the
automobile craze
*Cape May County
Museum*

OFFICIAL PROGRAMME.   7

EVENT No. 4
One kilometer for Gasolene Touring cars up to 40 h. p., driven by owner; moving
start.

No.	Car	H. P.	Owner	Driver
11	Winton	40 Gas	J. N. Wilkins, Jr	J. N. Wilkins, Jr.
12	Winton	40 Gas	C. J. Swain	C. J. Swain
14	Winton	40 Gas	J. H. Thropp	J. H. Thropp
15	Winton	40 Gas	J. A. Depew	J. A. Depew

Won by .... Second .... Time ....

EVENT No. 5
One kilometer for Heavyweight cars, 1432 to 2204 lbs ; moving start.
First Prize, Silver Cup, donated by J. Fred Betz, 3rd.
Second Prize, Silver Cup.

No.	Car	H. P.	Owner	Driver
1	Christie	130 Gas	Walter Christie	Walter Christie
2	Darracq	80 Gas	F. A. LaRoche Co.	M. Campbell
3	F. I. A. T.	130 Gas	Hollander and Tangeman	Louis Chevrolet
6	Ford	60 Gas	Ford Motor Co.	Henry Ford

Won by Darracq Second .... Time 27 .....

EVENT No. 6.
One kilometer. Special Event for Gasolene Cars; Flying Start Against Time
for the $500 Cape May Kilometer Trophy.

No.	Car	H. P.	Owner	Driver
1	Christie	130 Gas	Walter Christie	Walter Christie
2	Darracq	80 Gas	F. A. LaRoche Co.	Mr. Campbell
3	F. I. A. T.	120 Gas	Hollander and Tangeman	Louis Chevrolet
4	F. I. A. T.	24 Gas	Hollander and Tangeman	E. Cedrino
6	Ford	60 Gas	Ford Motor Co.	Henry Ford

Won by Christie. Second .... Time 23 .....

WE WILL GIVE YOU A 100-MILE DEMONSTRATION IN

The "Maxwell"

This is the Car that climbed the White Mountains and won the Gold Medal
for 2-cylinder stock cars.

16 H. P. Touring Car, $1,400.

Double opposed 5 x 5 motor, with mechanical valves under hood.   The three-speed
sliding gear transmission is in the same aluminum casting as crank case.   Water cooled natural
circulation. No pump. Pressed steel frame. All metal body.
Not one of our customers' cars have cost them a cent for repairs, and we will
gladly furnish name of every owner of a Maxwell for reference.
We will bring you down the Hudson, from our factory at Tarrytown, New York,
to your home in your own Maxwell Car, and if this demonstration is not satisfactory you are
not obliged to take the car.

KELSEY MOTOR CO.,
204 N. Broad Street,   -   -   Philadelphia, Pa.

Price 10 cents

**Official
Program**

AUTOMOBILE
RACE
MEETING

Cape May Beach
August 25th and 26th

Under the
Auspices of **Cape May Automobile Club**

THE HANDSOMEST AND MOST SERVICEABLE CAR ON THE MARKET

THE NEW SIDE - ENTRANCE WHITE STEAM CAR

COTTAGE WITH A FUTURE
This page, left: This three-story building on Ocean Street has a long and storied past. It was originally built as a summer cottage for the Gregory family and is now home to the nationally-acclaimed Queen Victoria B&B.
Don Pocher

THIS ONE'S FOR A PAR
This page, right: A golfer goes for the green on the ninth hole at the Cape May Golf Course on Lafayette Street
Cape May County Museum

A SMALL-TOWN STREET
Opposite page: The 300 block of Washington Street was home to a theatre, mechanic's garage, furniture store and other typical small-town shops
Don Pocher

a construction accident caused a portion of the building to collapse. Additionally, a large amount of bricks and other supplies purchased for the building disappeared during the evenings when the lot was empty.

The Cape May Real Estate Company celebrated the building of the hotel with a historic series of automobile races featuring Henry Ford, Louis Chevrolet, Alexander Winton and Walter Christie in August of 1905. The races were held on the beach, traversing from Sewell's Point to the Hotel Cape May on the new 'seashore track.'

One local story claims that Ford lost and had to sell his automobile to pay his hotel bill at the Stockton. While it is an entertaining tale, it is also untrue. Ford did lose his race against Christie, but money was not a concern. In fact, Ford later purchased a massive parcel of land

just outside of Cape May with the intention of using it for his new Ford Motor Company.

The most exciting news to come from the races concerned the stunning victory of a woman, Mrs Clarence Cecil Fitler, who beat all challengers in the race for gasoline touring cars up to thirty horsepower. Her victory made headlines all over the country and helped generate a good deal of interest in the East Cape May project.

When the Hotel Cape May opened for business in April of 1908 it offered accommodations for nearly 1000 people. With 330 rooms, spacious wraparound verandas and ornate grand ballroom, the hotel was considered the largest in the world. Unfortunately, it operated only six months before it was boarded up and closed, due to financial problems.

The closing of the hotel was just the beginning of problems for the new Cape May project. Within a year the president of Flinn's Cape May Real Estate Company, a man by the name of Peter Shields, resigned.

In the three years he was a part of the project, Shields dealt with a number of obstacles. Problems began during the construction of the Hotel Cape May. There was a strike among the workers, racial tensions with African-American laborers, the previously-mentioned collapse and the death of at least one workman, who fell from the partially-completed structure.

Meanwhile, Shields also had a large, Georgian-style home built a block down the road. His summer cottage, as he called it, was completed in 1907. Not long after the Shields cottage was finished, Shields and his family faced

BEFORE THE TRAGEDY
This page, left: Peter Shields and his family in their new automobile. Peter's son, Earl, who would lose his life at the age of 15 in a hunting accident, is behind the wheel.
Peter Shields Inn

A MOMENT ON THE PORCH
This page, right: Peter and his wife Cora pose for a picture on the front porch of their magnificent Cape May 'cottage', which is now the Peter Shields Inn. Shield was one of several prominent businessmen who tried, and failed, to save the ambitious East Cape May project.
Peter Shields Inn

a devastating loss from which he never fully recovered.

One fateful day, Peter's son, Earl, and some of his friends from the Cape May Yacht Club decided to go hunting in the unfinished swampland. Things were fine until the younger Shields tried to move from one boat into another.

Being only 15 years of age, Earl made a youthful mistake that turned fatal. He kept his balance by bracing himself on a rifle. Whether the gun misfired or the trigger was inadvertently pressed is unknown, but the rifle did fire and Earl was shot in the face.

Earl didn't die immediately and his friends carried him to the yacht club's headquarters, where doctors attempted to save him. The wounds were extensive and it was clear that he would not survive. His parents were summoned and four hours after the accident, Earl A. Shields breathed his last. His body was moved to the basement of the Shields cottage and then transported, the next afternoon, to the family's winter home in Bryn Mawr, PA.

Compounding Peter Shields's personal tragedy, the Cape May Real Estate Company was forced to declare bankruptcy amidst unpaid bills and a lawsuit from the architect who designed the Hotel Cape May.

Just as the company was in the middle of financial ruin its main harbor dredge was involved in an accident and sank. The dredge, which was christened the *Pittsburgh* at the beginning of the project to honor Flinn, sank to the bottom in front of Pittsburgh Avenue.

After Shields resigned in 1909 the new president, Frederick Feldner, promised to restore the project to financial prosperity. Only months after assuming the company's reigns, Feldner was involved in an horrific car crash. He and his wife, plus one of the primary investors in the Cape May Real Estate Company and his wife, along with the chauffeur, were killed instantly when Feldner's car was hit by an express train from Philadelphia.

The third president, Nelson Graves, also promised big things for the venture and initially he proved to be successful where his predecessors failed. Under his leadership the dredging of the harbor was completed and a new amusement park was built in Cape May. The park was known as the Fun Factory and it was located on the site of what is now the coast guard base.

Things were going a little more smoothly until, once again, fate dealt the project another crushing blow. In 1914 it was discovered that Graves had spent his entire fortune and was unable to resolve his personal debts. He declared bankruptcy and each of his financial holdings were leveraged to pay off his debts. Following Graves' lead, the Cape May Real Estate Company also declared bankruptcy and each of the lots were auctioned to pay back taxes.

With the remnants of the East Cape May project sitting idle on the eastern side of the island it appeared as if all the Cape May Real Estate Company's work was for naught. Even the celebrated Hotel Cape May had closed its doors. The immense building sat quiet and empty, a stoic reminder of what might have been.

All was not lost for the hotel, however, and eastern Cape May was about to be given a new purpose. In the summer of 1915 throngs of people flocked to the city's new harbor after word spread that the US Navy had sent a group of warships to Cape May. The rumors were partly true, as the navy had indeed decided to stage a battle group in the harbor.

It was a temporary situation, however, as the ships were actually on their way to the Philadelphia Naval Yard and only made a brief stop in Cape May. Nonetheless, the city was abuzz with talk over whether or not the navy would build a permanent home in Cape May. There

HAPPIER TIMES
The Shields family and friends enjoy the beach in front of the Pittsburgh businessman's summer cottage
Peter Shields Inn

**TICKET
TO RIDE**
This page, left:
Original tickets to
the theatre at the
East Cape May
Company's Fun
Factory at Sewell's
Point, which is now
occupied by the US
Coast Guard
Don Pocher

**HOUSE
OF FUN**
Opposite page:
The Fun Factory
shortly after
opening, with
patrons lined up
around the outside
of the tower. The
building was later
destroyed by fire
while being used by
the US Navy during
World War I.
Don Pocher

was a serious worry of invasion from Germany or one of the other warring nations involved in the conflict that would later be known as World War I. By November, the Cape May County Chamber of Commerce had formed a committee in the hopes they could convince the federal government to build a military base in Cape May.

The committee, led by Cape May Board of Trade President Luther Ogdon, met with the US Senate and congressional representatives from New Jersey and asked for their support. The government leaders readily agreed with Cape May's committee and pledged to take their concerns to the floor of the US Senate and House of Representatives.

Throughout 1916, state and federal officials negotiated the merits of constructing a military base in Cape May. There were significant strategic reasons, mainly the entrance to the Delaware Bay and Delaware River, along with the numerous munitions plants that were positioned along the Delaware River.

In Cape May, on what is now known as Higbee's Beach, the Bethlehem Steel Corporation maintained a testing facility for weapons and explosives. Bethlehem Steel had agreements to manufacture shells and other weaponry for a handful of nations, including the US.

Once a particular group of shells were ready to be tested, a special train would bring the munitions into the Cape May depot. They were immediately unloaded upon arrival and transported to the company's storage facility. At the appropriate time the shell or other explosive to be tested would be loaded on to a rail car and pulled on to the beach, where it would be detonated.

Keeping this and the security of the Delaware Bay in mind, lawmakers were eager to reach an accord that would provide military protection to the area. Their efforts were soon

hastened by two disastrous acts of German sabotage on strategic arms sites in New Jersey.

In the early morning of July, 1916, guards at an American munitions depot known as Black Tom encountered a handful of minor fires that appeared to have been intentionally set. The guards were not equipped to fight the fires, which quickly grew into one massive blaze. Shortly thereafter the entire depot was engulfed in flames and the munitions began exploding.

The explosions were so intense that they shattered windows 25 miles away and the repercussions were felt up to a hundred miles away.

Six months later, saboteurs attacked the Canadian Car and Foundry Company in Kingsland, NJ. Both attacks happened in the vicinity of northern New Jersey.

THE HEART OF CAPE MAY
This page: Jackson Street between 1905 and 1910. Note the cottage in the forefront, which later became the Inn at 22 Jackson. The street would fall into disrepair for many decades before dedicated and visionary B&B owners returned it to its former glories.
Don Pocher

FAMILY OF BEAUTIES
Opposite page: The Seven Sisters that make up an L-shaped collection of identical cottages on Atlantic Terrace and Jackson Street. The homes are still standing, but the front lawn was developed by former mayor Bruce Minnix into a food court known as the Akroteria.
Don Pocher

Jackson Str.   CAPE MAY, N. J.

Atlantic Terrace.   CAPE MAY, N. J.

Jos. K. Hand.

Hand-colore

A SHADY PLACE ON JACKSON
This page, top: An early 1900s view of the Carroll Villa shows striped awnings similar to those used today, which shade diners enjoying the food served on the porch by the hotel's famous Mad Batter restaurant
Don Pocher

GIANT FROM THE PAST
This page, below: The Baltimore Hotel was a behemoth that sat on the corner of Jackson Street on the parcel of land now occupied by the Tides condominiums. The Baltimore was demolished by the city in the 1960s.
Don Pocher

SAVING LIVES AT THE POINT
Opposite page: The lifesaving station at Cape May Point when it was still in use. The building to the left of the lighthouse was the foundation of the previous tower, which was covered and used for storage. It has since been washed away by the Atlantic.
Bunky Wertman

FROM THE ARCHIVES

A Bank Closes

The Philadelphia Inquirer, May 25, 1904

BANK AT CAPE MAY CLOSES ITS DOORS
Examiner Takes Charge of the Financial Affairs of the First National

THE appearance of a notice upon the doors of the First National Bank this morning, "Bank closed and in charge of the Controller of the Currency" caused considerable excitement. It is thought that the depositors are fully protected, but the loss is likely to fall upon creditors and stockholders. The deposits amount to $41,000.

The effect of the closing upon the business of the city and vicinity will be more disastrous than was at first supposed. One depositor excitedly threatened physical harm to the directors if payment was not made to him. Balances of businessmen will be tied up for some weeks of months and a general stringency is likely to result.

The bank began its career in the spring of 1901 and for a time attracted a considerable amount of business. Its first president was George W. Norcross, of May's Landing.

Later Dr Emlen Physick, a wealthy resident, invested a considerable amount in the bank and became its president. He interested some of the most conservative businessmen in the project, among whom was ex-Senator Robert E. Hand. Dr Physick planned to increase the capital stock from $25,000 to $50,000.

It is said that the recent discovery of loans amounting to nearly $10,000 upon paper considered to be worthless caused a halt in the plans and a special examination by the National Bank Examiner. Then it was decided to close the bank for the interests of all concerned.

U. S. COAST GUARD LIFE SAVING STATION AND LIGHT HOUSE, CAPE MAY POINT, N. J.

Exciting Plans For A Brand New City

The Philadelphia Inquirer, **December 1, 1902**

GREAT PLANS FOR A NEW CAPE MAY
Old Seashore Place to be Developed Into
an International Resort

ANNOUNCEMENT was made yesterday that documents were filed at Trenton Saturday incorporating the East Cape May Company, having for its object the improvement and development of Cape May, the oldest seashore resort in the country, to an immense degree. A gentleman interested in the project says Pittsburgh capitalists have bought over 4000 acres of land in and around the city and propose making changes that will revolutionize the resort.

Their plans include the building of a new city, which, they say, they intend to make one of the finest all-the-year-round resorts in the world. In this they declare they will be aided by the United States Government and the Pennsylvania and Reading Railroad Companies. Estimates of the cost of the project point to an ultimate outlay of $11,000,000.

For some weeks there have been rumors that a syndicate of which H. G. Frick, of Pittsburgh; George J. Gould, of New York; A. J. Cassatt, of this city, and prominent men of other cities were members, proposed making Cape May an international resort. Although those in the syndicate worked quietly, the project was of such magnitude that it was impossible to keep the facts from becoming public. An inkling of what is going on has come to the surface from time to time, but it was not until yesterday that the facts and real extent of the enterprises became known.

Prominent Men Interested
The operation was started several months ago by Anthony M. Zane, of Philadelphia, who was aided by Captain Frank G. Edwards, of Bristol, PA, owner of the steamer *Republic.* These were instrumental in interesting the Beechwood Improvement Company, Limited, of Pittsburgh, of which ex-Senator William Flinn is president. Mr Flinn is also the principal owner of the Sharon Steel Company, which last week consolidated with the Union steel Company, owned by A. W. Mellon and H. C. Frick, of Pittsburgh.

Mr Flinn made a number of trips to Cape May in the interest of the project, but in the details of management he was represented by Peter Shields, a real estate investor of Pittsburgh, who is secretary and treasurer of the Beechwood Improvement Company. The Pittsburgers have thus far extended $800,000 in purchasing land. They have bought 3000 acres in Cape May city and the adjoining county and they also bought 1000 acres on Two-Mile Beach and now own the beach exclusively. This beach adjoins Cold Spring Inlet and will be made a continuation of Cape May. The company has purchased the Cape May electric light plant for $100,000.

To Spend Millions
Following an outlay of millions of dollars for improvements, the projectors say the company will spend several millions more to attract people to Cape May, not only during the summer, but in the winter as well. In order to attract owners of yachts, deep waterways will be formed. The company intends constructing a lake for yachts with a water surface covering 600 acres. Conferences with government officials at Washington have resulted in promises to deepen Cold Spring Inlet so that the largest ocean-going yachts will be able to enter the lake. Around this lake will be scores of cottages for yachtsmen and their families and a substantial marine railway will be built for the use of yacht owners.

Between Cape May and Atlantic City, a distance of forty miles, there are waterways which are perfectly safe and navigable and over which yachts can be sailed without going to sea. It is proposed to improve these waterways and thus attract people from Atlantic City. Aided by the city, the Pittsburgers will pave all streets, lay new sidewalks and construct new sewers. The natural foliage for which the city is famous will be preserved and trees will be planted.

Pennsylvania and Reading Railroad officials are reported to have planned improvements in train service to and from the place. The Pennsylvania Railroad Company, it is stated, will relay eighty miles of track between Philadelphia and Cape May, and by putting on heavier locomotives, will cut down the running time to a little over an hour. The Reading Railway Company will also lower the time for fast express train service from Philadelphia to the new resort.

New Hotels Planned
It is planned to build two and perhaps three of the most modern seaside hotels. This winter 100 cottages will be built and they are expected to be ready for occupancy next June. The work of rebuilding Cape May will begin early in December, by which time the necessary land will be secured and contracts set. The 100 cottages will cost $10,000 each and will be built by a Philadelphia firm. The first hotel, for which plans have been completed, will cost $1,000,000. It will probably be located half way between Madison Avenue and Sewell's Point, on the beachfront. The second hotel will cost $600,000, and will probably be erected near Madison avenue. The projectors say three thousand men will be employed all winter on the improvements.

The Cape May citizens and public officials are reported to be co-operating heartily with the new enterprise. Councils have already voted $100,000 for a new boardwalk and bulkhead along the beach fronting their property. The city of Cape May has also agreed to rebuild the water works and has already expended $124,000 on this project. The Riparian Commissioners of New Jersey have granted all the necessary rights to the East Cape May Company and at their last meeting took steps toward getting the company similar rights to Two Mile Beach. A new style of sand dredge, designed by Senator Flinn, who is in the contracting business in Pittsburgh, will be used to construct the large inland lake. The sand from the lake will be used filling in the improved acreage fronting the ocean and lake.

The dredge *Pittsburgh* works to carve out the new harbor, a centerpiece of the East Cape May project *Don Pocher*
Opposite page: An aerial view of Cape May from 1921 shows the new convention hall and the Stockton Villa that was built on the site of the Stockton Hotel *Cape May County Museum*

LIFE'S A BREEZE
This page: The veranda of the Hotel Cape May was a great place for visitors to take in the cool ocean breezes while socializing with their fellow guests
Don Pocher

CLAIM TO FAME
Opposite page: The Hotel Cape May was considered the largest hotel in the world when it was completed in 1908
Bunky Wertman

CAPE CURIOSITY

The Hotel Cape May

THE STORY OF the Hotel Cape May story began in 1906 when construction commenced on the massive structure. The hotel was designed to be the anchor of a substantial development project, orchestrated by the newly-formed East Cape May Company. The plan was to build a landmark hotel, expand the present harbor, and sell more than 7,000 parcels of land on the eastern side of the island. Developers envisioned a ritzy, upscale community similar to Newport, RI.

The Hotel Cape May opened its doors in April of 1908, claiming that it was the largest in the world. The 350-room hotel was eight stories tall with a brick-and-concrete exterior, topped by a terracotta tile roof. Upon entering the grand foyer, guests were treated to an exquisite marble floor that seemed to go on for miles.

The word "luxurious" doesn't seem to do justice to the elegance that could be found throughout the hotel. The verandas and dining rooms were tremendous, the long, sweeping corridors were dripping with ornamentation, and the main lobby was bathed in the light of a gigantic, Tiffany-style stained glass dome.

The building appeared to be destined for greatness, a monument for the ages. However, the hotel was forced to close only six months after opening, due to structural problems that needed to be fixed. Within another six months, the East Cape May Company declared bankruptcy and its president, Peter Shields, quit.

Along with the financial problems of the company, Shields had also been dealt a devastating personal tragedy. Less than two years earlier, as the hotel was being built, his son was killed in a hunting accident. The bad luck seemed to rub off on his replacement, the new president of the East Cape May Company.

Not long after Frederick Feldner was appointed to the position, he and a major East Cape May investor, along with both of their wives and the chauffeur, were killed in a car wreck. Feldner was speeding on a road flanked by cornfields towards a rail crossing, where the Philadelphia-Cape May express train was bearing down on them. The tall corn stalks apparently shielded the train from Feldner's sight, and he also failed to notice a woman frantically waving to them from her porch. Newspapers graphically described the scene of carnage encountered by the rescue teams, who could do nothing for the five victims.

A gentleman named Nelson Graves stepped up and assumed control of the project. He didn't face any devastating personal loss, although he, too, was forced to declare bankruptcy in 1914.

The hotel was eventually taken over by the government and used as a military hospital during World War I. After the war the Hotel

Cape May changed hands once more and was renamed The Admiral Hotel. Things didn't work out so well and, in 1940, the City of Cape May bought the building at a sheriff's sale. The military returned to the property in World War II and the hotel was again used as a respite for wounded soldiers.

After the war the hotel passed through the hands of several owners until it was closed in the late 1950s for what many people thought was the final time – the hotel had begun crumbling and needed major repairs. Many entrepreneurs had tried to make a success of the old Hotel Cape May, but none had succeeded.

The devastating nor'easter that hit Cape May in March of 1962 seemed to seal the hotel's fate. The aging structure was battered by 75mph winds and the ocean surged more than 10 feet, causing waves as high as 20 feet. Tons of sand and debris were deposited inside the hotel through a number of broken windows. The storm caused a bad situation to get a whole lot worse, and all appeared to be lost.

Just as it appeared the ill-fated Admiral Hotel would be razed, she was given a reprieve. In October of 1962 a nationally-known minister named Carl McIntire purchased the building through his organization, the Christian Beacon Press.

McIntire quickly renamed it the Christian Admiral and spent hundreds of thousands of dollars bringing the old girl back to life. He was accompanied by legions of his followers, who worked with great determination and enthusiasm to put the hotel back together. Surprising many nay-sayers, McIntire opened the Christian Admiral for business in May of 1963.

Rather than operating it as a traditional lodge McIntire ran the Christian Admiral as a bible conference hotel, which meant that guests were prohibited to drink, smoke or fraternize on the premises. If a man and a woman wanted to reserve a room, the front desk staff was required to find out if they were married.

Reverend McIntire turned the aging hotel into a hotbed for christian fellowship. The Christian Admiral hosted religious seminars, large-scale revivals and its oceanfront library was the setting for Reverend McIntire's popular radio shows, which were broadcast all over the country.

As popular as the place was, the Christian Admiral never made a profit for Reverend McIntire. The hotel's daily operating costs and general upkeep proved to be much higher than the revenue it generated. Donations to McIntire's ministry and donations in kind from a handful of skilled craftsmen kept the Christian Admiral in business.

When Reverend McIntire opened the hotel

A LOCAL LANDMARK
This page, top: The Hotel Cape May was an imposing sight for passers-by on the boardwalk and ships at sea. Generations of sailors have told stories of using the hotel as a landmark to help guide them around the Island.
Don Pocher

SPLASHING TIME
This page, below: The hotel's swimming pool was originally filled with saltwater and it was one of the first pools on the island. The Hotel Cape May's employee dormitory is shown in the background.
Don Pocher

THE SHAPE OF THINGS TO COME
Opposite page: A rarely-seen artist's rendition of the Hotel Cape May that was drawn as the building was being completed for use as a promotional postcard.
Bunky Wertman

he was able to fund a large portion of the initial renovation through the sale of dedicated rooms. He offered his followers the opportunity to purchase a room for $1000. That fee would entitle the individual to decorate their specific room however they chose, with their own personal belongings.

A brass plaque would note who dedicated the room and each person who participated would be given free hotel stays for the rest of their life. The idea proved very successful and along with minimizing renovation costs it also provided guests with a relaxed atmosphere.

But the resourceful minister came unstuck in the 1980s when a disagreement with the Federal Communications Commission caused Reverend McIntire's show to be pulled off the radio. The indefatigable McIntire protested the decision by broadcasting from an old warship off the coast of Cape May, but he was fighting a losing battle. Many of his radio listeners moved on and those donation dollars disappeared quickly.

Without the donations to keep everything running smoothly, the buildings began to suffer. Routine maintenance was ignored due to the lack of funds and the operation began to fall apart. Reverend McIntire's Christian Beacon Press was forced to file for bankruptcy in 1990, with around $2.4 million owed on both the Christian Admiral and Congress Hall, McIntire's other bible conference hotel.

In February of 1996 steel cables were attached to the storied hotel and it was unceremoniously pulled to the ground by a bulldozer. Eventually, the majestic Christian Admiral was reduced to a pile of rubble. With each pull of the bulldozer, thunderous cracks were heard as the building struggled to stay standing. A storm of destruction then followed with the rain of bricks streaming through heavy clouds of dust.

O. L. W. Knerr, Pub.   NEW CAPE MAY HOTEL.

A LOCAL LANDMARK Opposite page: The attention to detail was especially evident in the Hotel Cape May's grand lobby. This 1930s photograph showcases one of the oversized marble fireplaces that flanked each side of the foyer, a few of the many (faux) marble columns that supported the ceiling and the ornate stained-glass windows that bathed the room in emerald, ruby and sapphire tones. Contrary to popular belief, the lobby's stained glass dome was not made by Tiffany, though the artisan who created it has never been identified. The dome was spared during the hotel's 1996 demolition. Prior to the building coming down, workers removed all 56 of the dome's stained-glass panels and placed them into storage, where they remain to this day.
Lynn Zettlemoyer

CAPE CURIOSITY

Preparing For The First Guests

This article was originally published in Greater Cape May Historical Society's July, 1996 newsletter.

JOHN P. Doyle walked nervously across the terrazzo floor and stared through the plate-glass doors toward the beach. As he watched the surf, he thought back over the months of hard work since he left the New Willard Hotel in Washington, DC to become manager of this, the finest hotel in South Jersey. Now here it was... Easter Sunday, 1908. Many noted people from Washington, Baltimore, Philadelphia and New York were to arrive shortly. At this very moment, members of Philadelphia's Quaker City Motor Clubs were driving in a procession down the dusty roads toward Cape May. This was the day Doyle had been working for all those back-breaking months... the Grand Opening of the Hotel Cape May.

There was just time for a final quick inspection. As he turned his back on the ocean, Doyle looked up at the stained-glass dome above his head. Sixteen wedge-shaped segments of colored glass sparkled beneath the sun, casting a warm glow on the Italian marble wainscoting. The two huge marble fireplaces, one on each side of the entrance lobby, were set with logs... ready to be lit should the April weather turn cold.

Yes, he thought, the pairs of brown-veiled columns throughout the lobby with their gold capitals added just the right touch of majestic dignity to this vast space. He wondered how many guests would ever tap one of those columns to find out it was hollow, really not marble but rather cast iron with a clever paint job.

Standing at the foot of the grand stairway with his hand on the ornately-designed banister, Doyle looked up toward the landing with its stained-glass windows set into the curving rear wall. In his mind he could picture the beautiful women in their elegant long gowns who would soon descend the 19 white marble steps to waltz merrily in the ballroom.

Turning west, Doyle walked down the corridor and through the French doors into the dining room. Two rows of columns supported the coffered ceiling. From each section hung a bronze fixture with fluted milk-glass globes. Half-round stained-glass panels surmounted the large windows that overlooked the ocean. The waiters were busy setting the tables to perfection. Each piece of silver flatware, stamped "Hotel Cape May", was carefully placed one inch from the edge of the table. Doyle picked up one of the plates, supplied by John Wannamaker of Philadelphia. Each one was embellished with the hotel's crest — a shield containing a lighthouse and three seashells flanked by two dolphins and topped with a mermaid. Beneath the shield was a banner containing the hotel name. It reposed beautifully on the white china in gleaming gold coin.

Crossing back through the lobby, Doyle passed the marble reception desk and glanced into the ballroom. Here the paired columns and pilasters were set against the walls, leaving the dance floor unencumbered. He stepped into one of the three waiting elevators. The uniformed operator closed the doors and a hydraulic plunger silently moved the cab upwards. There was not enough time to check each of the 350 bedrooms or even the five sleeping floors but there was time to spot check on one. Stepping off the elevator into one of the H-shaped corridors, he walked toward the oceanfront. At the end of the wide hall were French doors which could be opened to let the cool ocean breeze blow through.

Taking out his master key, Doyle unlocked the paneled door to one of the guest rooms. No detail had been left overlooked in its planning. The Colonial-style door knobs of glass had been used for reasons of sanitation. Decorated with pink wallpaper, each room boasted a brass bed that would not rust in the moist climate. On each dresser was a rectangular china brush tray with the gold hotel crest. A few steps down the connecting inner hallway between the two bedrooms was the bathroom, one of the 150 in the hotel. Looking in, he could see the big deep, clawfoot tub, the pedestal base wash basin, the toilet and the hexagon tiled floor... spotlessly white.

Back in the elevator and up to the top floor to check the roof garden, which had been inspired by the one at New York's famous Hotel Astor.

Now Doyle descended by the elevator to the ground floor. He entered a lobby below the main lobby, connected to it by the grand stairway. At the front of the hotel, uniformed doormen stood ready to help the expected guests from their autos when they arrived at the covered motor entrance under the broad front porch. Twin fireplaces also flanked the entrance hall here.

Doyle thought about the more than one million dollars that had been spent to build and furnish this great hotel, which he and Peter Shields, the president, had equipped with every luxury feature available to make a visit at Hotel Cape May memorable: billiard and pool rooms, a bowling alley, barber shop, tennis, cricket, 150 bath houses... all for the convenience and pleasure of the hotel guests. With its own power plant and steam heat, the hotel could stay open year-round.

Everything appeared to be in order, and just in time! A motorcar was pulling up to the entrance. John Doyle rushed forward to welcome the Hotel Cape May's first guests.

**THE PLACE
TO BE SEEN**
This page: The
beach and
boardwalk in front
of the Lafayette
Hotel was the
city's hotspot after
the iron pier was
demolished in 1910
Doug Miller

**LIGHTING UP
THE NIGHT**
Opposite page:
The Stockton Hotel
at night was quite
a sight, primarily
because each of
the rooms had its
own gas lines with
gas-lit lamps. While
other hotels were
relying on lanterns
and candles, the
Stockton designers
were planning
ahead.
John F. Craig House

FROM THE ARCHIVES

The Return Of Cape May

From *The New York Times*, July 28, 1912

W HEN NEWPORT was a fishing village, with a single tavern, Cape May was the most fashionable summer resort in America. In fact, it was practically the only summer resort by the sea anywhere on the Atlantic coast.

In the beginning of the eighteenth century, before the war of 1812, half a dozen families from Philadelphia and four from Long Island had discovered the attractions of Cape May. They found it possessed the most equable climate north of Key West, and the coolest summer climate on the Atlantic coast, that it had a perfect beach, without an undertow, high ground for building, and that it was easily accessible from all the large cities.

For half a century Cape May held its undisputed sway. Scores of summer cottages were built along the beach, a mile or so from the little town of 2,000 people, where resided the Captains of the coastwise sailing vessels, and which was 200 years old.

Even after Newport and other resorts to the north began to build up Cape May held its premature. For the generation that followed the civil war the "famous Stockton" was the beau ideal of all summer hotels.

The old Stockton was the last word in hotels in those days. There was a bath on every floor. Only twelve people were permitted at one table in the dining room, and each table had its separate plate of butter, its separate pitchers of water and milk. The Stockton is credited with originating the custom of placing ice in each separate glass instead of having it only in the water pitcher. Not only that, it was the first to provide bathing suits for its guests at a nominal rental, thus being the first to make convenient the visits of the weekenders, then in their incipient growth.

It was a truly wonderful hotel, with every up-to-date convenience and all modern contrivances- a palm leaf fan in each room and mosquito netting on all the windows. Its negro porter, who also blacked the boots and tended the front door, met every train, of which there was one each day and two on Saturday, and was personally acquainted with every visitor who had been there in twenty years. It was a marvelous place.

On Saturday nights the tables were cleared from the hotel dining room, the floor was smeared with bees-wax, old Hen Prouty came up from the village with his fiddle and the cottagers came in to join with the guests of the hotel in a dance. There was no thought of cliques, or social caste. Even introductions were dispensed with. Ordinary people or rowdies were not drawn to Cape May and our present dollar aristocracy had not arrived. Therefore, no one had any reason to shun any one else. Every summer meant the reconvening of a happy family.

Now times have changed. The old Stockton was torn down several years ago. Its final seasons had been exceedingly precarious and profitless. Other hotels had sprung up and they had their clientele, but it was not the fashionable

Hotel Stockton, Guerney St., Cape May, N.J.

clientele of the old Stockton.

Only four or five years ago it seemed that Cape May had had its day. The beach was still the same-the finest anywhere-the climate was still the same-as good as any, better than most-its accessibility was even greater, with improved railroad service; but the gay crowd, the polite crowd, the crowd that knows how and is able to spend money, and lots of it, had passed-perhaps for ever.

Then a group of Pittsburgh rich men took hold of Cape May. A very large sum of money was invested-several millions. A beautiful shore road was laid. A fine boardwalk, five miles long, was put down along the sea front. William Flinn, the boss who became a leader, built a row of cottages, which looked as if they had been turned out of a collender, or an Edison cement mold, and they were placed on the renting market at $500 a year. A real estate boom boomed-and collapsed.

The Pittsburgh era was short, spectacular, and of violent end. Most of the investors sold out at ten cents on the dollar. The masses would not come; the classes were irrevocably gone. One hotel manager, employed to lure the old patrons of the Stockton back, tersely told his proprietors after a few unsuccessful seasons that "the old Cape May habitués are either in heaven or in −, and you can't get into one place after them, and you don't want to go to the other."

Then five years ago a group of Philadelphians succeeded the Pittsburghers. They were led by Nelson Z. Graves, and they have apparently come to stay, with determination, patience, and plenty of money.

First, they built as fine a summer hotel as can be found anywhere in the world, the Cape May Hotel. It cost them over a million dollars, and possesses all the wrinkles of a recherché hostelry.

Individually they erected cottages, a score or more, not flashy, not pretentious, but commodious, homelike, up-to-date. They cost, on the average, $10,000 to $15,000. Not one cost more

than $50,000. They built a car line from Sewell's Point to Cape May Point, part of it with rails laid down on the very shore itself, between the Boardwalk and the beach. They put in a casino with a merry-go-round. Lastly, this Summer, they are putting in a "fun factory" at Sewell's Point, where they are spending $75,000 in duplicating a number of the odd pleasure devices at Coney Island "to amuse the kids." "Make the place attractive for the children and the adults will have to come," is their motto.

At first it was planned to make the Cape May Hotel an all-the-year-round resort. Climatically the place would be ideal for that, for, in the Winter time, there is no snow or ice, and one is never obliged to wear an overcoat. It is warmer than Norfolk, Va.

But transients will not go to Cape May in the winter time. The hotel was run at a loss for several seasons. Then, last year, it was open only for three months. Even that proved too long. While it was crowded in August the management lost in September all that it made the previous month. This year it did not open until the 22nd of June and will close the 1st of September, and this is the most prosperous year in its history.

Yet, through all these years, while Cape May has been having its ups and downs as a Summer resort, a comfortable number of the old established families have kept their homes there. Among them are few New Yorkers. Most of them are from Philadelphia, a few from Wilmington, and a few from Baltimore.

The dwellings of these faithful few are still to be seen, with their square frames, dormer windows, towers and cupolas, high porches, and boardwalks of a generation ago. No other well-known Summer resort on the Atlantic Coast has so few modern cottages.

In those plain, comfortable and commodious old homes the families to whom the appeal of fashion and the vogue of new places means little

one finds again this year, as before, the simple and wholesome hot-weather activities of a care-free summer colony. They have the "Cape May habit." They move to the Cape in May, and stay until November. Time was when no social record was complete without an account of Cape May doings. Now "society" is able to get along without a knowledge of what goes on there, while those who live there are indifferent as to whether "society" is interested in them or not.

Yet it is the hope and determination of the heavy investors who are building up the new beach that Cape May will "come back." They want the place to be again what it was in the halcyon days of the Stockton. For the last few days in July and the month of August they seem to be partly successful. On the hotel registers, even then, one does not read the names which one can find at Narragansett, but those who do go there are substantial and perhaps more discriminating than some who follow the crowd. At the present time one is unable to reserve a room for any time during August at the Cape May Hotel.

It is a great place for children. The air has been known to work wonders with little ones who were sickly. One of the leading children's specialists of Philadelphia has his home on the ocean front and brings as many of his patients as possible there for the summer. Philadelphians who otherwise would not visit so "slow" a place send their families there for a month or two and motor down for the weekends.

The population of the town itself leads a queer existence. It has no visible means of support. For ten months of the year it exists without turning its hand to any gainful occupation. Then, for two months, in the Summer, it decamps in a body into the woods, and turns its residences over to the influx of visitors. The two months' rent on a cottage will support an entire family of Cape Mayers for a whole year.

Even some of the newcomers have learned this

excellent economy. A Wilmington man two years ago built a cottage for $6,500 on a $4,000 plot of ground. This year he rented it for the season for $1,100.

Like any well-bred and self-respecting community, Cape May indulges in no hypocritical virtues, like the Atlantic City temperance Sunday. Once can get a drink there on the Sabbath day, if he is so minded, but those who have to have a drink on that day apparently do not think of going in that direction.

In one of the travel booklets on Cape May I find an enthusiastic account of the "Summer settlement which is not exclusive to the hotel contingent." The booklet adds that "this reciprocity of good-fellowship lends a note of sociability which is absent in larger resorts where the panorama of the season is more spectacular."

This statement is disingenuous. One must not expect to make casual acquaintances in Cape May and be picked up by them as he might be at Bayhead or Wildwood, where almost any well dressed man or any nice looking girl is likely to be invited to a picnic on a first introduction, or even without an introduction.

One could hardly expect this perfect "reciprocity" from those whose grandfathers and great-grandfathers has been in the habit of journeying to Cape May via stagecoach or lumbering private carriage, and who now, themselves, come down each Summer in motor cars to open the cottages which on the outside date back to the civil war, and on the inside present electric lights, tiled baths, Persian rugs, and electric fans.

No. The hotel "guests" do not, so easily as that, pick up their Summer acquaintances. One who enters the ballroom or the lobby uninformed of the etiquette of the place is likely to experience strange snubbing, which he may not perceive, but which will effectually squelch any desire, should he express one, to mingle freely with the society of the place.

It is quite bad form, for instance, for a new "guest" to take a place in certain groups of chairs which, by common consent, season after season, are occupied by certain regular habitués. One does not get a pleasant smile for such a mistake. Instead, he instantly finds himself alone, darkly frowned upon from a distance and severely ignored.

Therefore, few transients travel that way. It is not on the main line of resorting. There are no brass bands, nor shell games, nor unattached ladies, nor riotous young people where new adventures may be found readily. It is distinctly a family place, maintaining easily the prestige of time and quite satisfied with its own company. Not pretentious; merely possessing good taste.

Perhaps the former glories of Cape May will never return. Perhaps the millions that are being spent to bring it up to date will never find a return on their investment. At least, not from the summer tourist.

But there is a way in which Cape May will doubtless rise to greater glories than it has ever known. That will be through the new harbor which the Government is dredging there. Every visitor to the old resort remembers the acres of waste land-meadow and marsh-which lay between the old town and Sewell's Point, the ocean, and the creek. At the end of it is Cold Spring Inlet, where the Jersey fisherman find a livelihood. It is like those meadow marshes on which Atlantic City was built.

Five thousand four hundred acres of this waste land had been bought up and is fast being converted into a tract on which will be built a new city. At the same time the Government has appropriated $1,115,000 for the forming of a new harbor just off the Point.

This will doubtless be used as a naval base, and will be the only harbor of refuge between New York and Norfolk. It will be the best refuge on the Atlantic coast for yachts. It is believed that within a very few seasons it will be one of the principal yachting stations on the Atlantic seaboard.

This summer a yacht club house is being built at a cost of $25,000 and next year is expected to see Cape May in the beginning of a new grandeur which will be greater than the old. Then the old colonnaded hostelries, so popular in the seventies, now located several miles down the beach, will all disappear, and new stone and brick hotels will take their place. On the new-made land will be built larger cottages and into memory will pass the plain frame dwellings which were once so attractive.

But this season Cape May is in the hiatus. The old family life is lingering, steadfast and oblivious, dwelling in seclusion and quiet glory, like the lingering farewell of Indian Summer. The prospective yacht life, with perhaps its commercial accompaniment, with naval officers and their families, is still in the future.

It seemed peculiarly significant of both the history and the present status of Cape May that I should be shown about the prospective harbor and over the new-made land where is to rise the coming summer city by Capt. Alexander Hamilton Cruger. He is directing the operations of dredging and filling which are to herald the new era – a man's work.

Yet, in any other summer resort a man of Captain Cruger's type would be playing tennis or polo, yachting or dining, loafing or card playing. For the name he bears, while of great distinction, is not so distinguished as his blood; his great-great-grandmother being the sister of George Washington.

That describes Cape May – the descendant of Washington and Hamilton, while he enjoys his summer normally (his home is there) is yet planning and executing a vast scheme for the development of the land and sea.

CAPE CURIOSITY

Saving Lives For 100 Years

THE TRUE unsung heroes in the Cape May story can be found on any given summer day, sitting vigilantly atop red-and-white lifeguard stands. Year after year the resort's pristine beaches and miles of coastline are protected by the Cape May Beach Patrol.

Their record speaks for itself. In the nearly 100 years since the group was first founded, not a single person has drowned on a beach they were protecting. That's not to say there haven't been close calls — emergency situations arise nearly every day. In fact, the lifeguards have been put to the test more times than you might think.

Buzz Mogck, who became the fourteenth captain of the beach patrol in 1980, credits their spotless record on solid procedures, a good organizational structure and a dedicated team who are ready to handle whatever comes their way. "We've done things the same way for years and it seems to work well for us. Our backup systems have backups," said Mogck.

The notion of Cape May's Beach Patrol being able to handle anything has been tested over the years. One example is the crash of a US Navy helicopter just off the Cove in June, 1982. It was a day Mogck will likely never forget. "I remember sitting in my office, watching the helicopter hover in one spot before it just dropped out of the sky. It was the most devastating thing I can remember happening. If it would have fallen 40 or 50 more feet closer, it would have landed on a crowded beach."

Immediately after the helicopter hit the water, the beach patrol sprung into action. They swam out to the aircraft and worked to rescue the crew. Thanks to their efforts, seven of the eight member crew were saved.

Another notable example of the patrol's ability to function outside of the traditional lifeguard duties came in 2006 when a plane carrying an advertising banner crash-landed into the ocean off Broadway beach, about 500 feet from shore.

The distance made a standard beach rescue more difficult, but the lifeguards have boats and wave runners that were pushed into action. They quickly reached the pilot and brought him safely to shore.

On the afternoon of July 11, 2007 the patrol faced a very different scenario. A lifeguard noticed a strange object in the sand off the Cove. Few people would even consider the possibility of a bomb showing up on a public beach, but it appeared to be exactly what the squad faced that sunny afternoon. The lifeguard picked up the 18-inch device and carried it to the lifeguard headquarters so it could be examined. The danger was soon realized and while one set of guards contacted the authorities, another group evacuated the beaches and promenade. A bomb squad from Atlantic City was dispatched to the beach, while the patrol worked with the local police and fire departments to keep the area clear.

Once the bomb squad arrived, they were able to identify the object as a white phosphorous military flare. While it was proven not to be an explosive device, the flare was still considered extremely dangerous. The US military actually uses white phosphorous in battle as an incendiary device that can deliver shocking results.

BOYS OF SUMMER
This page, left: Arnold Cannone and Hugh Reilly, pictured as lifeguards in the 1950s. And below, Arnold (left) and his twin brother Harold. Their older brother Cleto was the captain of the CMBP from 1948 to 1980 and the beach at the lifeguard HQ is named after him.

THE MAN IN CHARGE
This page, right: Captain Buzz Mogck has been at the helm of the Cape May Beach Patrol since 1980.
Aleksey Moryakov

PUSHING THE BOAT OUT
Opposite page: Four ladies pull a Cape May Beach Patrol rescue boat along the sand in this 1941 promotional picture. It appeared on the inside cover of that year's Cape May guidebook.
Don Pocher

The bomb squad decided the flare was too unstable to transport away from the location and chose to detonate it directly on the beach. Witnesses reported a massive explosion with a cloud of smoke that plumed into the sky.

While the lifeguards have demonstrated impressive flexibility, it's important to remember their primary function since the beach patrol was founded in 1911 — keeping the beaches safe.

Back in the early days, registered nurses would assist the lifeguards by volunteering to spend hours in the headquarters, attending to anyone who needs their help. According to Captain Mogck, many of them were local women who worked at the hospital and had family members on the beach patrol.

As the times changed so, too, did the organization, and today there are no longer nurses stationed at the lifeguard headquarters. Instead,

every one of the patrol's lieutenants are trained and certified Emergency Medical Technicians. There's also a certified paramedic on the team, Lieutenant Jeff Rise.

This change has allowed a much quicker response time to victims on the beach, who no longer have to be transported to the headquarters to be seen by the nurse. Instead, the lifeguards can begin lifesaving measures right at the scene. If an individual needs to be taken to the hospital the patrol has six-wheel all-terrain vehicles to transport them to a waiting ambulance.

The Cape May Beach Patrol maintains a force of 70 guards to ensure that, on any given day, 58 of them will be available to keep Cape May's beaches safe. The city has done their part by equipping the lifeguards with state-of-the-art equipment and completing a thorough renovation of the beach patrol headquarters in 2008.

CHAPTER TEN
A Welcome Military Invasion

**WAR IS IN
THE AIR
This page: A soldier
stands on the
front walkway of
the Hotel Cape
May, which was
transformed into
a military hospital
during World War I**
*Cape May County
Museum*

**BROTHERS
IN ARMS
Opposite page:
Camaraderie was
strong at Navy
Section Base 9.
Soldiers and sailors
pose together in
a lifeboat for this
picture.**
*Cape May County
Museum*

**MONSTER
CONSTRUCTION
Previous page:
The largest blimp
hangar in the world
was built on the
Cape May Naval
Section Base to
house the dirigible
SSZ-23.**
Don Pocher

FOLLOWING German attacks on a New Jersey munitions dump and a foundry in 1916, a decision was made to secure the southern cape and in turn provide defenses for the Delaware Bay and river. The first step was to establish a naval base on the grounds of the Cape May Real Estate Company's defunct amusement park on the eastern tip of the island. The station was officially known as Navy Section Base No. 9 and the old Fun Factory's facilities were renovated to fit the needs of the military.

The navy base was given a duel task, as a training facility for aircraft and as a submarine port. Hangars were constructed for both airplanes and dirigibles, while docks were built for the submarines. While the navy was in the process of accommodating the submarines, additional docks were added for destroyers and other surface ships.

That same year, 1917, the navy built another base just north of Schellenger's Landing, across the harbor from the navy base. Construction began in June on Camp Wissahickon, or Wissahickon Naval Training Center as it was officially called. The training facility was a $1.5 million investment that consisted of 30 barracks, meant to hold 3,000 naval reservists.

Meanwhile, another of the Cape May Real Estate's most prominent holdings was taken over by the military. In January of 1918 the War Department entered into a lease with Nelson Graves to lease the Hotel Cape May for use as a military hospital. The terms were for full use of the hotel and its grounds, at a cost of $99,000 a year.

The War Department renamed it US Army General Hospital #11 and the 600-room hotel was turned into a treatment and training facility. Ballrooms were transformed into hospital

SENDING A MESSAGE
This page: A telegrapher at a typewriter in his room at the Cape May Army Hospital in 1919
Cape May County Museum

CAPE MAY CAMARADERIE
Opposite page, clockwise from top left:
Soldiers stand next to a coastal defense gun that was on the beach near the Navy Section Base
Cape May County Museum
Two soldiers pose with a life preserver from the pool at the converted army hospital
Cape May County Museum
A soldier from the Delaware Chapter of the Army Corps is introduced to another serviceman stationed at the army hospital
Cape May County Museum
Soldiers dig foxholes on the beaches at Sewell's Point and secure them with sand bags to help fortify the coast
Cape May County Museum

TELEGRAPHERS ROOM, S.B. STA. CAPE MAY N.J. SEP. 18. 1919.

wards, first-floor storage rooms were used for operations and the majestic lobby was partitioned for additional bed space.

On July 4, 1818, while sailors from the navy base were participating in Cape May's Independence Day parade, a fire broke out in the old Fun Factory. By the time flames were extinguished the amusement park section of the base was lost. The navy quickly rebuilt the facilities and there was relatively little disturbance to their operation.

By November, treaties were signed and the 'war to end all wars' had come to a close. Citizens of Cape May were worried about the economic damage to the city if and when the soldiers and sailors left. Their concerns were temporarily alleviated in 1919 when the navy built, at the base, one of the largest hangars ever constructed.

The hangar was built to hold the colossal SSZ-23 airship, which was designed and built by the British military for the US Navy. The airship lasted only a few months in Cape May before it was reassigned to another location.

There's been some confusion over the years about the fate of the airship — contrary to local legend it was not lost in a fire. There was a smaller blimp with the same call sign of SSZ-23 that was lost to a fire, but that happened overseas in late 1918.

Two years after Cape May's monster blimp was relocated, it was struck from the navy roster, deemed impractical due to its large size. Once the blimp was moved the navy continued to use the hangar for many years to store aircraft and another much smaller version.

In 1920 the citizens of Cape May saw their fears realized when the War Department began demobilizing military sections out of Cape May. Within three years the majority of navy, army and marine units had been transferred out of Cape May, leaving only a small

FIRE AT THE FUN FACTORY
This page: The devastation at the old Fun Factory, after a July 4 fire leveled the entire structure. There was very little manpower to extinguish the flames because most of the sailors were away from the base marching in Cape May's Independence Day parade.
Don Pocher

A CHANGE OF USE
Opposite page: The Fun Factory before the fire, converted for use as a Navy Section Base. The dance floor was used as a temporary dormitory and the old 'Barrel of Fun' was used as a brig.
Don Pocher

contingent of 150 men.

The egress of servicemen was capped by another huge economic loss that nearly proved tragic for the crew. The navy's newest and largest submarine, *USS S-Five*, was operating about 50 miles offshore of Cape May on September 1, 1920 when disaster struck.

The 230-foot long ship was performing an emergency test of the vessel's capability to crash dive, which meant submerging the sub to the bottom of the sea much quicker than normal. Unbeknownst to the 40-man crew, the main induction valve was left open as the submarine descended underwater. As a result the ventilation system that allowed the ship's crew to breathe fresh air while on the surface was effectively turned into an aquaduct.

Seawater began filling the sub from bow to stern and it appeared that all was lost. The ship violently lurched towards the ocean floor and hit it hard, knocking out virtually all of the sub's operating systems. While the crew hurried to stop the flooding and contain the water, the sub's captain, LCDR Charles 'Savvy' Cook, assessed the situation. He tried to execute a maneuver that would jar the vessel loose from the sea floor and then empty the air tanks to allow it to rise to the surface.

Cook's efforts proved fruitless, as did his next idea, to pump the floodwater out of the submarine. As the disaster went on its second hour, the crew began to accept the reality of their situation, stranded 180 feet below the ocean. It was in those dark moments that Cook devised an unconventional, but brilliant, plan.

Cook ordered almost all of the crew's remaining air to be forced into the rear ballast tanks. It was a risky move that would turn fatal if it were not successful, but he hoped the air in the ballast tanks would force the submarine to rise. Cook was only partially right and the result was immediate — the rear of the subma-

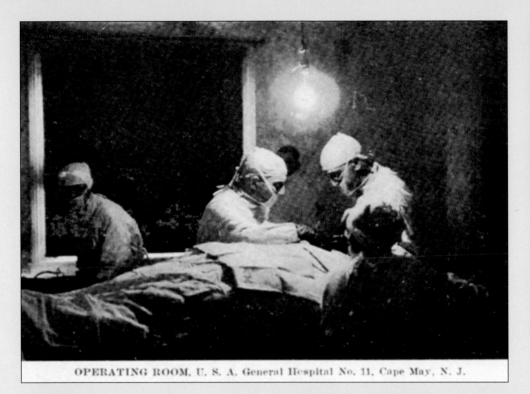

OPERATING ROOM, U. S. A. General Hospital No. 11, Cape May, N. J.

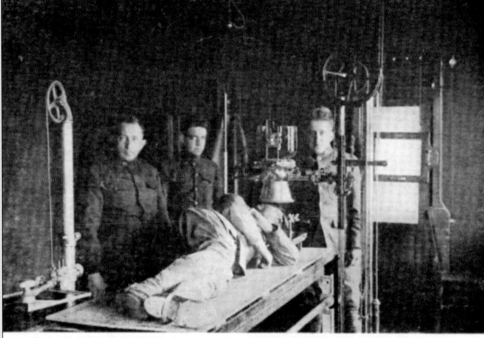

X-RAY DEPARTMENT, U. S. A. General Hospital No. 11, Cape May, N. J.

FROM THE ARCHIVES

A Unique Army Hospital

The Macon Daily Telegraph, August 11, 1918

The First Army Medical School is Opened in Cape May, NJ

THE first army medical school for the reconstruction of defects of hearing and speech of soldiers has been opened here under the division of physical reconstruction of the Surgeon General's office. It is a part of Army Hospital No. 11, located in what was formerly a luxurious hotel built by a land syndicate. Lieut. Col. Charles W. Richardson, of the Army Medical Corps, is the director of the school, said to be the first of its kind in the world.

Returned soldiers with hearing destroyed or impaired or suffering from partial or total loss of speech are to be educated physically and vocational. The school opened with a full corps of teachers and enough patients to occupy their time.

Lieut. Col. Richardson, who came here to establish the school, is professor of laryngology and otology in the George Washington University. He joined the army when this country entered the war.

A TRAGIC MOMENT
This page, top: The American World War I ship *Dorothy Barrett* was shelled by a German U-boat and sunk off the shore of Cape May
Cape May Point State Park

SINKING FEELING
This page, below: The American sub S-5 in her trial run after construction. Shortly after the picture was taken, the sub suffered a serious malfunction and sunk off the Cape May coast.
US Naval Historical Center

A HUGE UNDERTAKING
Opposite page: The enormous dirigible hangar that was built on the Navy Section Base. Although the hangar was demolished the site remains undeveloped and the concrete foundation remains.
Bunky Wertman

CONCIERGE TO CASUALTY
Previous pages: Postcards depicting the army hospital in the old Hotel Cape May

rine suddenly rose to the surface.

The front of the ship remained embedded in the ocean floor, however, and the submarine pivoted until it was nearly standing on end. At this point, the crew had been stranded for five hours and it seemed the vertical submarine was just another setback. The captain was all out of options when a startling report came that crewmen could hear waves splashing on top of the sub.

Cook suddenly realized that his ship was longer than the depth of water in which it was marooned, meaning that part of it was sticking out of the water. He immediately ordered members of his crew to begin drilling through the reinforced hull in an attempt to reach the open air. The work was hard and many members of the crew grew weary and lost consciousness due to the conditions.

As the remaining personnel worked on the hole, a passing ship caught their attention. Quick thinking led them to affix a T-shirt to a long copper pole and extend it out the small hole they had drilled through the exterior of the vessel. Luck was with them and the ship, the *SS Alanthus*, saw the makeshift flag.

The *Alanthus* came to investigate and when they learned of the sub's dire situation, their crew began to assist in the rescue operation. Meanwhile, the *SS General George W. Goethals* joined the scene. As the crew of *Alanthus* worked to free the sub's crew, the *Goethals* radiomen contacted the navy for assistance.

Navy ships began descending on the location, while the *Alanthus* and *Goethals* crews continued to work on the escape hole. It took more than 30 hours of hard labor, but the hatch was finally opened and 36 hours after the submarine sunk, the crew was rescued. Captain Cook was the last man to leave the disabled vessel and, under his leadership, all 40 submariners aboard the *USS S-Five* survived.

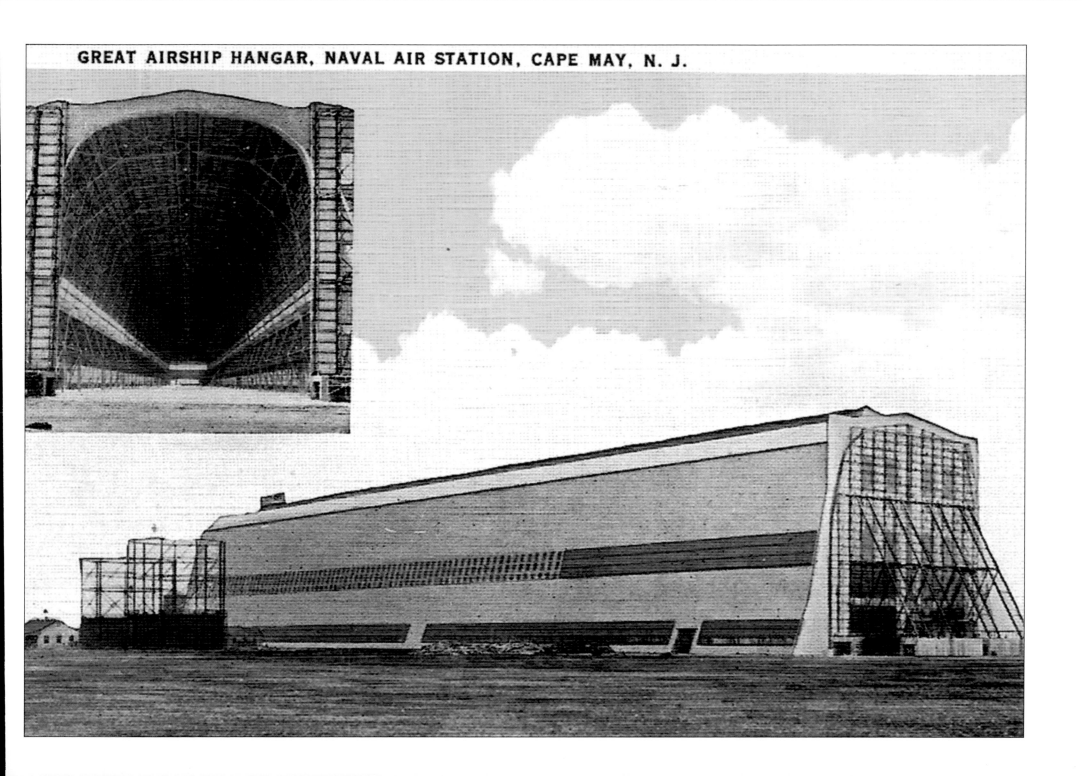

GREAT AIRSHIP HANGAR, NAVAL AIR STATION, CAPE MAY, N. J.

ALL THE TRIMMINGS
Soldiers and sailors stationed at the Navy Section Base at Thanksgiving in 1918 were well fed with a traditional holiday feast
Don Pocher

TAKING A MOMENT
Opposite page: Roommates at Navy Section Base No. 9
Don Pocher

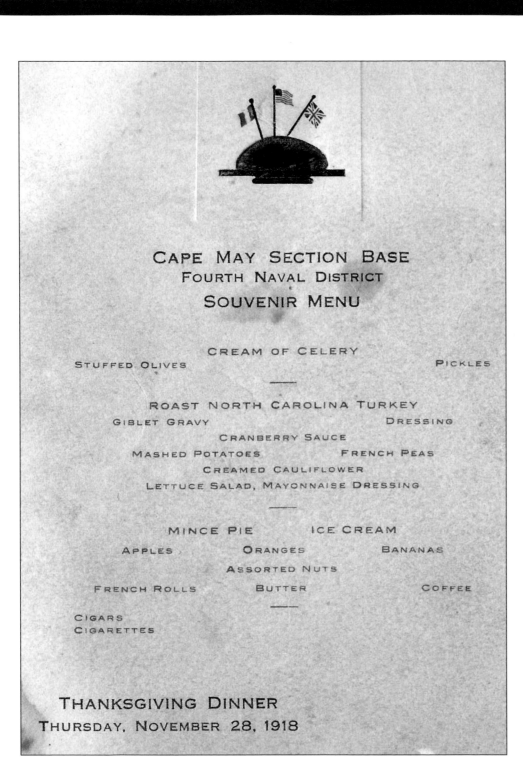

CAPE MAY SECTION BASE
FOURTH NAVAL DISTRICT
SOUVENIR MENU

CREAM OF CELERY
STUFFED OLIVES   PICKLES

———

ROAST NORTH CAROLINA TURKEY
GIBLET GRAVY   DRESSING
CRANBERRY SAUCE
MASHED POTATOES   FRENCH PEAS
CREAMED CAULIFLOWER
LETTUCE SALAD, MAYONNAISE DRESSING

———

MINCE PIE   ICE CREAM
APPLES   ORANGES   BANANAS
ASSORTED NUTS
FRENCH ROLLS   BUTTER   COFFEE

———

CIGARS
CIGARETTES

THANKSGIVING DINNER
THURSDAY, NOVEMBER 28, 1918

CAPE CURIOSITY

Cape May's Concrete Ship

THE SS *Atlantus* was launched on December 5, 1918. Originally, the ship was destined for World War I, one of 24 concrete ships planned to sidestep the steel shortage of the day. With the end of the war coming just one month before the launch of *Atlantus*, the government chose to build only 12 of these quirky vessels.

Joining the SS *Atlantus* in the concrete fleet were the *Cape Fear, Cuyamaca, Dinsmore, Latham, Moffitt, Palo Alto, Peralta, Polias, San Pasqual, Sapona* and the *Selma*. Of these, none were kept in service more than 10 years and none are afloat today.

The *Atlantus* was used to transport American troops returning from the war overseas and then as a coal transporter. She wasn't the most popular of the ships in the fleet, with many of the sailors who served referring to her as "the floating tombstone."

Because of the tremendous amount of fuel needed to move the gigantic vessel the *Atlantus* proved impractical and was retired in 1920, only two years after she was launched. Six years later the ship was purchased by a Cape May visionary named Colonel Jesse Rosenfeld, who was attempting to start a ferry run between Cape May and Delaware.

His plan was to use the *Atlantus*, along with two other concrete ships, to form a Y-shaped dock for his new ferry. Everything went smoothly as the *Atlantus* was towed to Cape May from a salvage yard in Virginia. However, what happened next would cement the SS *Atlantus* into the hearts and minds of Cape May visitors for many years to come.

U.S.S. "ATLANTUS"

REMAINS OF EXPERIMENTAL CONCRETE SHIP, ONE OF TWELVE BUILT DURING WORLD WAR I. PROVED IMPRACTICAL AFTER SEVERAL TRANS-ATLANTIC TRIPS BECAUSE OF WEIGHT. TOWED AND SUNK HERE AS WHARF IN 1926.

The sign says USS Atlantus, but you'll notice this book refers to the boat as the SS Atlantus. The correct title is 'SS' because 'USS' designates a Unites States ship commissioned by the military. The *Atlantus* was stricken from the US Navy record and sent to a salvage yard in 1920. The 'SS' designation is used for civilian steam ships, which the *Atlantus* was at the time it was brought to Cape May. *Don Pocher*
Opposite Page: The concrete ship shortly after it became grounded off Sunset Beach *Ben Miller*

One day in early summer, a monster storm hit the shores of Cape May. A treacherous surf created by the intense winds ripped the *Atlantus* from her moorings and she ran aground off the coast of Sunset Beach. Though Colonel Rosenfeld and others tried repeatedly to rescue the ship from her sandy tomb, they were never successful. The *Atlantus* was permanently entrenched in the sands off Cape May Point.

Around 1955 another problem was presented to the residents of Cape May Point when the ship began to show serious signs of decay. In addition to the ship turning on its side, the once-formidable vessel was beginning to split into two pieces.

It seemed the sea had finally secured its victory over the *Atlantus*, since no serious attempt to free her were made after that point. Instead, the ship was left to slowly melt away into the ocean, a few inches at a time.

Today's Cape May Diamond chasers at Sunset Beach can still see a small portion of the ship, although the majority of it is now buried in the sands.

Modern visitors to the Point, gazing at the small amount of concrete jutting out of the surf, probably have no idea exactly how big the ship actually was. The SS *Atlantus* was just over 250 feel long, 45 feet wide, with a hull that was six inches thick. All in all, the old frigate weighed more than 2,500 tons when she was launched.

THE FORGOTTEN STORM OF 1920 This page: Although most articles about Cape May's history concentrate on the hurricane in 1944 and the nor'easter in 1962, many other storms have battered the resort over the years. The damage seen in this 1920 picture occurred as the result of a minor hurricane that made landfall hundreds of miles away at Cape Fear in North Carolina. *Cape May County Museum*

A BUSTLING BEACH SCENE Opposite page: New-fangled automobiles are lined up on Beach Avenue near the equally-new Convention Hall and pier in this 1920 picture. Note the gentleman in a vintage swimming suit, waving at the camera in the bottom of the picture. *Cape May County Museum*

While the weary crewmen were recovering from their trial a coordinated effort was made to tow the submarine to the former Cape May navy base. An initial, unsuccessful attempt was made with the *SS Alanthus* before the tow lines were transferred to the much more powerful navy battleship *USS Ohio*. Even with the strength of the *Ohio*, the *S-Five* eventually broke free and sunk to the bottom about 15 miles from Cape May.

Following the departure of nearly all of the city's military forces, attention turned once again to the idea of a ferry linking Cape May and Delaware.

Since the late 1800s interest had been shown in developing a formal ferry service to expand upon the old steamship routes. In 1926, Colonel Jesse Rosenfeld took on the challenge of establishing the ferry service across the Delaware Bay. He developed a plan that involved purchasing three concrete ships that had been built by the navy during World War I.

Rosenfeld hoped to arrange the three ships in a Y-formation and use them as docks for the new ferry service. He had the first of the three vessels towed to Cape May in the beginning of that summer, a former concrete transport ship named the *SS Atlantus*.

Once the *Atlantus* was properly positioned, Rosenfeld planned to bring in the other two ships and complete the innovative dock. That never happened, however, because fate intervened in the form of a powerful storm.

The *Atlantus* had been docked off Cape May Point and at the height of the tempest the boat was ripped loose of its moorings and entrenched in a deep sandbar. Once the rains died down numerous attempts were made to free the *Atlantus*, but it failed to budge even an inch.

Eventually, Rosenfeld was forced to abandon his ferry plan. The decision was made to simply let the stricken *Atlantus* remain where it was, hopelessly stuck less than a hundred feet away from Sunset Beach.

Cape May County attempted to revive the ferry idea in the early 1930s with the creation of a Ferry Commission that was tasked with assessing the plan's viability. The commission's secondary purpose was to attract a private investor to help make the idea a reality.

Unfortunately, the group was unable to prove the viability of a ferry and although they had amassed a large amount of research the commission was eventually disbanded.

In the years following World War I, Cape May had turned into something of a ghost town. Even with the extensive advertising that was undertaken by the Cape May Real Estate Company years earlier, many summer vacationers considered the Victorian resort to be old-fashioned and out of date.

The local citizens attempted to modernize their aging homes and businesses by removing some of the ornate wooden millwork, known today as gingerbread. Another popular solution

was to paint over the old Victorian colors that were thought to be gaudy by 1930s' standards.

Throughout the city, marvelous shades of deep earth tones were painted a sterile white. Color was not entirely omitted, however, with many owners electing to paint their roofs the same tinge of green. Within a few years the streets were lined with white-and-green homes as far as the eye could see. The once vibrant city had become sanitized and dull, one cottage at a time.

Even with the modernization efforts and increased advertisements in Philadelphia newspapers, city leaders found it difficult to entice vacationers to return. The 1930s were a quiet time in Cape May and the city's future looked bleak.

At the start of the 1940s, businesses across the island faced hard times with fewer visitors making their way to Cape May.

Restaurants, hotels and shops all faced the difficult decision of whether or not they should

remain in business. Little did they know the city would soon become busier than it had been for half a century. The eyes of the world were on Europe and Asia, where post-WWI hostilities had reached a boiling point. Japan invaded China, Germany annexed Austria and Italy's leader, Benito Mussolini, began making promises of a new Roman empire.

A second great war was imminent, though the United States attempted to sidestep any involvement by remaining neutral.

A NEW FORCE IN CAPE MAY Camp Wissahickon was constructed on a parcel of land previously owned by Henry Ford, who hoped to build an automotive plant on the premises. It's not hard to imagine how different Cape May would be today if Ford's plans had gone through.
Bunky Wertman

FROM THE ARCHIVES

Constructing A New Navy Base

The Philadelphia Inquirer, July 27, 1917

WITH FIVE hundred carpenters and two hundred laborers working ten and twelve hours a day, Sundays and holidays included, the work on the new barracks for the naval militia at the Ford Farm is being rapidly rushed to completion.

This property covers several hundred acres of ground. This property will be used as the second big training department for the navy, and will quarter 2100 enlisted men in addition to several hundred officers and instructors.

The Navy Department has requested that the work on these buildings be pushed as rapidly as possible, and it was for this reason that Cramp & Co., of Philadelphia, who are the contractors, offered as high as $1.20 an hour for carpenters on some shifts. The man who is chiefly responsible for the quick time being made in the construction is Mr Lewis A. Wills, of Philadelphia, superintendent of the operation.

The entire barracks consists of forty buildings, which are chiefly constructed of wood. These buildings consist of twenty dormitories, six latrines, a receiving room, an officers quarters building, an administration building, an officers mess, a kitchen, two mess halls, a laundry, a storehouse, a boiler house, a 50,000-gallon

PASSED BY CENSOR.

CAMP WISSAHICKON, U. S. NAVAL TRAINING STATION. CAPE MAY, N. J.
Administration Building — Offices.

**SERIOUS
TRAINING**
This page:
Thousands of US
Navy Reservists
were stationed at
Camp Wissahickon
and trained in
everything from
rifle marksmanship
and large munitions
to military bearing
and seamanship
Don Pocher

**SHOWING
THEIR COLORS**
Opposite page:
Sailors from Camp
Wissahickon march
through the streets
of Cape May in 1918
Don Pocher

water tank, a concrete pump house with sunk pit, a hospital and a YMCA building.

The property is situated on the western side of the harbor, transportation being furnished by boats to a new dock on the harbor, and by railroad, the tracks of which were built by the naval reserves now here, and are connected with those of the Pennsylvania and Reading Railroads. This railroad is used for bringing supplies and construction material into the camp.

The buildings are the most comfortable that could be constructed for barracks purposes. Two rows of the dormitories, ten buildings in a row, form the two ends of the camp. Between these, the kitchen is situated. To the northern end of the kitchen are the buildings used by the officers and also the administration building. Still further to the north is the YMCA building, which is two stories in height, and contains rest rooms, a recreation hall and shower baths. Surrounding this building is a large drill ground and ball park.

Facilities for swimming have been erected at the edge of the harbor, so that in the warm months the men will be able to enjoy a swim in the harbor without losing a great amount of time.

The militiamen are expected arrive about the 1st of August and will come chiefly from Philadelphia and vicinity. Here the men will receive training in preparation for their work at sea. The *USS Chicago,* which was ordered here recently, will be fitted for a training ship and used exclusively in local waters.

The men will also be trained in manning large guns. Preparations are now being made with the Bethlehem Steel Company, who maintain a large proving ground here, for the men to receive their instruction in this line, at their plant.

The more important work in navigation will be taught by D. L. Brown, the government expert in charge of the local navigation school placed here by the United States Shipping Board.

CAPE CURIOSITY

The Birth Of Pennywise

SPEAK to a local or long-time visitor about *Pennywise* magazine and chances are you'll see a smile begin to form on their face as fond memories of the old publication come flooding back. It's a nostalgic, warm kind of feeling that comes with reminiscing about the good old days.

Pennywise was a wonderfully kitschy, down-home magazine, filled with witty advertisements and handwritten notes from the editor, Joe Barker. The journal was first published in 1931 and ran for more than 50 years, with the final copy hitting the streets in the late 1980s. It was produced weekly during the summer season in Cape May and, for a time, a second version was published monthly in New Hope, PA.

Over the years, *Pennywise* developed some fun traditions that would come to define the magazine. Each issue had its own theme, like the egg, key or Captain Mey editions, with accompanying handwritten drawings and puns added to all the advertisements.

Readers would see that Keltie News offered "A large sell-eggs-ion of period-egg-als and m-egg-azines also c-egg-ars and c-egg-arettes."

In the Key Issue, we learned that the Gazebo restaurant was, "An old-fashioned ice-key-ream parlor where you can get splendiferous sundaes and superific sandwiches."

The Huntington House's advertisement told us that "Cook-keys is the very best

buffet in Cape May," while the Winchester proclaimed "Even Francis-Scott-Key would have blown about our banner meals."

Another tradition was the welcoming of new businesses in the first *Pennywise* of the season. Those editions were especially popular because they included old stories from the editor's memories, which accompanied the new information.

A 1983 journal notes, "Frankly, if you haven't been here for a dozen years, you won't recognize the place – the mall, new hotels, and restoration of old Cape May has been great.

"Remember when all of Cape May was painted white with green trim and awnings, and how shocked everyone was when Christine McCloskey Croft Amore painted one of her houses on Congress Place a bright pink with white contrasting gingerbread and everybody jokingly called it 'the birthday cake' or 'The Pink House?'

"Since then it has been moved and made an 'historic landmark.' And now the style is to paint with Victorian color combinations, and we must admit personally, we rather like the 'rainbow village effect.' Others disapprove..."

Joe Barker produced *Pennywise* with the help of his partner and longtime business manager, Louis Pron, and a small support staff

From left to right: *Pennywise* founders Joe Barker and Louis Pron are shown in this undated picture – they became legends in the community with the publication of the frothy periodical *Julie Todd*
A page from the 'Captain Mey' issue in 1984
A typical collection of pictures from *Pennywise* *Julie Todd*
Issues from 1981 (the 50th anniversary) and 1956

made up of Carola Collings and W. Brinton Smith.

Sadly, all of the original *Pennywise* staff have passed away, although their legacy has not been forgotten.

The spirit of the publication lives on in *Exit Zero*, a weekly publication that was founded in the summer of 2003 by former New York magazine editor Jack Wright and local hotelier and developer Curtis Bashaw.

CHAPTER ELEVEN
The Storm To End All Storms

CAPE MAY'S SENTINEL
This page: Fire Control Tower 23 is Cape May's only remaining free-standing fire control tower. It's recently undergone a thorough renovation by the Mid-Atlantic Center for the Arts and is now open to the public.
Cape May Point State Park

LOOKING FOR SUBMARINES
Opposite page: Re-enactors demonstrate how soldiers used their azimuth and other tools to help target enemy ships
Cape May Point State Park

RIPPED TO SHREDS
Previous page: Cape May's boardwalk was torn apart by the nor'easter of 1962, dubbed by meteorologists as the Perfect Storm
Don Pocher

*A*FTER the German invasion of Poland in 1939 that officially sparked World War II, the United States began reconsidering its coastal defenses. German U-boats were wreaking havoc around the globe and their proliferation in the Atlantic Ocean was a serious cause for concern.

In 1940 the United States passed the Harbor Defense Program, which called for the installation of 150 armament batteries along the coast to protect against a naval attack or a full-scale invasion. Cape May was considered an important, strategic location for artillery and, in 1941 work commenced on Battery 223.

Federal officials chose to position Battery 223 along the coast between Cape May and Cape May Point to give its guns the ability to both defend the cape and help secure the Delaware Bay. Two sister installments named Battery Herring and Battery Hunter were built across the bay at Fort Miles in Cape Henlopen, DE.

Cape May's Battery 223 was built 900 feet from the ocean at high tide and covered with sand and sod to camouflage it. To ships on the sea, it appeared as just another sand dune. The structure was heavily reinforced with seven-foot-thick walls in the front and six-foot thick walls along the sides and back.

The bunker's firepower came from two panama gun mounts, with six-inch cannons. Each of the guns weighed 10 tons and had the capability of firing a 100lb armor-piercing shell more than 15 miles in all directions, every 90 seconds.

Battery 223 was supported by a series of four fire control towers that were erected in Cape May Point (Fire Control Tower 23), Cape May (Fire Control Tower 24), Wildwood Crest (Fire Control Tower 25) and North Wildwood (Fire Control Tower 26). The towers were used to spot targets in the Delaware Bay or Atlantic Ocean, then for-

**SECRET
MISSION**
This page, top:
After Bunker 223
was abandoned by
the coastal defense
forces a top-secret
underwater sound
surveillance system
was installed on
top of the concrete
structure and used
to track submarine
*Cape May Point
State Park*

**ROTTING
REMNANTS**
This page, below:
Remnants from the
bunker's panama
mount guns were
abandoned after
the war and left to
fall apart and decay
in the surf
*Cape May Point
State Park*

**READY
TO FIRE**
Opposite page:
Battery Herring
at Fort Miles, DE
was built to be an
identical twin to
Cape May's bunker.
With the exception
of the trees, this
is what Bunker
223 looked like at
ground level
*Cape May Point
State Park*

ward the positions to Battery 223.

Each tower utilized an Azimuth Scope and a Depression Range Finder, which allowed them to finely track a target's coordinates. Once the information was radioed to the bunker, an army specialist would use the coordinates from at least two of the towers to triangulate the position of the target, which was then given to the gunners.

Soldiers stationed at Battery 223 and at Fire Control Tower 23 were housed in St Mary's By the Sea, the Cape May Point summer retreat of the Sisters of St Joseph. Habits were replaced by uniforms as the nuns offered the 135-room building to the military for a temporary barracks.

The army also reactivated its former hospital in the old Hotel Cape May and leased a good deal of property in the city to use as military housing. At the same time, the navy and US Marine Corps returned to the former navy base and constructed a new airstrip to help train pilots to land on aircraft carriers.

Including the coast guard, which had taken over part of the base after World War I, Cape May was home to four of the five branches of the armed forces. The quiet town was perfect for the military's purposes and, while summer vacationers shunned the old-fashioned resort, the servicemen and their families loved the tight-knit community they had established.

For the duration of World War II Cape May resembled a large military base, complete with a USO and other entertainment facilities for soldiers and sailors.

In the midst of all the camaraderie and good times, the purpose for the military buildup of the Cape was never forgotten. People truly feared that Cape May would be attacked by enemy air forces or invaded from the sea. Vigilance was maintained at all times and air raid sirens were installed to alert the local populace of an impending attack. When those sirens sounded in the evening it was the responsibility of every citizen

SHOOTING PRACTICE
This page: The US Coast Guard practice firing breeches buoys, used in rescues, from shore to ship in this 1941 photo taken off Cape May Point
Cape May Point State Park

SPOT THE BUNKER
Opposite page: This is one of a handful of pictures that were taken of the Cape May bunker while it was in operation and the only one that is known to have survived. Because the bunker was camouflaged with dirt and sod, a yellow circle has been added to show its location.
Cape May Point State Park

CAPE CURIOSITY

History Of The Boardwalk

WHAT we recognize today as Cape May's boardwalk, or promenade as it's known in local circles, is a fancy version of a seawall. After two extremely powerful storms deposited many tons of debris throughout the city, Cape May chose to replace the traditional boardwalk with something a little more capable of keeping the Atlantic under control.

The Great Atlantic Hurricane in 1944 was the first of the two storms and it destroyed the original boardwalk. The wooden walkway was promptly rebuilt but less than 20 years later, in 1962, a powerful nor'easter tore it apart again.

The decision to replace the boardwalk with the promenade/seawall was made easier by the fact that the second storm turned planks of the boardwalk into wooden javelins and hurled them into buildings up and down Beach Avenue. It's been speculated that more damage was done to the city by sections of flying boardwalk than the actual flooding and wind damage.

When the promenade was constructed, it was built on a much smaller scale than the previous ones. The first boardwalk that was destroyed in 1944 extended almost the length of the island.

One of the earliest accounts of the boardwalk comes from West Jersey Railroad documents from the 1870s, which stated the old boardwalk was 10 feet wide and spanned approximately two miles.

In contrast, Atlantic City offered a smaller, minimal boardwalk in the 1870s which basically consisted of wooden planks resting on top of the sand. In addition, the walkway was not a

Cape May's boardwalk has always been an important part of the resort's success. This picture was taken in the 1940s and shows just how popular it was, even during the war years. *Cape May County Museum*
Opposite: Beach patrol members walk on the boardwalk in this 1950s shot *Cape May County Museum*

permanent fixture. After the summer season, the Atlantic City track was pulled up and taken away for the winter.

Cape May's boardwalk was extended to Sewell's Point during the early 1900s. This was during the exciting period of Cape May history when the harbor was dredged and the eastern section of the island was being developed into the "New Cape May".

In 1910 the city decided to enhance the boardwalk with giant arches, illuminating the walkway with hundreds of little electric lightbulbs. While other seaside resorts like Atlantic City appeared to cram their boardwalks with businesses and other amusements, Cape May kept much of it open. This minimalist effort allowed visitors to enjoy the sights and sounds of the Atlantic Ocean as they leisurely strolled the wooden planks.

Cape May's boardwalk did have its share of businesses and piers, extending the walkway out over the ocean. The main difference between the Cape and other resorts, however, was the way the city regulated the commercial sprawl and kept things well under control. In 1884, Cape May allowed the construction of a new 1000-foot iron amusement pier.

The iron pier was built where Decatur Street meets the beach and included two separate levels. Initially the pier was used primarily for dancing and the lower level for fishing. The dancing area was later covered, effectively turning the dance floor into a theatre that hosted operas, vaudeville and eventually movies.

In 1907 a fire erupted in one of the buildings on the wharf and, in a few short hours, the famous iron pier was destroyed. The structure

was rebuilt immediately after the fire and, with a few newer additions, proved to be even better than before.

Things went smoothly until 1909, when another disaster struck. Not fire this time, nor was it flooding from a storm... a ship carrying large stones actually slammed into the pier. Then, in 1944, the remaining section of the iron pier was destroyed by the Great Atlantic Hurricane.

The other major pier that extended the boardwalk over the Atlantic was located behind Convention Hall. Construction of the pier occurred at the same time Convention Hall was constructed, in 1917. The large hall and the buildings at the boardwalk end of the pier hosted assorted amusements and shops, while the wharf that extended over the ocean was used almost entirely for fishing.

In 1944, during the Great Atlantic Hurricane, the fishing pier was not-so-gracefully removed from the boardwalk by the churning ocean waves. Later, in the devastating nor'easter of 1962, the rest of the Convention Hall structure was swallowed by the ocean.

That particular area of the boardwalk was rebuilt with a new Convention Hall that was meant to be a temporary replacement. Though the seawall/promenade was constructed to replace the boardwalk after the nor'easter, Cape May decided to keep the spirit of the boardwalk alive by surrounding the new Convention Hall pier with wooden planks.

In the 47 years since the promenade was built the city of Cape May has weathered other powerful storms and hurricanes, but the concrete and blacktop walkway has done its job.

The ocean waters have still flooded over the promenade during a few especially powerful storms, but the promenade has always remained intact after floodwaters retreated back to the ocean.

**TIME TO
REBUILD**
This page, top:
After the 1944
hurricane hit
the city efforts
were started
immediately to
remove the debris
and rebuild the
boardwalk. By the
following season,
the city looked
better than it had
for years.
*Cape May County
Museum*

**A TOWN
DISAPPEARS**
This page, below:
The town of South
Cape May was
virtually wiped off
the map in the 1944
storm and what
little remained
was lost in the 1962
nor'easter
*Cape May Point
State Park*

**BURIED UNDER
THE SAND**
Opposite page:
Beach Avenue
was covered in
thousands of
tons of sand
during the 1944
hurricane, requiring
excavation
equipment to
remove it all
Don Pocher

to adhere to blackout conditions.

This meant that all visible lights had to be turned off, including street lights. If a home or business wanted to keep a light on inside the building they were required to have heavy, dark curtains covering all windows.

Local wardens patrolled the streets in the evening to make certain the law was followed. History documents few problems with compliance to the regulations, presumably because much of the town was made up of military personnel.

The lone attack that did hit Cape May on September 14, 1944 was nothing that any of the military installations could prevent. Coming not from an enemy force, the only real assault that Cape May faced during WWII came in the way of a Category Three hurricane.

The storm was known as The Great Atlantic Hurricane and when it reached Cape May that evening it unleashed force greater than any the town had ever faced. The hurricane did not actually reach landfall near Cape May but as it passed the island the eye of the storm remained just 30 miles off the shore.

For three hours the hurricane battered Cape May with winds of 85mph and gusts that reached 100mph. It came during high tide, producing 50-foot waves that crashed into the city.

The powerful winds were deafening, but the majority of destruction came from the tidal waves that crushed almost everything they hit. By the time the hurricane passed it had destroyed the boardwalk, ripped apart a number of ocean-front businesses and severely damaged private properties along Beach Avenue.

Once the floodwaters receded into the ocean the next day, the debris was four-feet deep in places. It was a tough break for the city of Cape May, but the large amount of soldiers and sailors on the island meant there was plenty of manpower to clear the wreckage and rebuild.

Cape May city fared much better than the bor-

**ROUND
OF DRINKS**
This page, top: The Congress Hall Bar and Lounge was introduced in the mid-1950s, a time when the hotel, and the resort, were in a deep slumber. It didn't last and was turned into a Howard Johnson. Now, it's Uncle Bill's Pancake House.
Don Pocher

**BLOWN
AWAY**
This page, below left: Hurricane Hazel did little damage to Cape May but it did tear sections off the Congress Hall roof in 1954
Forrest Laing

**A GRAND
ENTRANCE**
This page, below right: The Congress Hall ballroom is set up and ready for a function
Don Pocher

**DISTANT
MEMORY**
Opposite page: The 500 block of Washington Street was a different place in the 1940s, featuring the old Liberty Theatre and stores that have long since been demolished
Don Pocher

ough of South Cape May, which was destroyed in the storm. Much of the town had been washed away and even after the hurricane subsided, the floodwaters remained. The few houses that could be salvaged were moved into Cape May.

The city quickly recovered from the great storm and returned to the business of protecting the coast. With the exception of the hurricane the city made it through the war years unscathed and without incident.

When the end of World War II came in September of 1945 the people of Cape May worried, yet again, about the economic loss the city would face if the military left as it had after WWI.

Unlike then, soldiers did remain at Cape May Point to man the coastal defenses, but it was a much smaller support staff and the seaside resort returned to it sleepy status, much to the disappointment of local business owners.

Information that has just recently been declassified details a secret underwater sound surveillance installation that was moved to the Cape May Military Reservation, the official name for Cape May Point coastal defense site. According to the documents, the system was installed after the war and was used primarily to track submarines in the Atlantic and Delaware Bay.

Out at Sewell's Point, while the navy did move their entire contingent out of Cape May, they transferred ownership of the land to the coast guard. The switch was made in 1946, and the coast guard immediately went to work enlarging their new base. By 1948, all of the coast guard's east coast basic training was moved to Cape May.

After the war, Cape May city leaders again tried to entice summer sojourners to the island through a series of advertisements in papers around the region. Their efforts went relatively unnoticed and many of the cottages that had been used by the military for housing remained empty throughout the summer.

Following the two world wars Cape May faded

HEADING FOR HOME
This page: Two young ladies on Perry Street in 1941, at the end of their vacation in Cool Cape May. In the background is the Sevilla, now called Kings Cottage.
Dorothy Cann

MAKING MEMORIES
Opposite page: Author Ben Miller's great-aunt Jean Correll enjoys a moment on the boardwalk in the summer of 1941
Dorothy Cann

**LINING UP
TO SERVE**
This page, top: New
US Coast Guard
recruits line up at
the mess hall out at
Sewell's Point, on
the land that was
once home to Navy
Section Base 9
Don Pocher

**THOU SHALL
NOT PASS**
This page, below:
The lighthouse was
run by the Coast
Guard after the US
Lighthouse Service
was dissolved in
193 up until 1986,
and the entire area
was fenced off and
inaccessible to the
public
*Cape May Point
State Park*

**TRAINING
CAMP**
Opposite page: The
coast guard base is
shown in this late
1940s aerial picture
Don Pocher

into relative obscurity. Gone were the crowds of society's elite that once flocked to the island every summer. In their place came a new type of visitor that created a much different environment in the city. A dark cloud formed over Cape May and it would be years until it finally lifted.

Grand old hotels like the Windsor, Lafayette and Congress Hall fell into disrepair, forced to survive by renting rooms to visitors who had no respect for the buildings. Scores of Victorian cottages were partitioned into small apartment units and run as boarding houses, while others became broken down, abandoned shells of their former selves.

There was still a loyal group of visitors that returned to the Cape year after year, but they were small in number. Many vacationers found other watering holes to visit along the Jersey Shore, like the flashy new resort of Wildwood. In the late 1950s Cape May did see some new development in the form of a few modern motels along Beach Avenue, but it made little difference to the town's economy.

Even with the completion of the Garden State Parkway in 1957 Cape May had become stale and fallen into a rut. The 1950s and early 1960s found Cape May at one of its lowest points in history. Property owners were divided about how to turn the situation around. One faction believed that the only way Cape May would ever be able to compete with resorts like Wildwood and Atlantic City was to bulldoze the old buildings and replace them with more contemporary structures.

Another group that was primarily made up of apartment and boarding house owners felt that a hands-off approach was the way to go. Money was a big factor in their decision and few had the resources to simply knock their buildings over and start anew.

A third, much smaller group also existed which wanted to preserve the integrity of the

M R. JONES, average citizen of Cape May, was checking up on his expenses. For his gas and electricity, both of which were quite necessary, he paid $11 per month.

"Not so bad," he said.

But when he came to his tax bill, he roared with pain. His assessment was $2,500, and his bill $131.25! "WHAT DO I GET FOR THAT?" he demanded.

For $132 he got gas and electricity.

For $131.25 tax payment he got:

A good street to his home, well maintained.
A complete sewer system.
Every street in his town adequately lighted.
Police protection, 24 hours a day, every day.
Fire protection, 24 hours a day, every day.
Public health supervision.
Care of the poor.

H E THOUGHT of the great State and county roads and bridges, of our system of courts, of all the facilities operated for the common good, which we call the American Way of Life.

M R. JONES, falling asleep with a policeman patrolling his street, thought of the cost of these things. He would NOT do without them.

"Taxes are the biggest bargain we buy," he mused as he dozed into peaceful slumber.

The City of Cape May

Victorian structures because of their historical significance and inherent beauty. This faction was in the minority and had little power in the city, but their passion and enthusiasm would soon win over a great many supporters.

In March of 1962 Cape May faced another devastating storm that would prove to be even more damaging than the Great Atlantic Hurricane of 1944. It hit the cape on Ash Wednesday, with little warning. Local residents were aware of the impending storm, but they had no idea it would combine with another storm to become a deadly nor'easter.

Meteorologists would later deem 1962's nor'easter The Perfect Storm, due to a grouping of key atmospheric conditions, multiple storm fronts and unusually high tides caused by the Spring Equinox. The result for Cape May was three intense days of tempest, coinciding with a total of five very high tides.

When all was said and done, the city was torn apart. The boardwalk was ripped from its supports, with individual pieces of it propelled into houses and business all along Beach Avenue. Entire stretches of Beach Avenue were washed away and replaced with tons of sand and debris.

Cape May's renowned Convention Hall was dealt a fatal blow when tidal surges tore the pilings out from underneath it. Oceanfront businesses along the boardwalk were smashed into pieces and floodwaters carried the remnants as far as four blocks inland. The floodwaters remained in some parts of the city for almost a week afterwards, prompting residents to seek temporary shelters elsewhere.

The city worked hard to clean up after the storm and repair the damage, utilizing teams of laborers at different locations along Beach Avenue. Debris was taken away at an efficient rate and within a few weeks Cape May was ready to rebuild what had been lost.

IN NEED OF A FACELIFT
This page, left: Few readers would guess that the ramshackle cottage in the picture is the Pink House before it was restored and moved from Congress Place to Perry Street
Cape May County Museum

READY TO CRUMBLE
This page, top: The Cape May Point Lifesaving Station is shown in derelict condition, in the late 1950s, before it finally fell into the sea
Cape May Point State Park

REMEMBER GLORIA'S?
This page, below: The old Denizot Hotel when it was run as two lounges named Maureen's and Gloria's. The building now houses Cabanas and Martini Beach.
Don Pocher

BEHEMOTH BY THE BEACH
Opposite page: The imposing Colonial Hotel (now the Inn Of Cape May) in 1960, before the Avondale motel was built in front of it
Don Pocher

DEADLY DEBRIS
This page: The 1962 nor'easter was the most destructive storm that has ever hit Cape May. Boardwalk wreckage was scattered all over downtown, and flying debris caused as much damage as the storm itself – here, wreckage is strewn across Beach Avenue across from Decatur Street.
Cape May County Museum

CITY UNDER WATER
Opposite page: The storm surge brought ocean waters as far as four blocks past the boardwalk in places
Cape May County Museum

**THE END OF
THE HALL**
This page:
Convention Hall
suffered severe
structural damage,
with the rear end of
the hall torn away
from the rest of the
building. There was
no possibility to
repair the damage
and a temporary
convention hall was
built in its place.
That 'temporary'
structure stood
until 2010, when
it was demolished
to make way for a
new building, more
in scale with the
original.
*Cape May County
Museum*

**CEMENTING
THE FUTURE**
Opposite page:
Learning from the
mistakes of the
past Cape May
officials elected
to construct a
concrete seawall/
promenade instead
of replacing the
wooden boardwalk.
Although especially
rough storms have
flooded waters
over the seawall
at times, it has
protected the city
from more damage.
*Cape May County
Museum*

CAPE CURIOSITY

German U-Boat Is Captured

MARCH 11, 1945, saw the departure of *U-858* from its port in Kristiansand, Norway, setting course for the open seas of the Atlantic. The U-boat was one of 74 assigned to Germany's 33rd flotilla.

The original mission began in September of 1944, with the goal of bringing together all the U-boats that had been staged at French naval bases. Of the 74 U-boats in the flotilla, each was long-range, meaning they had the ability to create mayhem all over the globe.

Less than a month after *U-858* left Kristiansand, Germany's U-boat base at Kiel was attacked by the US 8th Air Force and a number of vessels were damaged. Soon after, another attack on the port was executed by Britain's Royal Air Force, which sunk one of Germany's most powerful heavy cruisers, the *Admiral Scheer*.

The 33rd flotilla had been underway for about six months when *U-858* began its final classified mission. There have been conflicting stories about the actual mission, but the prevailing belief is that *U-858* was not ordered to prowl the Atlantic with the other ships. Instead, she was believed to be one of six U-boats equipped with guided missiles that would be launched at specific American cities.

Four of the other suspected subs were sunk before they ever reached the United States. As each of the U-boats was destroyed, incred-

ible explosions shook the sea, much louder and greater in intensity than anything the Allies had seen before. This seemed to substantiate the claims of guided missile platforms on board and made the hunt for the two remaining subs even more intense.

Additionally, two German spies had been captured in Maine the previous November, after disembarking another U-boat and coming ashore. While being interrogated, they admitted to the mission of the six subs and bragged that the ships would destroy cities up and down the eastern seaport. They also elaborated on what the Allies

knew at that point, explaining that the subs were equipped with special snorkel gear, allowing the U-boat to be powered by its diesel engines while submerged.

In response to the threat, the US Navy set up a series of blockades off the coast of the northeastern United States. While effective in sinking *U-1235*, *U-880*, *U-518* and *U-546*, they failed to stop *U-805* and *U-858*. The two remaining subs made it past the US Navy and were en route to New England. Had the Germans not surrendered when they did it is quite probable that cities like Boston and New York would have been attacked.

AND IT'S OFFICIAL
Commander J. P. Norfleet accepts the surrender of *U-858* from the U-boat's commanding officer Thilo Bode. Commander Norfleet was buried at Cold Spring Cemetery.
Captain Jerry Mason, USN Retired

STANDING WATCH
Opposite page, left: A US Coast Guard sailor stands guard at the base's front gate with the help of a military dog
Coast Guard Historian's Office

A TIME TO REFLECT
Opposite page, right: A pensive-looking Thilo Bode after he was forced to surrender his U-boat to the United States
Cape May Point State Park

However, after Hitler died, Germany chose to surrender all military forces and all U-boats were given specific orders to get rid of their weapons and torpedoes, then hand over the vessels to Allied forces. Following orders, it is assumed that the crew of *U-858* unloaded the missiles from the boat and jettisoned them into the sea.

During daylight hours the commanders of the U-boat were also ordered to fly a black flag signifying their willingness to capitulate. In the night hours, the boats were to be fully illuminated with running lights, ensuring they were visible to Allied ships. It was just before 3am, on May 10, when crew members from *USS Muir* and *USS Carter* first laid eyes on *U-858*.

Two-thirds of the German crew were transferred from the sub to the American destroyer escorts *USS Pope* and *USS Pillsbury*. American sailors and marines assumed control of the U-boat and directed it to a rendezvous point about 40 miles off the coast of Cape May. Once the sub arrived at the location, in the early morning of May 14, the US Navy formally accepted the *U858*'s surrender and took possession of the ship. Most of the crew members were moved to an American ship and US sailors boarded the sub to bring it back to Fort Miles in Lewes, DE.

As the U-boat was brought to Delaware, residents of Cape May were afforded the opportunity to see the sub first-hand. The ship was escorted by contingents from the Navy and Coast Guard, with commercial fishing boats and other private crafts watching from the sides. The mighty *U-858* that held the Navy in such a fearful grasp towards the end of the war, was now under American control and the threat of a missile attack was thwarted.

It's interesting to note that while U-boats sank nearly 3000 Allied ships throughout the war with coordinated torpedo attacks, historians now believe *U-858* never damaged or destroyed any vessel. Previous reports of torpedoes being launched from the sub are said to be the product of mistaken identity and the boasting of German sailors. She was rumored to have held 14 torpedoes before her final mission but according to records none were ever launched.

In accordance with the rules of engagement, sailors from *U-858* were considered Prisoners of War and were transferred to a POW camp on Fort DuPont, also in Delaware. They remained there for about a year, before they were transferred to an England POW farm, where they worked for an additional two years.

The sub was stripped of all valuable assets and used for target practice off the coast of New England. Hit by a torpedo, *U-858* now rests at the bottom of the Atlantic Ocean.

CAPE CURIOSITY

The Long Fight For A Ferry

COLONEL Jesse Rosenfeld, a wealthy developer from Baltimore, purchased the *SS Atlantus* along with two other concrete ships, proposing to use them as part of a unique dock for a new ferry service. Unfortunately, fate intervened and a powerful storm ripped the *Atlantus* free of her moorings.

Because of this predicament the other two concrete ships were never towed to Cape May and the plan was scrapped. A few years later, in the early 1930s, community leaders established the Cape May County Ferry Commission to promote the idea of a ferry service from Cape May to Delaware and help find funding for the venture.

But the commission was unable to find adequate financial backing and another 10 years passed before the idea was revisited by the federal government. As Cape May received the coastal defense bunker it seemed the city was also going to get a ferry service, thanks to World War II. But when the war ended the government decided to scrap the planned ferry.

In 1953 New Jersey passed legislation to formally create the ferry service but the plans were scrapped when the Delaware legislature refused to accept New Jersey's terms.

A privately-held company, the Hudson River Day Line, offered to build and maintain a ferry service for Cape May in 1955, but this new proposal also failed.

Then, in 1957, the Garden State Parkway was completed, originating at the New York Thruway and ending in Cape May, and once again the decision was made to pursue a ferry service.

It didn't happen overnight, though.

It took until the formation of the Delaware River and Bay Authority, in 1963, for the project to actually proceed. With a solid plan to fund the $12.7 million necessary to establish the new ferry service, the DRBA also agreed to purchase four ships from the Chesapeake Bay and Tunnel District.

These four vessels, three running on steam and the other using a more modern diesel system, would make up the new Cape May-Lewes Ferry.

It took only one year to make the necessary preparations, build most of the necessary structures and ready the four ships for use. On July 1, 1964, the Cape May-Lewes Ferry officially opened for business.

Not so fast though... the string of bad luck wasn't quite over.

In a surprising turn of events, one of the ships was taken out of commission the day before the grand opening. The ferry service nearly faced a situation where only three of the four boats were able to participate in the opening day ceremonies. Apparently, the ship that was named to honor the city of Cape May was involved in an accident.

The previous day, as the *SS Cape May* was approaching the Lewes, Delaware docks, one of the ship's screws hit an underwater cable and it became hopelessly entangled in the engine.

Although July 1 was the official first day, there were many ferry crossings in the days leading up to it. Some were used for testing

and others were done to transport government officials and other financial backers between Delaware and Cape May.

All the officials who were on the boat were stuck in Delaware and another ferry had to be sent from Cape May to come pick them up, while crews worked to remove the steel cable and repair the ship.

Because of their hard work and dedication, the ship was fixed the same day and it set a course back to Cape May in time for opening ceremonies.

Judging by that misfortune, and the way the ferry struggled through its first years of operation, it seemed the Cape May–Lewes Ferry might just be destined to fail like the previous attempts.

The one main difference between this endeavor and the previous ones was the simple fact that the Delaware River and Bay Authority refused to lie back and take the loss.

The DRBA took a very aggressive approach to the problems by adjusting the rates for vehicles and passengers and nearly cutting the operating hours in half.

By instituting these changes and a few others, they were able to decrease the amount of money spent operating the ferry, while keeping the incoming revenue steady.

Their plan worked so well, in fact, that the DRBA was able to commission three new ships by 1972. Not long after, two more new ships were built for the Cape May–Lewes Ferry to increase the amount of passengers the ferry could transport.

Later, in 1994, plans were made to completely renovate and modernize all five of the newer ships, with the last one placed back in service by 1999.

One year later, a $12 million renovation plan was undertaken to improve the ferry's docks and terminals.

OFFICIAL TICKET

Cape May, New Jersey - Lewes, Delaware Ferry
PREMIERE TRIP   **June 29, 1964**

Nº 122

Leave Cape May   *Arrive Lewes*

1st boat - 11:40 A. M.   12:50 P. M.
2nd boat - 1:20 P.M.   2:30 P. M.

Delaware
Cape May
Tickets $10.00

S.S. CAPE MAY   TRIP TICKET

Lewes, Delaware, to Cape May, New Jersey

S.S. CAPE MAY   TRIP TICKET

Cape May, New Jersey, to Lewes, Delaware

Name

Address

CAPE CURIOSITY

The Fishing Industry

BEING A SEASIDE resort with beaches on both the Atlantic Ocean and Delaware Bay, fishing is an important aspect of the local culture. But fishing for sport is only a small part of the picture — Cape May offers the third-largest port on the eastern coast of the United States and processes between 50 and 75 million pounds of fish annually.

Cape May has been a hotspot for fishing, dating as far back as the 1700s. Early Dutch settlers tried to establish a whaling port prior to then, but their efforts proved fruitless. Even so, later colonists continued to pursue whale and while they, too, were unable to make it work, their rudimentary docks paved the way for today's modern port.

As colonial fisherman on the Cape abandoned their whaling dreams they embraced clamming and scavenging for oysters. This progressed to angling for smaller fish within sight of the land. That later evolved into fishing for larger species, which required boats to move farther from the coast.

A 1921 article in *The New York Times* recounted the tale of H. E. Derbyshire, who hooked one of the biggest sharks ever to be caught off the Cape May coast. The beast was nine feet long and weighed in at over 400lbs.

Derbyshire and his friends had been fishing for channel bass in the Delaware Bay, near Cape May Point. They secured their trophies to the boat,

allowing the fish to stay in the water while they continued to troll the waters. The shark, however, had other plans and began eating their catch.

Seeing the shark, Derbyshire used quick thinking and hooked it on to a fishing line. The article noted that Derbyshire and his friends fought the shark for more than an hour before it ultimately succumbed and they were able to bring it in to port.

Today's Cape May fishermen still catch shark just off the shore because of the island's natural contour that blends the Atlantic with the Delaware. Cape May waters are home to dozens of varieties of fish, including Atlantic croakers, black drum, blackfish, bluefish, clams, cod, crab, flounder, fluke, kingfish, lobster, mackerel, mahi mahi, marlin, menhaden, mullet, pollock, porgies, salt oysters, sea bass, sea scallops, speckled trout, squid, striped bass, swordfish, tuna and weakfish.

Amateur fishermen have the option to fish directly off the beaches, from rock jetties, on private boats and charter cruises. Though pier fishing was once quite popular in Cape May's illustrious past, there are no longer any municipal piers available for anglers. The top of the old military bunker was a favorite spot before the old cement structure became dangerously unstable.

These days the charter boats seem to be the most popular fishing outlet for visitors. The charter boat business is closely related to the party boat trade, with the main difference being the manner in which passage is secured. Charter boats

**REELING IN
A BIG BLUE**
This page, left:
A huge bluefin
tuna snagged in
the 1980s
The Lobster House

**FISHING FOR
PLEASURE**
This page, right:
The early 1900s
deep-sea fishing
boat *Vaud J.* was
a forerunner to
today's modern
charter boats
Don Pocher

**FROM THE DOCK
TO YOUR PLATE**
Opposite page: A
commercial fishing
vessel docks and
unloads at Cold
Springs Inlet in
the 1940s
The Lobster House

must be rented in full, ahead of the sailing date. Typically, a large group will charter a boat together or someone will charter a boat for themselves and their friends. Cape May is crawling with boats for hire and all it takes to find one is a trip to the local docks or a quick search on the internet.

In contrast, party boats allow passengers to buy their tickets on the same day of the voyage and anyone is welcome. Local party boats have a great reputation for living up to their name, getting like-minded people together for a fun day of fishing. They are typically larger than regular charter boats and offer additional amenities like bait, tackle and equipment rentals.

As popular as fishing is in Cape May, people are often surprised to learn that the island's commercial fleet is the second-largest in the country. The island's fishermen specialize in mackerel, fluke, sea scallops, flounder, sea bass and lobster.

Of those, the sea scallop industry is, by far, the largest and most prominent — Cape May scallops are shipped throughout the United States.

Although technological advances have changed the way modern fishermen secure their catch, the element of danger is ever-present. Commercial fishing has a mortality rate of 15% according to the National Bureau of Labor Statistics, considerably higher than any other occupation.

The risk is attributed to a combination of long hours, heavy machinery that is operated in all types of weather conditions, and the inherent dangers that come with working on the sea. Cape May fishermen are presented with additional worries, caused by the convergence of the Delaware Bay and Atlantic Ocean. The waters that surround the island are particularly notorious for their strong currents and unpredictable weather patterns.

From the first recorded fishing death of Andrew Jeffers in 1893, 75 fishermen have died in the waters surrounding Cape May. Generation after generation, the community has been forced to mourn the loss of beloved husbands, fathers and brothers who gave their lives to the sea.

Cape May residents again faced the duty of saying goodbye to friends and loved ones in

March of 2009. The tragedy occurred in the early morning of the 24th, when the scallop boat *Lady Mary* began taking on water. Within minutes, the 71-foot vessel had sunk, leaving the seven-man crew stranded 60 nautical miles from the coast.

By the time rescue crews arrived only one man was still alive, Jose Luis Arias. Coast guard helicopters airlifted two other men from the scene — Roy "Bobo" Smith Jr and Timothy "Timbo" Smith, but neither survived the ordeal.

The four remaining crew members were listed as missing and a massive search effort was undertaken. After days of fruitless searches, coast guard officials called off the search and acknowledged the deaths of Bernie "Tarzan" Smith, Jorge Ramos, Frankie Credle and Frank Reyes.

Near the Cape May harbor, at the end of Missouri Avenue, stands a monument to the many local fishermen who have lost their lives near Cape May. It's a fitting memorial that was dedicated in 1988 and includes statues of a woman and two children looking out over the harbor. The fishermen's names are etched into the base, along with an inscription from Psalm 107...

He hushed the storm to a gentle breeze, and the billows of the sea were stilled.

CHAPTER TWELVE
Battle For The Soul Of Cape May

**ANGEL OF
THE FUTURE**
This page, top:
One of the
Weightman
Cottages is moved
from its old
home next to the
Lafayette Hotel to
a new site behind
the Peter Shields.
The cottages are
now connected
and known as the
Angel of the Sea.
*Cape May County
Museum*

**BREAKING
GROUND**
This page, below:
The Morning Star
is shown in its new
location. It was so
large that when
movers tried to
bring it down Beach
Avenue its weight
caused the street
to collapse.
*Cape May County
Museum*

**MOVING
EXPERIENCE**
Opposite page:
The Evening Star
was also moved
from Ocean Street
and placed behind
the Morning Star,
although it has since
been demolished.
The engineer
perched on the pole
is Ed Hutchinson,
owner of the
Fairthorne B&B!
*Cape May County
Museum*

LOCAL LEADERS took a far-sighted approach in the city's post-hurricane construction. Instead of simply restoring everything to the way it was, they made significant upgrades that would protect the town from future storms. The most notable improvements were the storm sewers that were installed along the new Beach Avenue, the expanded rock jetties and the steel-reinforced concrete seawall that replaced the boardwalk.

The city also elected to replace Convention Hall with a much smaller, temporary building that would serve until a suitable replacement could be constructed (it only took 47 years for them to decide on a new building worthy of the cause). In addition, none of the ocean piers were rebuilt and with, the exception of the commercials spaces in front of Convention Hall and the small amusement building at the foot of Jackson Street, the city banned any further development along the new seawall.

In 1963 serious plans were finally put into action to construct the long-awaited Cape May Lewes Ferry. Colonel Jesse Rosenfeld's dream was finally a reality, at a cost of nearly $13 million. By July of the following year the first ferry crossed from the Cape May terminal in North Cape May to the terminal in Lewes, DE.

Along with the fierce nor'easter, 1962 also marked the arrival of Reverend Carl McIntire, a fundamentalist minister who would play a huge part in the coming resurrection of Cape May. McIntire made an immediate impact in October when he purchased the aging Hotel Cape May, or Admiral Hotel as it was known at the time of the sale.

McIntire headed an organization called The Christian Beacon Press, which he relocated to the hotel in 1963. The Christian Admiral hotel, as McIntire renamed it, served as a bible confer-

McIntire also used his organization to purchase Congress Hall, the Windsor and the Peter Shields Inn. Because each of his holdings were owned by the Christian Beacon Press, McIntire felt they should be considered tax-exempt. This caused tremendous friction between McIntire and the city leaders, sparking lawsuits and protests.

McIntire's battles with both Cape May and the federal government were legendary. At one point the FCC revoked his radio license and McIntire reacted by purchasing an old minesweeper and attempting to broadcast his show from international waters off the coast of Cape May. His Radio Free America broadcasts failed to work as planned, but it did gain McIntire and Cape May a good deal of media interest.

In the end, McIntire ended up writing a check to the city for $550,000 to pay for back taxes and public utilities. His organization faced tre-

ence and fellowship hotel, along with functioning as the backdrop for McIntire's national radio program, the 20th Century Reformation Hour.

In subsequent interviews and conversations with his followers, Reverend McIntire would describe his feelings towards Cape May as "love at first sight." He enjoyed the old architecture and considered the city a bastion of Americana. McIntire saw enormous potential in the town and believed it was the perfect location for him to expand his fundamentalist ministry.

One year after he opened the Christian Admiral, McIntire founded the religious Shelton College in a building he had constructed directly behind the hotel. McIntire also paid to relocate the Weightman Cottages (Angel of the Sea) and Morning Star/Evening Star buildings to the eastern side of town, adding to his organization's holdings and preventing each from being demolished.

THE SAVIOUR OF CAPE MAY
The late Carolyn Pitts was brought in by Cape May City Council to document every historic building but, unknown to them, she was secretly ensuring that the city's wonderful collection of Victorian architecture would be saved, against the council's wishes

CLEARING THE WAY
Opposite page: An aerial view of Cape May shows the city before Urban Renewal came to town. Many homes and businesses inside the circled area were demolished to create Carpenter's Lane, Lyle Lane and to extend Ocean Street to Lafayette Street. The clipping from the *Atlantic City Press* details the city's major demo project.
Beach Erosion Board and the Coastal Engineering Research Center

Harry Bellangy

mendous financial difficulty and all of his Cape May holdings fell into a state of neglect. McIntire faced widespread criticism for the terrible condition of his properties but without the necessary resources to maintain the aging buildings, there was little that he could have done differently.

The buildings were eventually sold off to private investors, with the exception of the Windsor Hotel, which burned down in 1979, and the Christian Admiral, which was demolished in 1996. The Windsor fire was deemed arson by the local fire marshal and almost immediately accusations were made as to who was responsible.

Some in town placed the blame on McIntire himself and remarked that much of the hotel had been emptied before the fire. Those on McIntire's side responded by pointing out that some of the most valuable pieces from all of his Cape May properties were being stored in the Windsor at the time of the fire. Priceless antiques from the Hotel Cape May, Congress Hall and the Windsor were lost.

McIntire blamed officials in the local city government for the fire. He believed they did it out of spite and to collect the unpaid back taxes that were due to the city. The hotel had an insurance policy that covered fire, but there was a caveat that required McIntire to pay any debts to the city before he received the remainder of the money.

While McIntire was fighting to save some of Cape May's landmark hotels and cottages, another group of concerned citizens were preparing to wage a battle of their own. Throughout the 1960s developers had begun buying up properties in town under the banner of Urban Renewal. Their intention was to demolish the Victorian structures and replace them with new hotels and motels.

The original Urban Renewal idea was to create a Victorian Village in the center of town,

with an outdoor pedestrian mall on Washington Street as the village center. It was thought that the Victorian theme could be used as a sort of gimmick to attract tourists, who would then stay in the new hotels and motels outside of the Victorian Village area.

This plan was endorsed by the city's leaders, who in 1963 applied for federal money from the Urban Renewal Administration to make it a reality. The application was approved and Cape May was given nearly $3 million to create their Victorian Village. Developers were overjoyed at the decision because it bolstered their plans to build up the beachfront and areas outside the designated village boundaries.

Meanwhile, a handful of Cape May cottagers grew incensed at the apparent lack of respect for the town's history and atmosphere. They began meeting in the late 1960s to discuss ways to halt development outside the small Victorian Village area and preserve as much of the city as they could. As the cottagers met, developers contin-

SOUTH JERSEY

SECOND SECTION

Atlan

ATLANTIC CITY, N

LANDMARK TO GO —This hotel, the Baltimore Inn, one of historic landmarks in Cape May, is among some 70 buildings scheduled to be torn down in city's Victorian Village renewal project, but city at present has no place to dispose of debris.

(Press Photo)

BUT NOWHERE TO DUMP THEM

Cape Is Razing 70 Buildings For Victorian Village Project

By JOHN ANDRAS
Press Staff Writer

CAPE MAY — It's no easy task to put up a building, but tearing one down is hard too. When 70 buildings meet the wrecking ball, the situation can become downright difficult.

During the next three and a half years, officials here hope to demolish 70 structures as part of the city's urban renewal Victorian Village project.

There's just one problem: Where to put the buildings after they are torn down.

"Here we are in the throes of demolition," John S. Needles, urban renewal director, said about the next buildings to come down, "but no place to put them."

Needles was referring to the fact the city cannot simply dump and burn rubble from demolished buildings. State health laws prohibit open burning.

Currently, the municipality is in consultation with state health authorities and, according to Needles, the state has promised to provide a dumping and burning site within the area, so demolition can continue.

BOARDWALK SNAPSHOT
This page, top: From the 1980s, Ocean Deck restaurant, now known as Henry's on the Beach
Don Pocher

AN OLD HAUNT
This page, below left: Palmer's Marine Bar was a popular hangout near the Lobster House. The building has since been demolished.
Don Pocher

SANDWICH SHOP EATEN UP
This page, below right: Urban Renewal also claimed the home of Regina's Subs on Lafayette Street. The site is now home to Oyster Bay restaurant.
Don Pocher

THE OTHER LOOKOUT TOWER
This former World War Two sentinel took pride of place on the eastern side of Beach Avenue before a new hotel, the Golden Eagle, was built around it in 1970. The hotel is now called The Grand, and the tower is still in there!
Don Pocher

**ARLINGTON
TO ALCOTT**
This page:
This Cape May
landmark has gone
by a few different
names in its life
– it started out
as the Arlington,
one of Cape May's
plushest hotels
when it was built,
then became the
Huntington House
and now it's the
Hotel Alcott,
also home of the
gourmet restaurant
La Verandah
National Archives

A PALE IMITATION The old McCreary Cottage, on Columbia Avenue, had been 'modernized' with white paint and green roofs during the 1930s. When Jay and Marianne Schatz purchased the property in 1979 and transformed it into the Abbey B&B they restored the Victorian look to the building and utilized a multi-colored paint scheme to highlight the architectural features and millwork. It's now one of Cape May's best-loved and most distinctive buildings. *National Archives*

ACCIDENTAL DISCOVERY
This page, top: Cape May's first B&B, the Mainstay Inn on Jackson Street. The dark blue asbestos shingles hid the cottage's original cedar shake siding until, one day in the 1980s, the new owners were doing construction work on the house and the cedar was discovered. Sandy and Owen Miller, who renamed the property Windward House, then removed the shingles and restored the cedar to its original luster.
Sandy Miller

A THING OF BEAUTY
This page, below: One of the grand interiors of the second Mainstay Inn after owners Tom and Sue Carroll took the name with them when they moved from Jackson Street to Columbia Avenue. They turned the Mainstay into a national attraction.
Maciej Nabrdalik

ued to move forward with their plans and valuable pieces of Cape May's storied past were bulldozed to the ground.

Each time one of the city's storied hotels or homes were lost the cottagers gained more supporters. Their biggest advocate became a woman named Carolyn Pitts, who had actually been hired by the city leaders to help establish the Victorian Village.

One contingency that came along with the federal grant money was a requirement that the city bring in an architectural historian to document every building in the designated village area. When the city hired Pitts they failed to check into her background and never learned that she was a longtime Cape May enthusiast who favored preserving all the town's Victorian architecture.

As Pitts went about her job cataloging the buildings within the boundaries of the city's planned Victorian Village, she also took the time to document a large number of other properties throughout Cape May. By the time she was done, she had amassed hundreds of pages of research on local buildings.

When the mighty Elberon Hotel was leveled to make way for the Victorian Motel on the corner of Congress Place and Perry Street in 1969, the cottagers received a visit from Pitts. The time had come to make a stand and Pitts had an unconventional, but promising, idea.

Pitts and the cottagers organized all of the data that had been collected on the buildings in town and created a portfolio showing Cape May's architectural and historical significance. Without notifying any of the city leaders or gaining their approval Pitts petitioned the federal government to have the entire city of Cape May placed on the National Register of Historic Places.

The plan was successful and, in 1970, the city was added to the register and gained federal pro-

tection from further development. Remarkably, the move was made without the knowledge of anyone in the local city government, the region's congressman or even the state governor!

By the time they found out about it, the designation was already made and it was too late to change anything. The government leaders were furious with Pitts and tried desperately to reverse the decision. They condemned the historic designation and their lack of knowledge about the proceedings. Once it became clear the decision would not be overturned the city's mayor, Frank A. Gauvry, threatened to sue anyone involved in filing the paperwork.

Pitts and the cottagers gave local leaders the opportunity to announce the news to the public but after they failed to make a proclamation the cottagers gave the story to *The Philadelphia Inquirer*.

In the years immediately after Cape May was placed on the National Register of Historic Places Pitts and her group of cottagers faced another struggle. Developers had purchased the abandoned Emlen Physick Estate and planned to knock it down to make way for tract housing.

The once-grand mansion had been left to rot and it had become a haven for vagrants and mischievous local schoolchildren. Nonetheless, the house was a historic building, perhaps one of the most significant in the city, and the cottagers sought to preserve it.

The cottagers formed a new organization, the Mid-Atlantic Center for the Arts, with the intention of saving the building so that it could be used as a Victorian museum. They applied for more federal funds to purchase and rehabilitate the property with help from Pitts, but this time the city government was not caught off guard.

When the federal government approved the request and prepared to transfer the money to the city, the mayor promptly refused it. The city petitioned the federal government to rescind the

THE B&B PIONEERS Mainstay Inn owners Tom and Sue Carroll pose for *Americana* magazine in 1979
The Carrolls

IT'S A DIRTY JOB
This page, top left: Dane Wells works in the main parlor during the restoration of an old guest house into the pristine Queen Victoria B&B, which he and his wife Joan owned for 24 years
Queen Victoria

PREVIOUS EXISTENCE
This page, top right: When Dane and Joan Wells purchased the cottage at 102 Ocean Street, it was the Beverly Guest House
Queen Victoria

TAKING A SAMPLE
This page, below: Joan Wells on the roof of the house with an analyst from Sherwin Williams, who took paint samples and used them to match the original colors of the house.
Queen Victoria

SHINING JEWEL
Opposite page: The finished product, a gorgeous B&B that remains one of the most acclaimed in the country
Queen Victoria

money and in the process angered local citizens who perceived their actions to be retaliatory and not in the best interest of Cape May.

Mayor Gauvry was voted out of office in the next election and replaced by Bruce Minnix, one of the principal founders of the Mid-Atlantic Center for the Arts. Under Minnix's leadership, the city accepted the grant money and the Emlen Physick Estate was saved from demolition.

Minnix and his administration were also responsible for Cape May being named a National Historic Landmark in 1976. This additional designation cemented the city's historical legacy for generations to come and fostered Cape May's rebirth as a premier seaside resort.

Following the news that Cape May was officially named a National Historic Landmark, restoration projects began cropping up all over town. The streets lined with drab, white and green houses, were slowly transformed into

vibrant neighborhoods. One by one, old buildings that were considered eyesores were renovated into Victorian masterpieces.

Cape May was alive again, ready to reclaim her throne as Queen of the Seaside Resorts and the summer vacation crowd took notice. For many years each new season brought nearly double the crowd of the previous one. Cape May also began welcoming visitors during the off-season as community-wide celebrations were founded.

One of the most significant changes for Cape May was the new bed and breakfast business that was started by Tom and Sue Carroll. The Carrolls purchased an ornate old home at 24 Jackson Street that had been separated into apartments and run as a boarding house.

Throwing caution to the wind, the Carrolls removed all the apartments and began renting rooms with the added amenity of breakfast in the morning. They named their inn The Main-

GOODBYE TO ALL THIS

Top left: The massive Elberon Hotel once sat along Congress Place on the site of what is now the Victorian Motel. Like the other buildings on these pages, it was demolished in the name of Urban Renewal.

Top right: This view of the 400 block of Washington Street shows A. E. Smith's Little Shop, next to Joe Drogo's barber shop and Hebenthal's Cigar Shop & Pool Room, which was accessible through the door under the E & W Taxi sign.

Bottom right: Brown's Hardware Store lost its giant billboard when this building on the corner of Lafayette and Jackson Streets was razed and replaced with a much smaller shop that now houses All Irish Imports.

Bottom left: Another view of the 400 block of Washington shows Titleman's Liquor Store and the Savoy Bar on a property that is now inhabited by the City Centre Mall.
Don Pocher

MORE VINTAGE BUILDINGS LOST

Top left: The old Cape May High School was situated along Lafayette Street, where the Acme now stands. The Acme side-loading dock marks the spot of the school's front doors.

Top right: The southern side of the 300 block of Washington Street was home to Hunt's Theatre, which was demolished to make way for a "Victorian" strip mall.

Bottom right: Locals fondly remember this pharmacy on the northwestern corner of Perry Street and Congress Place. As well as medications, the pharmacy provided an extensive candy selection for kids.

Bottom left: Congress Hall's garage sat next to the pharmacy, across the street from the hotel. The building you see on the left is now known as the Pink House. It was spared demolition and moved to 33 Perry Street, a site that had just been cleared by the demolition of Cape May's VFW building.

Don Pocher

FALLEN GIANT
The aging Baltimore Hotel on Jackson Street was built following the fire of 1878 and survived for nearly a century. It was put to the sword as part of Cape May's Urban Renewal project and was replaced by the Seaport, which later became the Tides condominiums.
Greater Cape May Historical Society

A GEM ON JACKSON
When the Kulkowitz family purchased the Carroll Villa on Jackson Street in the 1970s they turned the rundown property into a bed and breakfast inn. This picture, from the mid-1970s, shows the property before the Mad Batter restaurant was added on to the front porch. The building to the left of the Carroll Villa is an old rooming house which is now the boutique Virginia Hotel, also home of the Ebbitt Room restaurant which, along with the Mad Batter and other excellent venues, prompted *The New York Times* to call Cape May the "Restaurant Capital of New Jersey."
National Archives

FOR THE LOVE OF PHYSICK
This page: A group of re-enactors perform during one of the first Victorian Week celebrations in the early days of the Mid-Atlantic Center for the Arts. Kneeling is Bruce Minnix, an award-winning TV producer from New York who became a leading light in the fight to save the Emlen Physick Estate and who later became mayor of Cape May after the voters showed their unhappiness at the previous occupant, who had tried to stop the city being granted National Historic Landmark status.
Mid-Atlantic Center for the Arts

WALKING THE WALK
Opposite page: Tourists are led down Congress Place during one of MAC's first walking tours. Notice all the buildings in the background are painted white.
Mid-Atlantic Center for the Arts

stay and when they chose to move to a bigger building on Columbia Avenue in 1977 they took the name with them.

Cape May's first bed and breakfast inn was then purchased by Sandy and Owen Miller, who renamed it The Windward and joined the B&B business themselves. Across the street, Poor Richard's Inn and the Carroll Villa had already opened. Soon, B&B inns began sprouting up all over town and Cape May became informally known as the B&B capital of America.

The 1980s and 1990s saw the continued growth of Cape May as a premiere seaside resort – and the unofficial designation of another desirable status for the city. In an August, 1996 column about the resort's culinary offerings, *New York Times* columnist and noted author, Fran Schumer, labeled Cape May "The restaurant capital of New Jersey."

That honor was thanks to a culinary coup d'état that swept through the city, led by the Kulkowitz family, who blazed a trail with the Mad Batter, on Jackson Street. In the late 1970s, the family patriarch, Harry Kulkowitz, decided

RETURN OF A FIERY CURSE
Cape May suffered several fires in the 1970s, 1980s and 1990s, a century after the inferno that destroyed 40 acres of beachfront land. Two of the most devastating were at the Devonshire condominiums on South Lafayette Street (this page left) and the Windsor Hotel, which was destroyed in 1979 (this page, top right and opposite page). In 1997, there was a major scare at the Virginia Hotel, but the Cape May Fire Department were able to save the boutique hotel, following a blaze that begun in the hotel's chimney (this page, below right).
Cape May Fire Department

COLORFUL CUISINE
This page, left: The Mad Batter was the trailblazer of Cape May's restaurant scene. Chef Lisa Shriver is pictured with owners Mark Kulkowitz and Pam Huber at the restaurant's renovated bar.
Aleksey Moryakov

MASTER OF THE EXOTIC
This page, right: Another major player in the restaurant revolution was Steve and Janet Miller's 410 Bank Street, whose chef Henry Sing Cheng has been creating edible masterpieces from the day the restaurant opened in 1984.
Aleksey Moryakov

to open a restaurant that was unlike any others in town. His new eatery offered patrons an upscale menu with non-traditional dishes that contrasted with what Cape May diners were used to eating.

It was a risky decision but the gamble paid off almost immediately. The restaurant was continually booked and people began traveling to Cape May specifically to eat at the Mad Batter. As Philadelphia and New York City papers hailed the eatery, local restaurateurs took notice. It was not long before more fine dining restaurants began appearing around the island and the city quickly earned a reputation as a gourmet dining mecca. In 1984 Steve and Janet Miller opened 410 Bank Street, which offered a French-Caribbean menu

that delighted the critics, while Curtis Bashaw added to the town's stock with The Ebbitt Room, housed in the Virginia Hotel, revamped and re-opened in 1989. The other culinary giant that added to the city's growing reputation was the Washington Inn, opened in 1978 by Toby and Rona Craig.

A 2004 *New York Times* review of the local restaurant scene, entitled, "How Cape May Became a Culinary Capital", acknowledged the Mad Batter's place in Cape May history. The article spoke of the restaurant's founding and noted, "A generation later, Cape May — at the southernmost tip of New Jersey — is considered one of the East Coast's culinary capitals. While shore fare elsewhere still seems to be stuck in

that stuffed-flounder and crab-cake mode, at least a dozen high-end restaurants here are destination spots for food lovers from New York to Washington and beyond."

The city has also become known for its abundance of natural wonders and, in July of 1992, The Nature Center of Cape May was opened. The center is still functioning today with the same goal of educating children and adults about the environment.

Cape May had faced a grim reality in February of 1996 when the historic, but ill-fated-from-the-start Hotel Cape May/Christian Admiral was demolished. There were few people in town who wanted to see the building knocked down, but it had been allowed to

deteriorate so badly that it was beyond rescue.

As a consolation, the loss of the Hotel Cape May paved the way for a restoration of another landmark Cape May hotel, Congress Hall. The hotel's signature yellow paint was faded and chipping off, while the prominent three-story columns had become warped and rotted. Renovations on the legendary hostelry were completed in July of 2002, at a cost of $22 million.

December of 2006 marked the beginning of a difficult path for Cape May's Beach Theatre, the only remaining movie theatre in town. Frank Enterprises, owners of the theatre, announced they were closing for good and that the property would be redeveloped. Original plans called for the theatre to be demolished and replaced with condominiums.

Almost immediately a group of concerned citizens organized and formed a non-profit foundation to save the theatre. They pointed to the historic significance of the theatre, which was designed by noted architect William H. Lee in the 1950s. Their Beach Theatre Foundation began a fund-raising campaign to secure enough money to temporarily lease the property from Frank Enterprises.

Through the work of the Beach Theatre Foundation and a number of volunteers the theatre was able to reopen for business in November of 2007. In the meantime, however, Frank Enterprises moved forward with their redevelopment plans and were granted a demolition permit for the building by Cape May's Historic Preservation Committee.

The Beach Theatre Foundation continued to operate the movie house throughout 2008, with the hopes of being able to raise enough money to buy the property outright.

However, Cape May's Planning Board officially approved Frank Enterprise's plans for the six condominium units in December of 2008 and the Beach Theatre Foundation faced their final setback when it was forced to close the movie house around the same time, due to electrical and heating problems.

Their lease expired on March 31, 2009 and they were nowhere near being able to meet Frank Enterprise's asking price of $12 million.

The Group That Saved The City

THE bitter struggle between developers and historical preservationists had reached a boiling point in the late 1960s, with the future of the quiet little resort resting on the outcome. If the developers had won the battle, Victorian Cape May would have been bulldozed over, to be replaced by modern hotels and glitzy, neon-covered motels.

Two major properties in the city had already succumbed to that fate – the Lafayette Hotel and the Elberon. The gorgeous old Lafayette was swiftly replaced with the contemporary Marquis de Lafayette and the Elberon was demolished to make way for the Victorian Motel.

As an added blow to the preservationists, additional historic properties were cleared on the city's main commercial thoroughfare, Washington Street. In their place was built Victorian Towers, a modern high-rise tower for senior citizens. It appeared that the future of the jewel of the Jersey Shore was going to be cemented in modernization, at the expense of Cape May's Victorian charm.

However, everything changed once the entire town was suddenly listed on the National Register of Historic Places. Few knew how it happened, because the entire plan was veiled in secrecy until it was completed. Regardless, once the honor was bestowed upon the city it created a huge roadblock for the developers.

The front entry hall of the Emlen Physick Estate is a beautiful sight to behold *Mid-Atlantic Center for the Arts*
Opposite page: Bob Heinly (aka Dr Physick) joins a fellow re-enactor for a game of croquet *Maciej Nabrdalik*

To make the situation even more hopeless for those who favored a more modern resort just over five years later the City of Cape May was officially named a National Historic Landmark. This great honor was granted in 1976, and it recognized Cape May as "possessing exceptional value or quality in illustrating or interpreting the heritage of the United States."

Ask anyone who has ever visited the legendary city of Deadwood, South Dakota or colonial Williamsburg, in old Virginia – National Historic Landmark status is a serious business. Once Cape May secured the title the future of the island became clear. The city would no longer be known as just another seaside community, with plummeting property values and problems attracting tourists.

Instead of being regarded as outdated the buildings were considered vintage and rather than describing Cape May as old-fashioned, the city became Victorian. The same qualities that once drove tourists away in favor of resorts like Atlantic City and the Wildwoods began bringing them back in droves. People longed for a relaxing getaway from their fast-paced lives and they found comfort in the Victorian allure of Cape May.

Throughout the resort, rundown boarding houses were painstakingly restored and transformed into charming bed and breakfast inns. The pedestrian mall on Washington Street became tremendously popular, with both visitors and full-time residents. A new group of dedicated Cape Mayas began taking the town by storm, spreading the Victorian history of the resort through walking tours and trolley rides.

This collection of residents and vacationers called themselves the Mid-Atlantic Center for the Arts and formed in late 1970. Their organization had been active throughout the years leading up to the landmark status and they were largely responsible for the honor.

Originally founded to rehabilitate and restore the Emlen Physick Estate, one of the finest examples of Victorian architecture on the island, MAC also introduced Victorian Week (it was only a weekend in the early days and now spans 10 days) and the candlelight house tour at Christmas time. As for the rehabilitation project, it was extensive and consumed hundreds of hours along with plenty of money.

The money problem was covered by government grants – after the city leaders declined to use existing HUD funds for the project. The original plan called for the municipal government to assume ownership of the Physick Estate, with MAC managing the restoration and maintaining the property.

Just as the battle over redevelopment was intensifying in the early 1970s, Cape May's mayor and other city leaders decided they were not comfortable with the arrangement. Instead of going forward with the initial plan, the mayor refused to accept the grant and called a halt to the project.

However, the mayor failed to file the papers properly and the grant was never officially refused. Not long after the debacle, the mayor was voted out of office and replaced with a new leader, who promptly signed on the dotted line for the money.

With the money in hand and the labor force in place, renovation work began immediately on the Emlen Physick Estate. Along with the construction work on the house itself the grounds were restored and many of the original furnishings were refurbished and placed throughout the mansion. When the venture was completed the estate became a shining example of the Victorian era and a showplace for the community of Cape May.

The Mid-Atlantic Center for the Arts, meanwhile, has evolved from a group of enthusiastic volunteers into a cultural organization that employs 160 professional staffers and utilizes a volunteer army of nearly 300 people.

SAVED FROM THE BULLDOZER A before and after display of the Emlen Physick Estate, one of Cape May's greatest architectural masterpieces. The picture on the left shows the damage that years of neglect had wreaked on the house, which was slated for demolition before a determined group of Cape May cottagers and local business owners formed an organization called the Mid-Atlantic Center for the Arts and eventually saved the structure. In the picture on the right it is apparent that their restoration efforts were worthwhile. The house is just as grand now as it was when it was first constructed for Dr Emlen Physick. *Mid-Atlantic Center for the Arts*

Cape May Star and Wave

Serving New Jersey's Only National Historic Landmark City

142nd YEAR NO. 9   CAPE MAY, N.J. 08204   TWO SECTIONS   THURSDAY, FEBRUARY 29, 1996   PHONE 884-3466   50 CENTS

Here we see the walls of the Christian Admiral give as the building is "pulled" to the ground by large cables connected to a single bulldozer. The large yellow letters HRISTIAN start their fateful descent to the ground.

The letters STIAN remain intact as they plummet to the ground amidst the bricks and boulders. Spectators were ordered to stay far away from the Monday morning's demolition attempt by Winzinger workers who warned of bricks flying every which direction.

A great wall of dust rises as the rest of the east wing settles to the ground. Too thick to see through, workers and spectators alike had to wait several minutes to see what was, and what was not, left of the Christian Admiral.

photos by Jennifer Kopp

Christian Admiral begins fall by faithful crowd's eyes

By JENNIFER KOPP
Star and Wave Correspondent
CAPE MAY — "You're watching history go away, kid" says the

Major structural demolition began the previous Wednesday afternoon just as warmer temperatures brought fog billowing in

ing creaks and cracks and finally lets go.
"It's stubborn. (It) doesn't want to come down," says security

ogle.
Ralph Cornwell, born in Rio Grande ("we used to call it 'Rior' Grande back then") in 1921, re-

By 8 a.m., onlookers dot the beach front, most with sure-shot and video cameras, waiting and watching the demolition crew for

tant to leave to get more in fear of missing something.
So the waiting continues.
The wait can be long. Though

The country's original seaside resort reached a landmark milestone in 2009, when Cape May proudly acknowledged its 400th anniversary. A year of festivities was planned to commemorate the occasion, beginning with the coronation of a king and queen to preside over the revelry.

Cape May's new royal family consisted of King Charles "Bud" Swain and Queen Patricia Milligan. Swain is a local businessman whose family roots extend back into Cape May's illustrious past. His family has owned and operated Swain's Hardware since 1896.

Milligan grew up in Haddonfield, NJ and began her love affair with Cape May in 1957, when she first vacationed on the island with her family. Forty years later, she moved to the cape permanently and has been a community fixture ever since.

Following the coronation in December of 2008 the anniversary festivities kicked off in style with the Half Moon Gala Ball at Congress Hall on February 19, 2009. Amongst the historical lectures, art shows, theatre events and a beard-growing contest that was inspired by a similar contest during the 350th anniversary celebrations of 1959, the city played host to a special grand opening in spring of 2009.

In March, 2009 the Mid-Atlantic Center for the Arts (MAC) unveiled their $1.3 million renovation of Fire Control Tower 23. Prior to the restoration, the aging WWII lookout tower had fallen into a state of disrepair and was in danger of being lost forever. No measures were taken to preserve the structure when the military abandoned it decades ago and the tower did not age gracefully.

MAC officials recognized the historical significance of Tower 23, which was placed on the New Jersey Register of Historic Places in May of 2003. Just as they did 20 years earlier with the lighthouse, the organization renovated the tower to pristine condition and opened it up to

A BRAND NEW MALL Washington Street saw a rededication ceremony in June of 2008 when the newly-renovated mall was officially re-opened. Mayor Jerry Inderwies cuts the ribbon. Third from the left is Frank Gauvry, who, as mayor 40 years earlier, opposed a plan by local preservationists to save the Emlen Physick Estate. Gauvry was also against the idea of Cape May being granted National Historic Landmark status, favoring instead more modern developments in town.
Aleksey Moryakov

RETURN OF A SENTINEL Opposite page: On March 27, 2009 Veterans Marvin Hume and Vince Panzano were on hand for the opening of Fire Control Tower 23, which was restored by the Mid-Atlantic Center for the Arts and opened to the public
Aleksey Moryakov

the public. The first visitors and representatives from the media climbed the spiral staircase on March 27.

Cape May has been reborn through a combination of the resort's new B&B business, the reinvigoration of the city's restaurant trade, the infrastructure investments made by city leaders and the commitment of the Cape May's many hotel, motel and condominium owners.

With a showpiece new convention hall set to open in 2010; a thriving cultural scene that includes a top-class jazz festival, film festival and a beautifully-renovated theatre featuring Broadway-class drama from Cape May Stage; beaches that are among the most desirable on the east coast; and a group of veteran, and rookie, hoteliers and restaurateurs who are in a relentless pursuit of excellence, the city is as popular

now as it has been for more than a century.

This island at the tip of New Jersey was primed for greatness from the start. The Kechemeche indians treasured the peace and tranquility they found here. Standing on the same beaches as they did, staring off into the same horizon that captured their gaze 400 years ago, it is apparent that while so much has changed over the years, the spirit of Cape May has never faded.

HAPPY BIRTHDAY TO CAPE MAY!
On August 29, 2009 the city of Cape May celebrated its 400th anniversary with a parade through town, which followed a number of events that were organized throughout the year. The date marked the arrival of Sir Henry Hudson's Dutch sailing vessel *Half Moon* at the southern tip of New Jersey.

Aleksey Moryakov

CAPE CURIOSITY

The Return Of Congress Hall

HUNDREDS OF onlookers witnessed Congress Hall's rebirth in June of 2002 in a scene that brought to mind the story of the phoenix. The famed hotel may not have perished in flames the way the phoenix (or the original Congress Hall) did, yet many had written off the old hotel.

Decades of neglect had taken its toll on the structure of this Victorian masterpiece, which had slowly deteriorated into a crumbling relic. Though the casual onlooker could see little more than a few broken windows, some peeling paint and a sagging roof, those intimate with the building's condition knew the sad truth.

Underneath all the exterior embellishments and many layers of weathered paint lay something approaching a house of cards. The building was structurally unsound and, unless something was done to secure it, Congress Hall could have collapsed. Even if the structure were to be stabilized a thorough rehabilitation was needed to make it a viable hotel again.

Luckily, that is what happened. The massive project was undertaken by Curtis Bashaw, grandson of Congress Hall's former owner, Reverend Carl McIntire. Bashaw attracted a group of friends and investors in 1998 to join him in his attempt to resurrect the iconic hotel.

Among those friends was Craig D. Wood, who had partnered with Bashaw to form Cape Advi-

**BEACH TENTS
CAUSE A FLAP**
This page:
Congress Hall
faced controversy
in town when
they first erected
cabanas on the
beach in front
of the hotel in
2006. There were
differing views over
whether or not
they conformed
to planning
regulations. A
compromise was
reached and the
hotel installed
smaller versions.
dbox

**A BIG NOISE
IN TOWN**
Opposite page:
Today's Congress
Hall is around half
the size of the
original Big House
that once stood on
the property, but
it is also a whole
lot more beautiful
and inviting than its
more rudimentary
predecessors. The
2002 renovation
cost nearly
$25 million, and
the result was
nothing less than
extraordinary.
Here, the hotel and
its grounds host
the annual Fourth
Of July fireworks
display.
Aleksey Moryakov

**GOING
GREEN**
The hotel's grand
lawn is not as
large as it once
was, but beautiful
landscaping has
made it a favorite
spot for weddings.
The lawn also
hosts the annual
Fourth Of July
celebrations.
dbox

sors in 1995. The Congress Hall development would put the relatively new partnership to the test as the two were presented with a series of obstacles from the start.

Before the Congress Hall plans were drawn up, Cape Advisors were forced to deal with an intense backlash caused by the razing of the Christian Admiral on the east side of town. It was public knowledge prior to the demolition that Cape Advisors, who owned both Congress Hall and the Christian Admiral, would be unable to save both hotels.

Each of the hotels required extensive work that would cost far more than they were worth. Cape Advisor's initial plan was to sell the Christian Admiral to another preservation-minded developer and use the revenue from the sale to fund the renovation of Congress Hall. The fatal flaw proved to be the sheer size of the Christian Admiral and the huge amount of money it would take to save it. Bashaw led dozens of developers through the building, but to no avail.

A handful of offers were made by local residents and developers, but they were negligible. None came close to matching the value of the hotel and the prime beachfront land. In early 1996, the Christian Admiral was brought to the ground by a team of bulldozers, while scores of local residents and cottagers fumed.

They blamed Bashaw and his grandfather personally for the loss, making wild accusations of underhanded deals with the local government and lamenting the years of neglect under the reverend's ownership. Threats were whispered around town that because of the demolition, Cape May was in jeopardy of losing its National Historic Landmark status, although the National Parks Service never made such a claim.

With the Christian Admiral gone, attention turned to Congress Hall. Some of the same challengers of the Admiral's demolition began to line up in opposition to the proposed renovation of Congress Hall. Critics took umbrage with many aspects of the project and fought especially hard against Cape Advisors' plans to build an underground parking garage and conference center.

Legal challenges were issued and again the specter of the town losing its landmark designation was raised. Even after a representative from the National Park Service publicly stated that there was no danger of the town being removed from the list, opponents pressed on.

It took two years before the initial hurdles were overcome and construction could begin. At that point, lawyers for both sides continued to wrangle in court while the Cape Advisors construction teams stripped the hotel down to its bare bones. Passers-by on Perry Street and Congress Place were afforded the experience of looking directly through Congress Hall to the ocean.

Over the course of the next two years the hotel was systematically rebuilt. Congress Hall's signature three-story wooden columns were reinforced with steel, along with the roof and support structure. In fact, a total of 75 tons of steel were added throughout the hotel.

Along with the steel came 10 miles of plumbing, 50 miles of electrical wires and 2,400 gallons of paint. In addition, 158,000 bricks were removed from the hotel, cleaned and put back into place. Cape Advisors took pains to reuse as much of the original materials as possible and managed to incorporate many rescued pieces from the Christian Admiral.

Cape Advisors backed away from their proposed additions in the face of continued legal challenges and chose to focus all their resources on the hotel.

In the end, the project cost more than $22 million and the result was nothing short of remarkable. Congress Hall had been rebuilt from the basement up and is, once again, the reigning queen of Cape May.

The Launch Of Exit Zero

CAPE May's riotously-popular weekly magazine, *Exit Zero*, was inspired, like many good ideas, by a conversation in a bar. In this case, the Brown Room in Congress Hall. The date was early 2003 and the conversation was between Curtis Bashaw, a principal owner of Congress Hall, and Jack Wright, a magazine editor who had quit his job in New York to spend the previous summer in Cape May – Bashaw had offered him the job of managing the re-opened hotel's pool cabana.

After the 2002 summer season ended Bashaw had commissioned Wright to produce a book about the history of Congress Hall. While researching the book Wright had read through many issues of *Pennywise* magazine, which delighted generations of Cape May locals and visitors from its launch in the 1930s to its demise in the 1980s.

Bashaw and Wright agreed that Cape May needed to bring back the jaunty spirit of the legendary publication. Instead of returning to New York and resuming his national magazine career, Wright bought a ramshackle fixer-upper on the island and launched, with Bashaw's support, a weekly rag full of advice, information and humor – for both tourists and locals.

The first issue of *Exit Zero* (so named because Cape May has no exit on the Garden State Parkway) was published on July 4, 2003, containing just 24 pages. It was an instant hit and quickly grew in size and stature.

Wright was helped by David Gray, a friend he had worked with on a newspaper in Scotland in the early 1990s. Gray had initially come to Cape May for a five-day trip but stayed on for

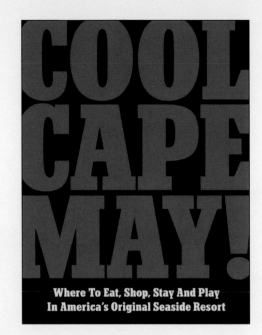

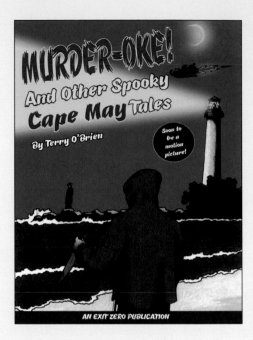

a five-week odyssey. He helped with the design and began writing a humorous column called The Old Fogey which has appeared in every issue since.

The two were joined that first summer by Maciej Nabrdalik, a young Polish computer science student who had met Wright when he worked as a lifeguard at the Congress Hall pool in 2002. Nabrdalik was teaching himself photography and became *Exit Zero*'s first photographer, quickly making a name for himself with his candid, high-quality shots.

In 2004, Wright and Bashaw reached an agreement that allowed Wright to buy out Bashaw's share in the magazine and he became sole owner. At the end of the year, Jason Black added a much-needed layer of professionalism when he joined as Advertising Manager (and later became Wright's business partner).

As well as providing information on how to enjoy Cape May, which is the magazine's main mission, *Exit Zero* has also launched several promising careers.

Maciej Nabrdalik returned to Poland and polished his skills so successfully that he became one of the most sought-after photographers in the country. He won awards in four national contests in 2007 and 2008, including Picture Of the Year in 2007 for a stunning portrait of the outgoing Polish president. In 2008, he took part in the New York Photo Festival and was nominated in their annual photography awards.

Terry O'Brien's cultish Undertow column made its debut in 2004 and a couple years later he began writing short stories which were serialized in *Exit Zero* and then turned into a book of short stories in 2008. The collection, *Murder-Oke! And Other Spooky Cape May Tales*, was featured on National Public Radio and on the front page of *The Philadelphia Inquirer*. A second book of O'Brien's stories is planned.

Craig McManus, a psychic medium, began a column called The Ghost Writer, which he then parlayed into a series of books titled *The Ghosts Of Cape May*, all of which have become local best-sellers.

And Ben Miller started out with a photo-based column titled The Way We Were, which became the inspiration for the book you are reading now.

Exit Zero Publishing also produces *Cool Cape May*, an annual guide book that is distributed to most of the hotels, motels and inns, and recently released a popular little book called *The Exit Zero Guide To Cape May*. More Cape May-centric books are planned in the future, as are other titles of national interest.

In 2005 the company opened a retail store on Perry Street, producing a wide range of souvenirs bearing the *Exit Zero* logo, as well as selling the books produced by the company.

Local business owners and community leaders credit *Exit Zero* for not only exuberantly promoting Cape May as a desirable tourist destination but for bringing together the community through its photographic coverage of everything from major social events to individual birthday parties, weddings, and scenes from the local bars and beaches.

EXIT ZERO

Cape May, NJ   A sprightly sheet full of the sprays of the old ocean   July 4, 2003

WELCOME TO A NEW VOICE IN CAPE MAY

YOU can buy T-shirts in town featuring the slogan, "Cape May, A drinking town with a Victorian problem." Leaving aside the obvious point that those kinds of T-shirts, like novelty answer-machine messages, stop being funny after around a tenth of a second, they still provide the kernel of a thought. Cape May doesn't have a Victorian problem, but we at *Exit Zero*, the town's new weekly entertainment newspaper, think it has something of an image problem.

The pioneering folks who saved Cape May in the 1970s by getting together to preserve its Victorian heritage, in the face of a blinkered city council, cannot receive enough praise, and their legacy lives on through the good works of the Mid-Atlantic Center for the Arts. In fact, it's hardly a legacy since most of them are still alive, kicking and contributing as much as ever.

However... Cape May is more than just the finest collection of Victorian architecture in the country. It's America's original beach resort, and we think that's an image that needs to be cultivated. Not to the detriment of the Victorian message, but in conjunction with it. We often hear people in this town waxing on about Martha's Vineyard, the Hamptons and Key West. And to be sure, they're all beautiful beach resorts. But think about it: what do these places have that Cape May lacks (okay, we'll give Key West the nod for total hours of sunshine)?

As well as boasting a Victorian wonderland that ranks among the finest

Continued on Page Two

TRAINING DAY: D. J. Draus and Greg Oldham of Cape May Beach Patrol.   By staff photographer Maciej Nabrdalik

Cape May's Sprightly, Effervescent, Unmissable Journal ★ May 26, 2006 ★ Vol. 4, No. 16

EXIT ZERO

Opposite page: Some of the Cape May-centric books produced by Exit Zero Publishing which are aimed at spreading the good word about America's Original Seaside Resort
Left: The first cover of Exit Zero, from July 4, 2003, featured lifeguards D. J. Draus and Greg Oldham.
Above: This amazing painting by local artist Victor Grasso (which many thought was a photo) graced one of the special glossy color issues produced every summer by Exit Zero Publishing

CAPE CURIOSITY

Building With A Stormy History

THE CITY'S first convention hall was constructed between 1917 and 1918, across from the majestic Stockton Hotel. In addition to the expansive dance floor and convention area, the grand edifice also provided a number of commercial spaces. Over the years it housed a luncheonette, dress shop, fabric store, pharmacy and a movie theatre.

Behind the hall a long fishing pier was constructed that quickly grew popular among locals and visitors. It served the public well until the Great Atlantic Hurricane of 1944 smashed it to pieces. Luckily, only the pier and the boardwalk in front of it were destroyed, with the convention hall escaping relatively unharmed.

Eighteen years later, during the Ash Wednesday nor'easter of 1962, the building suffered a much different fate. A powerful, churning Atlantic Ocean battered convention hall and the floor was ripped out from underneath it. The whole south end of the structure was chopped apart, leaving no possibility for repairs.

Cape May's city officials recognized the importance of having a convention hall in town, so the decision was made to quickly construct a replacement.

Due to the widespread destruction done by the storm, including the loss of the boardwalk and much of Beach Avenue, the city found itself

in a tough situation. There was not enough money to both repair all the damage and rebuild convention hall to its previous grandeur.

The solution was to construct a temporary hall on the site, with the intention of replacing it when the necessary funds became available. Local government leaders estimated that would take approximately 10 to 20 years.

As it turned out, that second, temporary convention hall stood on the Cape May beachfront for 47 years, one year longer than the original. A movement was started in 2007 to finally replace the building with a much larger, multifunctional hall, though it met with stiff resistance from some members of the community.

There was still some ambiguity as to the future of the temporary hall until a 2008 inspection found it to be unstable. City leaders held a series of public meetings to discuss the possibility of a replacement building, with many different designs and plans presented to the public.

Even so, there were still members of the city who vehemently opposed the building of a new convention hall, arguing that the costs involved (around $10 million) were unnecessary and that a smaller-scale building would suffice.

Others called for the new center to look exactly like the original, even though the architects pointed out that this was not a practical

design for a beachfront location.

The city declined to make a final decision and instead placed a referendum on the ballot in the November 2008 election, asking residents if they supported the proposed replacement.

The results were clear and the local electorate overwhelmingly voted in favor of a new hall. As a result, the city began the process of demolishing the existing structure and building the new one.

Cape May's third convention hall will include 32,000 square feet of commercial spaces, a large auditorium, city offices and community meeting rooms. At the time of writing, it was scheduled to be completed by the summer of 2011.

CAPE CURIOSITY
The City Of Many Festivals

ASIDE from being a storied seaside resort Cape May has become a festival destination. From music and food to Victorian customs, Cape May hosts 11 annual festivals throughout the year, along with other family-friendly events and theme weekends.

The season starts in March with the Singer Songwriter Festival, which was founded in 2008. By its second year, the event had already blossomed to include 150 different musical acts, showcased on 15 separate stages around town. In addition to the live music and jam sessions, the SS Cape May, as it's called, includes a series of music clinics and workshops held at Congress Hall.

Next on the schedule in the highly-acclaimed Cape May Jazz Festival, held twice each year in April and in November.

After the jazz music comes one of the community's favorite celebrations, the Spring Festival. Once upon a time it was called the Tulip Festival and the Chamber of Commerce of Greater Cape May organized the event. Every year, visitors would flock to Cape May to look at thousands of brightly-colored tulips. Seeing the popularity of the tulip festival, the Mid-Atlantic Center for the Arts (MAC) decided to create their Spring Festival. They added food tasting, trolley tours, garden tours, classes and seminars. Eventually, the two celebrations merged into one event.

Tulips blend into melodious tones when the Cape May Music Festival, which celebrated its 20th anniversary in 2009, takes hold of the town at the end of May.

This page, left: Chris Barron, formerly of the Grammy-winning Spin Doctors, played at the second annual Singer Songwriter Cape May in March, 2009 *Aleksey Moryakov*
Right: Fashions from Victorian Week *Maciej Nabrdalik* **Opposite: Cape May Jazz Festival** *Aleksey Moryakov*

As the music festival comes to a close in early June it's time for the West Cape May Strawberry Festival to begin. Residents of Cape May have a perennial date with strawberry shortcake the first Saturday of each June. The event includes much more than just strawberries, offering an assortment of seafood and fresh produce, along with arts and crafts.

The city founded Harborfest in June of 2008 and it was regarded as an instant success. Harborfest is a celebration of the seas and seaside culture in general. There is plenty of fresh seafood to be enjoyed, a scallop cook-off between some of the city's best chefs, live entertainment and ecological seminars.

Cape May's restaurant industry gears up each September for the Food and Wine Festival, sponsored by MAC. The event was founded in 1997 and offers food tasting at a variety of local restaurants, winery tours and tasting, cooking classes, seminars and the People's Choice Chowder Contest.

October is a huge month for festivals with Jackson Street's Octoberfest, West Cape May's Lima Bean Festival and the one that started it all, Victorian Week. Octoberfest is an opportunity for friends, neighbors and visitors to come together on Jackson Street and turn the avenue into a little German village. Traditional German food, a beer garden, music, dancing and crafts round out the celebration.

Over in West Cape May, the lima bean takes center stage as the town recognizes the area's rich agricultural history. A Lima Bean King and Lima Bean Queen are crowned and the under-appreciated bean is available in many different food choices.

The name Victorian Week is a bit deceptive, since the festival lasts 10 days. Back in the 1970s, the group that founded MAC conceived of the festival to celebrate the town's Victorian heritage and help reinvigorate the local tourism industry. Since then, Victorian Week has introduced Cape May to many new visitors, especially after endorsements like the one from the American Bus Association, which named Victorian Week one of the Top 100 Events in North America.

Rounding out the festival season is the New Jersey State Film Festival, which occurs each November. The event was founded in 2002 to highlight New Jersey films and is sponsored by the Cape May Film Society. Academy Award-winning actress Susan Sarandon appeared at the festival in 2003, when she was honored with the New Jersey Governor's Award for Outstanding Contribution by NJ Governor James McGreevey.

In addition to the annual festivals, Cape May also offers a number of special events and community celebrations. Some have quite a long lineage, like the Queen Maysea Coronation and the Baby Parade, which were both founded in 1932.

Each year on the Fourth of July, Congress Hall offers residents and visitors a spectacular fireworks display.

And come Christmas, the town is transformed into a Charles Dickens wonderland for a variety of tours, special events and the annual West Cape May Christmas Parade, which comes directly through the city of Cape May.

There are also Sherlock Holmes weekends, chocolate buffets, arts and crafts shows, fishing tournaments, sand sculpture contests and the annual beachfront run.

Practically every season of the year offers something different. More now than ever before, Cape May is a year-round vacation destination.

Epilogue

AS WE celebrated Cape May's 400th anniversary in 2009, we witnessed an exciting time in the town's history. There were parades, balls and a beach party to celebrate the occasion, all while city leaders worked to preserve Cape May's future.

The city-wide celebrations may have faded, but the best is yet to come. There are a number of projects on the horizon that will help preserve the resort's Victorian heritage while ushering in a new standard of hospitality.

The most prominent change will be the new Convention Hall that should be completed in the coming years. Architectural designs show it will be a gorgeous addition to the Cape May beachfront, with majestic two-story windows on all sides, multiple community rooms, plenty of hall space for large events, and panoramic views of the Atlantic Ocean.

City leaders are also planning changes in the way the Cape May markets itself to visitors, with a comprehensive public relations plan that should appeal to all demographics. The newly-renovated Washington Street Mall was turned into a Business Improvement District in 2009, allowing merchants to work together to keep the mall in tip-top shape.

Local officials have been working with the federal government to ensure that the beach replenishment program will continue to be fine tuned, allowing the beaches to be preserved without sacrificing the safety of beachgoers. The city is also taking measures to make the beaches more handicapped accessible so that all visitors will be able to enjoy Cape May's 'sugar sands.'

The age-old struggle between preservation and modernization continues, with the fight to save the 1950s Beach Theatre in the forefront. The owners have applied to knock the theatre down and replace it with commercial spaces and condominiums. Elsewhere in town, some of Cape May's most attractive Victorian homes and B&Bs are also being divided into condominiums at an alarming rate.

Even so, the future of Cape May's B&B trade seems secure, with the arrival of several new innkeepers. Their energy is contagious and is attracting large numbers of young travelers. It appears the most prosperous inns have found a way to balance modern amenities with the Victorian charm that makes Cape May so special.

The city's hotels have also found success, even in troubling economic times. Travelers may be staying for shorter periods of time, but the allure of Cape May keeps bringing them back, year after year. Our future is never certain, but if history has taught us anything, it's proven that Cape May will endure whatever the fates allow.

Our Sponsors

WE would like to acknowledge the assistance of the following businesses, which not only supported the production of this book, but in doing so, continue to fly the flag for Cool Cape May, America's Original Seaside Resort. Thank you, one and all!

ACCENT ON BEAUTY

This is the place for facials, massage, body treatments, manicures, pedicures and haircare. They were the 2009 winners of the "Best Day Spa on the Jersey Shore", by myfoxphilly.com's hot list. Skincare therapist/owner Jeannette Cohen feels a deep obligation to provide clients with the best services, products and technicians. The staff take their craft to a higher level with continuing education, research and understanding the importance of a smile. Accent on Beauty is NOT your typical salon. They do in-depth consultations, have a short wait time, and deliver dramatic results. Book early, appointments fill quickly! *128 Sunset Boulevard, West Cape May, (609) 884-7040, www.accentonbeautycapemay.com.*

ALEATHEA'S

The magnificent Inn of Cape May is home to Aleathea's… a truly family-run business. The inn and restaurant are run by the Menz family and the restaurant is named after Thea, who bakes desserts. Take a stroll around the lobby, packed with antiques and gifts for sale. Then enjoy an aperitif at the bar, with ocean views. Stroll out to the porch, where you can sit in a rocking chair and enjoy a cocktail or hors d'oeuvres. The atmosphere is floral, fresh, summery, and intimate – yet the tables are placed far from one another, so diners need never fear being overheard or bumped. *7 Ocean Street, Cape May, (609) 884-5555, ext. 226, innofcapemay.com.*

A PLACE ON EARTH

Browse for quality bath/body products lovingly crafted on the island, with beautiful packaging. So what's the difference between the soaps in the supermarket aisles and the soap Canyon Allen and his mother Rose make? They come in amazing scents like Coconut Ice, Strawberry Shortcake, and Lemon Poppyseed; are hand-stirred, cured in wooden molds, and hand cut. Only plant life is used to make them – olive, coconut palm and other vegetable-based ingredients. The scents come from essential oils and are tested on family and friends – not Fido or Thumper. *526 Washington Street Mall, Cape May, 866-400-SOAP, www.aplaceonearth.com.*

AQUA TRAILS

Paddle through wetlands, your kayak illuminated by dazzling pinks and purples that trail across the skies as the sun descends. Aqua Trails has been running kayak tours since 1994, offering regularly-scheduled tours in the wetlands, plus full moon and sunset tours. Experienced kayakers guide the two-hour tours; so don't worry if you need a few pointers. It's a great way to experience the wetlands, as well as interacting with herons, oystercatchers, egrets, sandpipers, and other marsh life. Reservations suggested. *1600 Delaware Avenue at The Nature Center, Cape May, (609) 884-5600, www.aquatrails.com.*

ATLANTIC/CAPE MAY PARASAIL

Few experiences are more thrilling than soaring 500 feet over the shore. Not sure how parasailing works? It's a flight over the ocean with a boat towing you – the boat doesn't have to go fast since the wind does most of the work. Cape May and Atlantic Parasail are celebrating their third decade in business and they are the original parasail company in New Jersey. They have two 2008 Ocean Pro Parasail boats that are inspected and certified by the USCG. The company has a 100% safety record and can carry kids as young as five. Reservations required. *Ocean Drive at Two Mile Landing, Wildwood Crest, (609) 522-1869, www.atlanticparasail.com.*

BACKSTREET

Loved by locals and visitors alike, Backstreet is a hidden gem located a short walk or drive from Cape May. The specials will provide you with a wide variety of culinary surprises, such as baby lamb chops or jumbo lump crab imperial. Everything is made from the freshest of ingredients and the specials are often more extensive than the menu. Chef Theresa studied at the Culinary Institute of America, and brings 20-plus years to the kitchen. Backstreet is "simply delicious", reasonably priced, with plenty of free parking. *600 Park Boulevard, West Cape May, (609) 884-7660, www.backstreet-capemaynj.com.*

BAYBERRY INN

Location and reputation for quality have earned Bayberry Inn awards for "Most Perfect Stay" and "Best For Walking To Shops & Restaurants" by *Arrington's B&B Journal.* They were also featured in *Travel Smart* and *South Jersey* magazines. Guests are treated to a different three-course breakfast each day and specialties include gourmet stuffed French toast. Each room has wireless internet, private bathrooms, and AC. Some have fireplaces & TVs. Park your car at the Inn and leave it, since you can walk everywhere from the Bayberry! *223 Perry Street, Cape May, 877-923-9232, (609) 884-9232, www.bayberryinncapemay.com.*

BEACH SHACK / THE RUSTY NAIL

The name says it all. When you dream about your beach vacation all winter long, you dream about a place that is casual, relaxed and a stone's throw from the beach. That's the Beach Shack, a completely re-furbished motel style resort where you can wear you flip flops all day and all night. The focal point of the Beach Shack is the Rusty Nail, Cape May's iconic surfer bar and restaurant that features Cape May's longest bar, coldest beer, grooviest entertainment, and the best outdoor eating and drinking space surrounding a fire pit. *205 Beach Avenue, Cape May. 1-877-SHACK07. www.beachshack.com.*

THE BIRD HOUSE OF CAPE MAY

Since 1995, The Bird House of Cape May has offered the most complete selection of quality birdhouses, feeders and nature gifts in the area. Classic, contemporary, Victorian and eclectic styles abound. Handmade of cypress, cedar, mahogany and copper, these designs will enhance your backyard haven for years to come. A fun collection of durable natural gourd birdhouses in many shapes, sizes and colors is available, too. The Bird House also has garden accents, wrought-iron pieces, nature-inspired home decor and gifts for nature-lovers of all ages. *109 Sunset Boulevard, West Cape May, (609) 898-8871, www.birdhouseofcapemay.com.*

THE BLUE PIG TAVERN

The patio is a delightful spot to start your day with Congress Hall's signature Benedict – cheddar scallion biscuit with pancetta, poached eggs and white truffle hollandaise. Or linger over lunch with a crab cake salad as you sip iced tea and people-watch. Whether you sit indoors by the fireplace in the winter or outdoors on the patio or garden, you will enjoy a distinctive Cape May ambiance. Each of the dining rooms provide a different mood, but both serve the signature American tavern fare, utilizing local seafood and produce in creative, accessible ways. *251 Beach Avenue, Congress Hall, (609) 884-8422, www.congresshall.com.*

BY THE SEA REALTY

Located in the heart of Cape May this is a full-service real estate office offering a wide range of services. Their agents offer prompt, friendly, professional services to all of their customers and clients. Cape May's Victorian charm, fabulous restaurants, large fishing ports and appealing accommodations make this southern New Jersey shore town a must. Along with sale listings, they maintain a large inventory of rentals, and are here to assist you in planning your vacation in Cape May and surrounding areas. Contact By The Sea Realty for all of your real estate needs. *315 Ocean Street, #2B, Cape May, (609) 884-3050, www.capemaybythesea.com.*

CAPE ISLAND BIKE RENTALS

Historic Cape Island is a beautiful place to explore – it's not that large, and it's very flat, too. Which means, guess what? Riding a bike is the best way to see it all! Cape Island Bike Rentals have two locations, at either end of town, to serve you. And they are known for their friendly, helpful service. They have bikes for everyone, from kids to seniors – there are beach cruisers, surreys, tandems and Alley Cat kids' tandems. They also rent beach chairs, carry-alls and wheelchairs. Now THAT is versatility! *727 Beach Avenue and 135 Sunset Boulevard, Cape May, (609) 884-8011 or 898-7368.*

CAPE MAY BIRD OBSERVATORY

Cape May was picked by *Natural History* magazine as one of the world's top 50 spots for natural treasures – monarch butterflies in autumn, fall hawk migration, spring shorebirds and horseshoe crabs, songbirds, owls and more. NJ Audubon's Cape May Bird Observatory is nature HQ. The Northwood Center, overlooking Lake Lily in Cape May Point, is the spot for all your nature needs – year-round activities, a huge selection of binoculars, clothing, books, and nature items. Open daily, 9:30am-4:30pm. *701 East Lake Drive, Cape May Point, (609) 884-2736, www.birdcapemay.org.*

CAPE MAY SANDAL SHOPPE

Any and all manner of gear for the tootsies await the fashion-savvy shopper. They've got you covered for your summertime flip-flop needs, Rocket Dog beach shoes, and sexy sandals. You'll also love the comfy Emu boots, fuzzy Lala Lew slippers, as well as a selection of lovely pumps and dress shoes. And there is no sense buying the fabulous shoes without an equally fabulous handbag – the affordability factor here lets you manage both. And why not reward yourself for being such a sensible shopper with a nice piece of funky jewelry while you're at it? *108 Jackson Street, Cape May, (609) 898 3547, www.capemay-sandalshoppe.com.*

CAPE MAY VETERINARY HOSPITAL

We love our cats and dogs, which is why you want to be absolutely certain they are in world-class hands when they are feeling under the weather or are in need of more serious treatment. So it's a good thing that Cape May Veterinary Hospital is here. Not only are the veterinarians super-friendly and great to get along with, but they also know their business inside out. Dr Panaccio, Dr Moffatt and Dr Link really DO care… and it shows. From routine checkups to pet emergencies, Cape May Vet has the knowledge and experience to help. *694 Petticoat Creek Lane, Cape May, (609) 884-1729, www.capemayvet.com.*

A Cape May beach scene from 1906
Don Pocher

CAPE WINDS FLORIST & GIFT SHOP

They recently moved to a larger location in beautiful West Cape May, at the corner of Stimpson and Broadway. This means the experience of discussing flowers with the friendly, knowledgeable staff is pure pleasure. Need a special gift? They have SO much to choose from. Forget searching for parking – there is plenty – so you can get straight to the good stuff. Brides-to-be will love visiting and picking out their schemes in this romantic, elegant, yet relaxed setting. Every time you see a beautiful floral design and ask, "Who did the flowers?" you get one answer more than any other. **860 Broadway, West Cape May, (609) 884-1865, www.capemayflowers.com.**

CARPENTER'S SQUARE MALL

Art galleries, boutique shops, cappucino bar and dining under the stars... enjoy stunning photos at Spirit Catcher. Across the hall, refresh yourself with a Green Mountain organic coffee at MagicBrain CyberCafé, and check your emails or surf the web. You will then be attracted to the shiny baubles and fun jewelry at Dorothy's. More treats are in store at No. 5 Trading Co., where you'll find jewelry and accessories from around the world. Then, you'll be inspired at Art Decor gallery, which specializes in Antique Prints, and SOMA NewArtGallery, which showcases emerging local and regional artists. Finish with lunch or dinner at Gecko's. **Carpenters Lane and Perry Street, Cape May.**

CELEBRATE CAPE MAY

You can't visit Cape May without making a visit to the Washington Commons Mall, home of Celebrate Cape May. They specialize in all things Cape May! Get the most fun souvenirs in town, plus the best selection of T-shirts and sweatshirts, cool jewelry, magnets, shot glasses, and Cape May decals for your car! Celebrate Cape May carry thousands of other beachy items and the most extensive selection of hermit crabs on the island. Buy any hermit crab habitat and take your favorite crab home on them – that means FREE! **315 Ocean Street, Washington Commons, Cape May, (609) 884-9032, www.celebratecapemay.com.**

CHRIS CLEMANS SOTHEBY'S

Chris Clemans & Company opened in 1990 and set the standard of excellence for the real estate profession in Victorian Cape May. Chris and her team are well trained and knowledgeable about all aspects of the exciting market in our nation's oldest seaside resort. The agents live here, work here, raise their families here, and take the business of helping others do the same very seriously. Whether looking for a summer home, new residence, investment property, B&B, or the perfect summer rental, look no further than the professionals at **Chris Clemans Sotheby's International Realty. 1159 Washington Street, Cape May, (609) 884-3332, www.chrisclemansSIR.com.**

COLDWELL BANKER SOL NEEDLES

In 1901 a gentleman by the name of Sol Needles opened the first real estate office in Cape May. Now, 109 years later, it remains a leader in the market. While benefiting from its affiliation with a national company, Sol Needles Real Estate is still independently owned by fourth generation family members and maintains the feeling of a small town, family-run business. It is a leader in both residential and commercial sales and offers the largest selection of summer rentals in the city. When you deal with Coldwell Banker Sol Needles, you KNOW you are getting the best service possible. **512 Washington Street Mall, Cape May, (609) 884-8428, www.coldwellbankercapemay.com.**

CONGRESS HALL HOTEL / SEA SPA

Set amidst a sweeping lawn overlooking the Atlantic Ocean, Congress Hall offers a vibrant atmosphere with modern-day comforts in a lovingly renovated 19th-century hotel. Guest rooms, which range from doubles to luxurious suites, include state-of-the-art amenities in an environment of timeless calm. Congress Hall's L-shaped design affords many rooms glorious views of the beach. Congress Hall is a wonderful year-round vacation destination. Enjoy the decadence of the Sea Spa, the coziness of The Brown Room bar, and the nightlife at the Boiler Room. **251 Beach Avenue, Cape May, 888-944-1816, www.congresshall.com.**

CUCINA ROSA

Locals love this place, and given that every second local in Cape May seems to be either a server, a chef or both, that's a ringing endorsement. The food is Italian at its best. Among the favorite appetizers are shrimp rosa – a pancetta-wrapped shrimp baked on a spinach and ricotta; crawfish fra diablo – Louisiana crawfish tails sautéed in spicy marinara sauce; and homemade Italian sausage. Specialty dishes include twin pork chop Rosa – two six-ounce pork chops marinated and grilled, topped with sautéed red peppers. Dine on the patio on warm evenings. **301 Washington Street, Cape May, (609) 898-9800, www.cucinarosa.com.**

DR ARLENE HUGHES GORNY

Dr Arlene Hughes Gorny, an optometric physician, has been here since 1996 to help with one of our greatest assets... our vision. She offers comprehensive eye exams, treatment of eye-related problems, contact lens fittings, a nice selection of frames, and quality sunwear. Christine Peck, optician, and Linda Hadrava will assist you with all of your needs. They truly care how patients will look in their new glasses and provide a personalized process of frame selection, lens design and hands-on fitting. Not only do you get the latest in lens technology, they will accessorize your face, too! There is an optical lab on the premises. **937 Columbia Avenue, Cape May, (609) 898-0800.**

EAST LYNNE THEATER COMPANY

This Equity professional company, founded in 1980, received the New Jersey Theatre Alliance's Achievement of Excellence Award for "30 years of celebrating America's heritage through productions and educational programs." The blend of world premieres and American classics can't be seen anywhere else! Programs include a mainstage season from June-December and March, touring shows, and educational outreach for all ages. Most performances are Wednesday-Saturday at the ADA-accessible First Presbyterian Church. **500 Hughes Street, Cape May (609) 884-5898, www.eastlynnetheater.org.**

FAIRTHORNE B&B

Built in 1892 by a whaling captain, the graceful, ultra-romantic Fairthorne, in the heart of Cape May, features a beautiful wraparound verandah with rockers, striking antiques, air tubs for two, king beds with luxurious linens and fireplaces. Each morning, fresh, seasonal fruits, juice, and delicious breads and muffins accompany a mouth-watering breakfast entrée. In the afternoons, innkeepers Ed and Diane invite you for tea and home-baked cookies. In the evening, watch horse-drawn carriages from the verandah, or sip a glass of sherry by a crackling fire. **111 Ocean Street, Cape May, 800-438-8742, (609) 884-8791. www.fairthorne.com.**

410 BANK STREET

Slowly spinning fans stir the aromas of French New Orleans cooking, as seafood and steaks grill over mesquite. Dining outdoors in the garden, or on the veranda, the dream continues with the cuisine of Chef Henry Sing Cheng, whose creations range from local-caught tuna and swordfish in fabulous sauces to smoked, grilled and blackened roasts and prime rib. *The New York Times* writes, "People drive down to Cape May just to eat at 410 Bank Street, and it's worth it." And 410 Bank was once again voted "Best Restaurant in Southern New Jersey." BYOB or try a selection of regional wines. **410 Bank Street, Cape May, (609) 884-2127, www.410bankstreet.com.**

FRESCOS SEAFOOD TRATTORIA

Voted "Best Italian Restaurant in Southern New Jersey" by *New Jersey Monthly*, and tops in the state by *ZAGAT*. Stroll to Frescos down historic gas-lit Bank Street, dine on the veranda, or in the Tuscan-inspired dining rooms of this 1880 Victorian, and you could just as well be somewhere in Europe. And the food? "Divine" says *ZAGAT*. "Exceptional" says *The NY Times*. The cuisine is inspired by the diverse regions of Italy and the fresh seafood of Cape May. Award-winning chef Joseph Badger brings an incredible creativity and richness to the menu. Frescos is BYOB, but has regional wines available. **412 Bank Street, Cape May, (609) 884-0366, www.frescoscapemay.com.**

GABLES

The Gay Group doing Good Things for the Entire Community was established in 1995, dedicated to a vision of improving the quality of life through encouragement, aid and support for individuals and groups of Gay, Lesbian, Bisexual, and Transgender persons. GABLES supports GSANI - for youth by youth, and many other local organizations. Based on a network of volunteers and partnerships, GABLES presents annual events to promote understanding and cultural diversity. As publisher of The Rainbow Directory GABLES won an "Excellence in Tourism" award, the first gay organization in the state to have that honor. **(609) 861-1848, www.gablescapemay.com, www.gsani.com.**

GAIL PIERSON GALLERY

Summer 2009 saw the successful opening of the gallery, in the heart of the historic district. This fine art gallery is a fresh take – providing high-quality access to the work of artists of varying styles, in a charming downtown setting. Open all year, the gallery introduces new artists and art lovers to Cape May. In 2010 the gallery welcomes residents and visitors to a calendar of receptions and events, with opportunities to meet the artists. Art in education and interactive technologies will be a year-round focus. Owner Gail Pierson is proud to support continuing arts and education development. **658 Washington Street, Cape May, (609) 884-2585, gailpiersongallery.com.**

GECKO'S

The only place in town for southwestern cuisine, Gecko's was voted Best Mexican in Southern New Jersey by *NJ Monthly* for the last five years. *Philadelphia* magazine included it in their "Best Of The Shore 2006", while the *Press Of AC* called Gecko's "excellent." Try chile-rubbed ribeye; chiles stuffed with shrimp, jicama, pumpkin seeds and cheese; and the three sister quesadilla, quite possibly the best veggie dish in town. Then there is Gecko's famous house salad. With its sweet-and-tangy taste, and some seriously fresh veggies and crisp greens, you'll probably agree it's the best salad you've tasted. **Carpenter's Square Mall, Cape May, (609) 898-7750.**

GOOD SCENTS

The aroma of candles and incense floats you through the door, the twinkling of jewelry and giftware delight your eyes; and soon you are swaying to classical jazz, new age and world grooves. All kinds of unusual goodies are around every corner, like mini-massage tools that fit your thumbs; the Shot Carver, turns any piece of fruit into a shot glass; the Zents collection of fragranced body products; Naked Bee natural sun screens and skin care; irresistible all-natural soy blend or beeswax candles; and the Möbius Strip Bracelet, a symbol of infinity, engraved with special sayings. **327 Carpenter's Lane, Cape May, (609) 884-0014, www.sensia.com.**

**The underside of Denizot's
Pier after a fierce ice storm**
Cape May County Museum

HARBOR VIEW RESTAURANT

With its wide-angle view of the skyline of Cape May, the harbor, and the wetlands, you might expect Jimmy Buffet to appear, summoned by the laidback vibe, good food, and bands that play out on the deck on summer nights. Enjoy delicious food, along with raw bar and sushi favorites. Harbor View is locally famous for their she crab soup, clam chowder and char-broiled burgers. The outside bar is the place to be if your tastes to run to the Caribbean way of life. Lunch and dinner daily, and breakfast on Saturday and Sunday. *954 Ocean Drive between the Garden State Parkway and Wildwood Crest, Cape May, (609) 884-5444, www.harborviewcapemay.com.*

HARPOON HENRY'S

The restaurant has great sunset views, and a fun menu. Whether you want a lazy lunch or a night out, Harpoon Henry's has the right ingredients. There's a huge deck, three bars, and a lively crowd with just the right kind of entertainment – think Key West. There are entrées like coconut-fried grouper or Bahamian swordfish, and tasty sandwiches like the jerk chicken breast, or crab cake. Sitting at the outside cabana bar, enjoying one of 150 frozen drinks, you'll wish your stay could go on forever. There is a giant sandbox, where the kids can have a blast. *Beach Drive and Browning Avenue, North Cape May, (609) 886-5529, www.harpoonhenrys.net.*

HENRY'S ON THE BEACH

You might see dolphins in the surf, whether you come for breakfast, lunch or dinner. There are plenty of seats inside and out, on the beachfront deck, so large parties are no problem. The eatery is family oriented and reasonably priced. Take a morning stroll through the historic streets of Cape May and end up at Henry's for a homemade biscuit, eggs, and pancakes. Or head on over later in the night for chicken mascarpone, while your kids nosh on chicken fingers. You can bring your own wine and beer, and they also offer a selection from Cape May Winery. *702 Beach Avenue, Cape May, (609) 884-8826, henrysonthebeach.com.*

HENRY SAWYER INN

This jewel sits in the historic district, where it's easy to forget what century you're in. The Henry Sawyer will gently remind you of the present with its modern amenities… before lulling you back into the past with cozy fireplaces, meticulously-decorated rooms, and the breezy veranda. Beach-goers will find chairs, towels, hot and cold aprés-beach showers, while antique lovers will be impressed by the collection, and history buffs will appreciate how much care has been put into researching the house. Book a room with a private veranda, or make new friends on the porch. *722 Columbia Avenue, Cape May, 800-449-5667, (609) 884-5667, www.henrysawyerinn.com.*

HIENKEL ELECTRIC

Electricity is a beautiful thing… we can all agree on that. We can also agree that it's not the kind of thing that even the most enthusiastic DIY-er should mess around with. That's why you need an electrician you can trust to do the following things: 1. Turn up on time; 2. Clearly communicate what the problem is (if you don't already know); 3. Supply you with a fair estimate that WON'T suddenly change without good warning or good reason; 4. Carry out the job in a very friendly and efficient manner. Bill Hienkel, a retired local police officer, does all of these things. *North Cape May, (609) 886-9015.*

HOMESTEAD REAL ESTATE

It's not just a "place" you're looking for; it's a feeling, too. HomeStead understands that and is dedicated to serving home owners, sellers, buyers and renters with integrity and professionalism. With a full-time, first-class rental department they have instituted a convenient drive-thru check-in/out, 360° virtual tours and online reservations on all rental units, accepting Visa and MC to book vacation rentals. HomeStead also provides property management services to those who may be out of the area, or aren't handy with a hammer and nails. Come blog on www.HomeSteadCapeMay.com. *846 Broadway, West Cape May, (609) 884-1888.*

HOTEL ALCOTT

This gem has old world charm everywhere – in the 31 guests rooms and suites, on the rocker-lined verandah sprinkled with flowers and plants, in the courtyard with its gurgling fountain, and its quietly elegant decor throughout, inviting you to step back and relax. The Alcott's rooms and suites are luxuriously appointed with pillowtop mattresses, custom down duvets, plush European linens, in-suite robes and slippers, flat-screen LCD TVs, free wireless internet, continental breakfast and refreshments. Known as a premiere location to host wedding and special events. Featuring La Verandah for three star award-winning dining. *107-113 Grant Street, Cape May, (609) 884-5868, www.hotelalcott.com.*

ISLAND GRILL

Although the Island Grill is located in the heart of historic downtown Cape May, it offers a little slice of the Caribbean, from the playful decor to the exciting food. Examples: the macadamia nut-encrusted chicken breast, and chile-crusted pork chop with ancho-orange vinaigrette. The Island Grill serves breakfast, lunch and dinner, and you'll be sorely tempted by some of the delicious lunchtime sandwiches, like the Cuban, a ham, cheese, pork, dijon-mayo, and dill pickles masterpiece, which is grilled to perfection. *311 Mansion Street, Cape May, (609) 884-0200.*

MAD BATTER

This famed eatery on beautiful Jackson Street has been serving delicious and innovative food for four decades. Customers who have waited in line for the amazing breakfasts are now returning with their children. Dinner options are inventive, and the seafood is extraordinary. The Batter recently installed a beautiful new bar, so now you can enjoy a martini, great food and linger over happy hour. Other recommendations: try a scrumptious dessert on the porch and eat in the sky-lit dining room or secluded garden terrace (a special treat that you should enjoy often!). *19 Jackson Street, Cape May, (609) 884-5970, www.madbatter.com.*

MISS CHRIS FLEET

Surrounded by water, Cape May has some of the best fishing on the coast. For a great fishing experience, call the Miss Chris Fleet. Cape May's premier fishing boats enjoy the ability to fish the ocean or bay – wherever they are biting. The fleet offers full, half-day and night fishing trips, with free parking, bait, and instructions. Fish-cleaning and rods are available. Bring the kids – young anglers are a specialty! Separate accommodations available for women. Boats have twin engines and first-class safety and fish-finding equipment. Boats and crew undergo coast guard inspections and testing. *3rd Avenue and Wilson Drive, Cape May, (609) 884-3939, www.misschris.com.*

MODEL CLEANERS

Model Cleaners may well provide a vital service to Cape May's restaurant industry, but it's also popular with locals and visitors, too. Why? Because it's way more than just a dry cleaner! And while dry cleaning is a part of their business (and by the way, they are the only dry cleaner in Cape May County who use environmentally-safe solvent), they also offer expert alterations on clothing, coin-operated laundry facilities, garment storage and even tuxedo rentals. And Model Cleaners is open every day! *411 North Route 9, Cape May Court House, (609) 465-4101, www.modelcleanersonline.com.*

NAVAL AIR STATION WILDWOOD

This is a place where brave young men trained to fly the Helldiver. Surrounded by undeveloped wetlands, they dive-bombed over rivers and fields before heading to the South Pacific, where the Helldiver sank more enemy ships than any other warplane. Their presence is still felt today at the NASW Aviation Museum, at the county airport, a few minutes from Cape May. Get up close to the F14 Tomcat, UH-1 Huey, the T-33 Thunderbird, and a coast guard rescue helicopter you can sit in, along with interactive exhibits and videos. The museum is a blast for the whole family. *500 Forrestal Road, Cape May Airport, (609) 886-8787, www.usnasw.org.*

OCEAN VIEW RESTAURANT

A classic family restaurant which locals (and, therefore, smart tourists) love. Although famous for its breakfasts, it's also an excellent, wallet-friendly, venue for dinner. A favorite dish is Chicken Of The Sea, which is chicken breast stuffed with crabmeat and topped with shrimp sauce. There are some superb lunch choices (the reuben sandwich and paninis, for example) and, for dessert, you HAVE to try Boston Cream Pie. One other highlight: take a look at the name again. Do you think maybe the view is among the best in town? You'd be right. *Beach and Grant Avenue, Cape May, (609) 884-3772, www.oceanviewrestaurant.com*

THE ORIGINAL FUDGE KITCHEN

There's always a smiling employee outside their stores, with a tray full of treats. After you get a taste, stroll in and soak in the smells of freshly-whipped fudge and feast your eyes on the candies and chocolates. The fudge is whipped in the front window and is the same recipe that's been used by the Bogle brothers for four decades. There are also chocolate-covered strawberries, pretzels, licorice allsorts, chocolate truffles, candy seashells, sour patch kids, malt balls, almond clusters, and coconut clusters. Open every day. Or shop online. *513 Washington Street Mall, 728 Beach Avenue, Cape May, 800-23-FUDGE, www.fudgekitchens.com.*

OUT OF THE PAST ANTIQUES

Think of anything hard to find, so unusual and distinctive it's hard to imagine a store that could carry it. Then come here! Everywhere you look there are lovely surprises that would have been found in bedrooms, bathrooms, kitchens, and lounges from the first half of last century. If your granny kept a collection of boxes in the attic filled with kitchen items, reading materials, decorations and other household goods, and you discovered all of those treasures and placed them in a cute, friendly store… well, that's what Out of the Past is like. Off season, They are open on weekends, but call first to check. *394 Myrtle Street, Cape May, (609) 884-3357, www.outofthepastantiques.com.*

PATRICIA RAINEY STUDIOS

Patricia has painted most of Cape May's historic buildings, and plenty of stunning landscapes. Her work can be seen at shows and exhibitions throughout the town, but they're best enjoyed in your home, or the home of a friend or family member who loves Cape May like Patricia does. Unlike some more "precious" art, Patricia's detailed and lovely prints are just as happy brightening a note card or mouse pad as they are nestled on a wall of your home. Look out for her beautiful book, *Patricia Rainey's Victorian Wonderland*, which features 80 of her gorgeous paintings; and her 14-month calendar. *(609) 886-4863, www.patriciaraineystudios.com.*

PINK

Looking for a fabulous cocktail dress? The latest party pants and tops? And some Frye boots and shoes or Crystal sandals? Then you'll need a jacket to top off the whole ensemble. Plus a to-die-for handbag! Oh, and a belt, maybe a hair accessory, a scarf or a hat? No matter the season, no matter the trend, Pink has got it, courtesy of the discerning tastes of the Papendick sisters, Julie and Jen. Coco Chanel said it best: "Dress shabbily, they notice the dress – dress impeccably, they notice you." From denim to linen, cotton sundresses to satin cocktail dresses, Pink is one-stop shopping for day-to-night fashions. *33 Perry Street, in the Pink House, Cape May, (609) 898-1113.*

PROFESSIONAL PROPERTY SERVICES

Like the name says, the emphasis is on 'professional.' They're a full-service property management company located in Cape May, available for residential, commercial and condo associations. You name it, they'll do it – from floor installation or plumbing and electrical work, to the routine tasks like lawn care and taking down (or putting up) those pesky storm windows and screens. So tear up that honey-do list and put a professional to work for you. If Cape May is your home away from home, Professional Property Services will also keep an eye on your place while you're gone with weekly property checks. *(609) 770-8357, www.professionalpropertyservice.com.*

THE QUEEN VICTORIA B&B

Welcome to one of the country's finest B&Bs. Thirty-two inviting rooms and suites with private baths are decorated with Victorian antiques. Every day, guests enjoy a hearty breakfast and a British afternoon tea. Enjoy the facilities of four impeccably-restored 1880s buildings with picturesque porches, parlor with a gas-log fireplace, and pantry areas with beverages, ice, hot chocolate, teas and coffees. For the ultimate in indulgence, The Queen Victoria B&B presents the Crown Jewel, two stories of luxury that take you beyond the best Victorian tradition into a new dimension of sophistication. *102 Ocean Street, Cape May, (609) 884-8702, www.queenvictoria.com.*

SEAN'S RESTAURANT

You will ALWAYS receive a warm welcome from Sean Conners, who has been working in the restaurant business in Cape May for two decades, as a cook, waiter and front-of-house. Sean is well known to many for his dazzling smile and winning personality. Now he has his own charming beachfront restaurant, with his partner Jennifer Papendick (who runs Victorious, a wonderful jewelry and soft furnishings store in Congress Hall). Sean is in the kitchen, cooking up some downhome treats and when you realize he cooks as well as he smiles, you'll know you're in for a treat. *Beach Avenue between Perry and Jackson, (609) 898-0017.*

SOMA NEWART GALLERY

Cape May's fine art gallery showcases the exciting work of new and emerging artists from Southern New Jersey, Philadelphia and New York. Gallery owner Janet Miller is proud to have brought the first SOHO-style urban gallery to Cape May, and to offer the talented artists of our region a sophisticated venue. Each month the gallery hosts a highly anticipated opening night "meet the artist" reception. Visit the gallery website for this season's schedule. SOMA is in Carpenter's Square Mall, along with a photography gallery, vintage print shop and several stores and cafés. *31 Perry St, Carpenter's Square Mall, Cape May, (609) 898-7488 www.somagallery.net.*

SUMMER STATION

It's almost too easy to wake up in one of their comfortable, spacious rooms and roll directly from your bed on to the beach. The view is hard to beat, too. For those of you who take vacationing very seriously, it's an even lazier option for spending a sunny summer day. The beautiful deck feels private, but looks out over the promenade, giving you the best of both worlds. The comfy suites, with kitchen units, are perfect for spending the week with the family. And there's high-speed internet in the lobby – in case you need to stay in touch with the real world. *217 Beach Avenue, Cape May, (609) 884-8800, wwww.summerstationhotel.com.*

SUNSET BEACH

This is the home of one of the most enduring Cape May traditions – the lowering of the American flag every night at sunset to the strains of Kate Smith singing "God Bless America". Don't even think about leaving Cape May without witnessing the sunset at the Concrete Ship. And don't worry that your kids will be bored. A beautiful mini-golf course opened in 2007, and more fun can be had browsing the three gift stores. When you're hungry, Sunset Beach Grille serves burgers, dogs and other staples. Come an hour or two before the ceremony and search for Cape May Diamonds. *Sunset Beach, Cape May Point, (609) 884-7079, www.sunsetbeachnj.com.*

TOMMY'S FOLLY COFFEE BAR

Paying homage to Cape May's original host (Thomas Hughes built the original Congress Hall hotel in 1816, ignoring local skeptics who thought it was a foolish idea), Tommy's Folly Coffee Bar and Boutique, located in Congress Hall, is the "in place at the inn" where people stop by for a cappuccinos and to-go treats, and to browse Cape May's broadest selection of newspapers, unique gifts and clothing that you just cannot leave behind. A bonus? They serve cupcakes and old-fashioned ice cream cones in the afternoon. *251 Beach Avenue in Congress Hall, Cape May, (609) 884-6522, www.congresshall.com.*

UNCLE BILL'S PANCAKE HOUSE

Ever walk by a restaurant and get hungry? Perhaps you were just sightseeing, but then the smells hit you, your appetite was sparked, and the tummy started rumbling. This is what happens when you pass by Uncle Bill's, where people patiently line up for breakfast, brunch and lunch. These guys have been in business in Cape May for over 45 year and you'll find out that the hearty meals don't disappoint. As for the circular building that houses the restaurant, it was built by Congress Hall in the 1950s to house a cocktail bar. It later became a Howard Johnson before being turned into the pancake playground it is today! *Beach Avenue & Perry Street, Cape May, (609) 884-7199.*

UNION PARK DINING ROOM

Union Park offers one of the finest dining experiences in South Jersey. The menu is contemporary with timeless classics intertwined. Appetizers like foie gras, raw bar-style seafood plateau, classic Caesar salad and crab cakes set your taste for the delicate creations on the entrée selection – the South African lobster tail is rightly famous. Union Park, which is housed in the elegant beachfront Hotel Macomber, is open year-round, is BYOB, dressy casual, and provides the perfect venue for weddings, rehearsal dinners, family reunions and corporate meetings. *Beach and Howard Street, Cape May, (609) 884-8811, www.unionparkdiningroom.com.*

VICTORIOUS

It's hard not to be hypnotized by the stunning selection of new and estate jewelry at Victorious. The jewelry runs the gamut from ornate and older to right-this-minute and fabulous, and they specialize in rare platinum and diamond pieces. Manager Jen Papendick is a gemologist, ready to explain all that VVS, VS, and SI stuff to you, as well as helping you pick an amazing new or antique ring, bracelet, earrings, or necklace. They also have stylish goodies like Hobo handbags, sweet clutches, and a wide variety of accessories. *251 Beach Avenue at Congress Hall, Cape May, (609) 898-1777, www.victoriousantiques.com.*

VIRGINIA HOTEL & EBBITT ROOM

This beautiful boutique hotel occupies a prime spot on Jackson Street, half-a-block from the beach. It features stunning rooms decorated with a mixture of elegance and whimsy, and one of the finest restaurants in South Jersey, The Ebbitt Room. The food is as good as the critics say – rated by ZAGAT 2009/2010 as "extraordinary" and "perfection". This is fine dining at its best. Allow yourself to be spoiled. The restaurant makes great use of seafood sourced locally and from along the Atlantic seaboard, as well as fresh produce from Cape May's Beach Plum Farm. *25 Jackson Street, Cape May, 800-732-4236, www.virginiahotel.com.*

WEST END GARAGE

The ultimate oasis for retail therapy, the West End Garage is an 80-year-old building that has been transformed into an indoor exhibition space featuring multiple vendors of art, antiques, collectibles, vintage clothing, jewelry and nibbles. The West End Garage opened last summer and quickly became the number one shopping destination in town. You can lose yourself for hours browsing the various stalls. Make it a regular stop – vendors replenish inventory weekly and you never know what you'll find – or miss. Truly the discerning shopper's paradise! *484 Perry Street, Cape May. 609-770-8261, www.thewestendgarage.com.*

WHITE DOVE COTTAGE B&B

This is the ultimate escape, especially in the offseason, when Cape May is at its most romantic. Relax, dream, read, stroll, clear your head – miles away from rush-hour traffic and deadlines. The White Dove is tastefully furnished with American and European antiques, along with modern conveniences like private bathrooms and AC. The veranda is furnished with rocking chairs and shaded by old sycamore trees on quiet, gas-lit Hughes Street. And you'll be glad to know that the beach, shops, theater, concerts, movies, tours and superb restaurants are only blocks away. *619 Hughes Street, Cape May, 800-321-DOVE, (609) 884-0613, www.whitedovecottage.com.*

WILSEY REALTY

Located in downtown historic Cape May, Wilsey Realty has combined the latest technology in real estate sale and rental marketing in a completely-renovated office building (which won an award from the Historic Preservation Commission). Wilsey offers downtown parking along with an experienced sales team to provide their clientele with unmatched professional and personalized service. Wilsey Realty's user-friendly website assures sellers and rental property owners that their properties will be highly exposed on the internet. *501 Lafayette Street, Cape May, (609) 884-1007, 877-884-8907, www.wilseyrealty.com.*

ZOE'S BEACHFRONT EATERY

Zoe's has delicious homemade pancakes that might be the best in town. For lunch, there are freshly-made sandwiches, hoagies, salads and burgers that make the perfect beach treat. Then there's dinner – maybe you skipped lunch and you realize as you walk off the beach that you can't wait until you've showered and changed and you want to eat right NOW. If so, go to Zoe's, sit on the patio (dog-friendly, by the way), order a grilled chicken caesar and enjoy that wonderful late afternoon light. Or get it to go. Also, Zoe's vegetarian section includes superb veggie burgers made from scratch. *Beach Avenue at Stockton, Cape May, (609) 884-1233.*

DRESSED APPROPRIATELY
A Victorian beach outing in Cape May – no skimpy swimwear for them!
Don Pocher

Bibliography

Cape May County, New Jersey, The Making Of An American Resort Community
By Jeffrey M. Dorwant, Rutgers University Press, 1996

Geology of The County of Cape May, State of New Jersey
By Geo. H. Cook, Rutgers College Press, 1857

Images of America, Cape May in Vintage Postcards
By Don and Pat Pocher, Arcadia, 1998

South Jersey, A History, 1664-1923
Edited by Alfred M. Heston, Lewis Historical Publishing Company, Inc., New York and Chicago, 1924

The History of Cape May County, New Jersey from Aboriginal Times to the Present Day
By Lewis Townsend Stevens, Cape May, 1897

The New Jersey Coast in Three Centuries; History of the New Jersey Coast with Genealogical and Historic-Biographical Appendix
Edited by William Nelson, The Lewis Publishing Company, 1902

The Summer City By the Sea: Cape May, New Jersey, An Illustrated History
By Emil Salvini, Rutgers University Press, 1998

This is Cape May, America's Oldest Seaside Resort
By Jean Totten Timmons, Timmons Guides, 1974

Tommy's Folly
By Jack Wright, Beach Plum Press, 2003

The original Congress Hall, destroyed in the fire of 1878 that swept through Cape May, was twice the size of the current building
Congress Hall Archives